SRA Reading Mastery Plus

Presentation Book C

Level 3

Siegfried Engelmann
Susan Hanner

SRA

A Division of The McGraw-Hill Companies

Columbus, Ohio

Table of Contents

www.sra4kids.com

SRA/McGraw-Hill

A Division of The McGraw-Hill Companies

Copyright © 2002 by SRA/McGraw-Hill.

Send all inquiries to:
SRA/McGraw-Hill
8787 Orion Place
Columbus, OH 43240-4027

Printed in the United States of America.

ISBN 0-07-569119-1

1 2 3 4 5 6 7 8 9 BCH 06 05 04 03 02 01

Lessons 101–105 · Planning Page

Looking Ahead

	Lesson 101	Lesson 102	Lesson 103	Lesson 104	Lesson 105
Lesson Events	**Vocabulary Review** Reading Words Vocabulary Review Story Reading Paired Practice Alphabetical Order Independent Work Workcheck Writing-Spelling	Vocabulary Review Reading Words Story Reading Paired Practice Alphabetical Order Independent Work Workcheck Writing-Spelling	Vocabulary Review Reading Words Story Reading Paired Practice Alphabetical Order Independent Work Workcheck Writing-Spelling	Reading Words Story Reading Paired Practice Alphabetical Order Independent Work Workcheck Writing-Spelling	Reading Words Story Reading Glossary and Guide Words Reading Checkouts Independent Work Workcheck Writing-Spelling
Vocabulary Sentence	#25: She <u>commented</u> about the <u>still</u> water.	#25: She <u>commented</u> about the <u>still</u> water.	sentence #23 sentence #24 sentence #25		
Reading Words: Word Types	–s words –ed words mixed words	modeled words mixed words	modeled words mixed words	words with endings mixed words	mixed words
New Vocabulary	packed	block count on mean	receive	ashamed honest let somebody down harm rise	remains loss
Comprehension Passage					
Story	_Andrew Begins to Change_	_Andrew Plays Harder_	_The Titans Play Harder_	_Andrew Leaves the Team_	_The Championship Game_
Skill Items	Alphabetical Order	Alphabetical Order	Alphabetical Order Vocabulary Sentence	Alphabetical Order Vocabulary Sentences	
Special Materials					Thermometer charts
Special Projects/ Activities					

Lessons 101—105 · Planning Page

1

Lesson 101

Materials: Each student will need a copy of textbook 3 which contains a student glossary.

EXERCISE 1
VOCABULARY REVIEW

a. **Find page 342 in your textbook.** ✓
- Touch sentence 25. ✓
- This is a new vocabulary sentence. It says: She commented about the still water. Everybody, read that sentence. Get ready. (Signal.) *She commented about the still water.*
- Close your eyes and say the sentence. Get ready. (Signal.) *She commented about the still water.*
- (Repeat until firm.)

b. When you **comment** about something, you quickly tell about that thing. Everybody, what's another way of saying **She quickly told about her illness?** (Signal.) *She commented about her illness.*
- What's another way of saying **They quickly told about the weather?** (Signal.) *They commented about the weather.*

c. Another word for **silent** or **peaceful** is **still.** Here's another way of saying **The children were silent: The children were still.**

d. Your turn. What's another way of saying **The animals were peaceful?** (Signal.) *The animals were still.*
- (Repeat step d until firm.)

e. What's another way of saying **The air was silent?** (Signal.) *The air was still.*

f. Listen to the sentence again: She commented about the still water. Everybody, say the sentence. Get ready. (Signal.) *She commented about the still water.*

g. Everybody, what word means **silent** or **peaceful?** (Signal.) *Still.*
- What word means **quickly told about something?** (Signal.) *Comment.*
- (Repeat step g until firm.)

EXERCISE 2
READING WORDS
Column 1

a. Find lesson 101 in your textbook. ✓
- Touch column 1. ✓
- (Teacher reference:)

1. <u>reporters</u>	4. <u>practices</u>
2. <u>themselves</u>	5. <u>chances</u>
3. <u>members</u>	

- All these words end with the letter **S.**
b. Word 1. What's the first syllable? (Signal.) *re.*
- What's the whole word? (Signal.) *Reporters.*
c. Word 2. What's the first syllable? (Signal.) *them.*
- What's the whole word? (Signal.) *Themselves.*
d. Word 3. What's the first syllable? (Signal.) *mem.*
- What's the whole word? (Signal.) *Members.*
e. Word 4. What's the first syllable? (Signal.) *prac.*
- What's the whole word? (Signal.) *Practices.*
f. Word 5. What's the first syllable? (Signal.) *chan.*
- What's the whole word? (Signal.) *Chances.*
g. Let's read those words again, the fast way.
- Word 1. What word? (Signal.) *Reporters.*
- (Repeat for words 2–5.)
h. (Repeat step g until firm.)

Column 2

i. Find column 2. ✓
- (Teacher reference:)

1. noticed	4. squeezed
2. realized	5. frightened
3. dressed	

- All these words end with the letters **E-D.** Those letters make different sounds in the words.

j. Word 1. What word? (Signal.) *Noticed.*
   • (Repeat for: **2. realized, 3. dressed, 4. squeezed, 5. frightened.**)
k. (Repeat step j until firm.)

Column 3

l. Find column 3. ✓
   • (Teacher reference:)

1. **packed**	4. **awful**
2. **still**	5. **commented**
3. **comment**	

m. Word 1. What word? (Signal.) *Packed.*
   • When things are squeezed into a small space, they are **packed.** Here's another way of saying **People were squeezed into the car: People were packed into the car.**
n. Your turn. What's another way of saying **People were squeezed into the car?** (Signal.) *People were packed into the car.*
   • (Repeat step n until firm.)
o. What's another way of saying **People were squeezed into the stands?** (Signal.) *People were packed into the stands.*
p. Word 2. What word? (Signal.) *Still.*
   • (Repeat for words 3–5.)
q. Let's read those words again.
   • Word 1. What word? (Signal.) *Packed.*
   • (Repeat for words 2–5.)
r. (Repeat step q until firm.)

Column 4

s. Find column 4. ✓
   • (Teacher reference:)

1. **Handy Andy**	4. **newspapers**
2. **firing**	5. **holler**
3. **towel**	

t. Number 1. What name? (Signal.) *Handy Andy.*
u. Word 2. What word? (Signal.) *Firing.*
   • (Repeat for words 3–5.)
v. (Repeat steps t and u until firm.)

Individual Turns

(For columns 1–4: Call on individual students, each to read one to three words per turn.)

VOCABULARY REVIEW

a. Here's the new vocabulary sentence: She commented about the still water.
   • Everybody, say the sentence. Get ready. (Signal.) *She commented about the still water.*
   • (Repeat until firm.)
b. Everybody, what word means **quickly told about something?** (Signal.) *Commented.*
   • What word means **silent** or **peaceful?** (Signal.) *Still.*

STORY READING

a. Find part B in your textbook. ✓
   • The error limit for this story is 15. Read carefully.
b. Everybody, touch the title. ✓
   • (Call on a student to read the title.) *[Andrew Begins to Change.]*
   • What's going to happen to Andrew? (Call on a student. Idea: *He's going to change.*)
c. (Call on individual students to read the story, each student reading two or three sentences at a time. Ask questions marked **1**.)

> • (Correct errors: Tell the word. Direct the student to reread the sentence.)
> • (If the group makes more than 15 errors, direct the students to reread the story.)

d. (After the group has read the selection making no more than 15 errors, read the story to the students and ask questions marked **2**.)

Andrew Begins to Change

   The newspapers were filled with stories about Andrew. They called him "Handy Andy, the man who does it all for the Titans."

2. Everybody, what was Andrew's nickname? (Signal.) *Handy Andy.*
2. What does that mean, does it all for the Titans? (Call on a student. Idea: *He runs and he kicks.*)

Andrew was very busy. He had to go to the practices. He also had to talk to reporters. And when he left the practice field every day, a group of fans would be outside. They wanted him to sign his name in their books.

2. Why were the fans outside the practice field? (Call on a student. Ideas: *They wanted Andrew's autograph; to see Andrew.*)

Andrew didn't daydream anymore. His life was like a great daydream so he didn't have time for anything except living.

2. Why didn't he daydream? (Call on a student. Ideas: *Because his life was like a great daydream; he was too busy.*)

He worked very hard. And the other members of the Titans started to work hard, too. They started to become proud of themselves and proud of their team.
Before Andrew had come around, people would say to the other players, "Oh, you play for that awful team, the Titans." Now the people would say, "Wow, you play with the Titans. They are the hottest team in football."

2. What does that mean, the hottest team in football? (Call on a student. Ideas: *The most popular team; the best team.*)

The players wanted to show the fans that the team wasn't just a one-man team. They wanted to show that there were 11 good football players on the field when the Titans played.

2. What did the players want to show the fans? (Call on a student. Idea: *That the team wasn't just a one-man team.*)
2. How could a player show that he was important to the team? (Call on a student. Idea: *By doing his job well so the team played well together.*)

When the players played better, the coaches didn't yell as much. Before Andrew came along, you would never hear Denny say, "Good job." But now, he would frequently holler to his players, "That's the way to run that play. Good job."

2. Everybody, did he used to say things like that? (Signal.) *No.*
2. Why was he saying nice things now? (Call on a student. Idea: *Because the team was playing better.*)

And the people who owned the Titans didn't tell Denny they were thinking of firing him. Instead, they asked things like this: "What do you think our chances are for winning the championship?"

2. Everybody, were the owners still thinking of firing Denny? (Signal.) *No.*
2. What were they asking about now? (Call on a student. Idea: *What the Titans' chances were for winning the championship.*)
2. What do you think: Did the Titans have a chance to win the championship? (Call on individual students. Idea: *Yes.*)

Denny would reply, "Our chances of winning the championship are pretty good if we keep playing the way we're playing."
And the fans were happy. The people who lived in Andrew's city felt that the team was their team. They talked about the team. People who didn't know each other would talk on the bus or in the grocery store. "Did you see Handy Andy and the Titans last Sunday?" they would say. Then they would start talking about the game.

2. Everything has changed since Andrew came to the Titans. How have the players changed? (Call on a student. Idea: *They play better.*)
2. How have the coaches changed? (Call on a student. Ideas: *They're happier; they're nicer to the players.*)

2. How have the owners of the team changed? (Call on a student. Ideas: *They're happier; they don't want to fire Denny.*)
2. How have the fans changed? (Call on a student. Ideas: *They like the Titans; they're happier.*)

Every Sunday the stands were packed. There were no empty seats. And when the Titans came onto the field, the fans would cheer. The fans would think, "That's my team and it's the best team there is. Yea for the Titans."

For five Sundays, it was the same. Andrew would come onto the field when the team couldn't move. He would either kick the ball or run with it. When he kicked, he would usually make a field goal. When he ran with it he would always make a touchdown. Nobody could stop him. Sometimes three or four players would hit him at the same time. For those players, running into Andrew was just like running into the side of a truck. They bounced back and Andrew kept going.

But then on the sixth Sunday, Andrew felt strange. When he was getting dressed for the game, he noticed that his hands and feet were tingling.

1. Everybody, had they ever tingled before? (Signal.) *Yes.*
1. When? (Call on a student. Idea: *At the Magnetic Research Company, when he walked into the room full of electricity.*)

He had the same feeling that he had felt earlier at Magnetic Research Company when he had walked into the room filled with electricity.

Now he was sitting on the bench in front of his locker putting his shoes on. Suddenly, he realized what was wrong. He grabbed the locker handle and squeezed it as hard as he could.

1. Why do you think he did that? (Call on a student. Idea: *To test his strength.*)

Instead of bending it like a piece of clay, he put a tiny dent in it.

1. What was happening to his strength? (Call on a student. Idea: *It was fading.*)

He tried again. The outcome was the same.

1. What does that mean? (Call on a student. Idea: *He could only put a little dent in the locker handle again.*)

Andrew Dexter was losing his super strength.
He was still strong, perhaps as strong as a quarter horse, which meant that he was probably as strong as five or six very strong men.

2. How strong was he now? (Call on a student. Ideas: *As strong as a quarter horse; as strong as five or six very strong men.*)

But he didn't have the strength of an African elephant anymore.
He was frightened. If he was getting weaker and weaker, he would soon lose all his super strength. He would just be plain old Andrew Dexter again. Mean George walked by the bench and slapped Andrew on the back. "Big game today," Mean George said. "You're going to do it for us again today."

2. He said, "You're going to do it for us again today." What does he think Andrew will do? (Call on a student. Idea: *Win the game for them.*)

"George," Andrew said, looking up at the huge man. "I . . . I don't think I'm going to be . . . I don't . . . "

2. What is Andrew trying to tell George? (Call on a student. Idea: *That he (Andrew) is losing his super strength.*)

"What's the matter, man?" George said and sat next to Andrew. The bench bent down under the weight of Mean George.

2. Why did it bend down? (Call on a student. Idea: *Because Mean George weighed a lot.*)

"Andy, you look sick."

1. Go back to the beginning of the story. Follow along while I read.
2. Read the rest of the story to yourself. Find out how the Titans could win without Andrew. Raise your hand when you're done.

> **Andrew said, "You guys are going to have to help me out. I don't think I'll be able to run or kick as well today."**
>
> **"You've got to," George said. "Without you, we're just a bunch of bums."**
>
> **"No," Andrew shouted. "Don't you say that. You guys are great. You just don't know it. You can do it without me. You just have to tell yourselves that you can."**
> **MORE NEXT TIME**

2. (After all students have raised their hand:) Andrew told George that the Titans could win without him. What would they have to do? (Call on a student. Idea: *Tell themselves that they can win.*)
2. Everybody, did George think the Titans could win without Andrew? (Signal.) *No.*
2. Everybody, was the author's purpose in this story to inform, entertain, or persuade? (Signal.) *Entertain.*

EXERCISE 5

PAIRED PRACTICE

You're going to read aloud to your partner. Today the **B** members will read first. Then the **A** members will read from the star to the end of the story.
(Observe students and give feedback.)

End-of-Lesson Activities

INDEPENDENT WORK

Now finish your independent work for lesson 101. First do the worksheet. Raise your hand when you're finished.
(Observe students and give feedback.)

WORKCHECK

a. (Direct students to take out their marking pencils.)
 • We're going to check your independent work. Remember, if you got an item wrong, make an **X** next to the item. Don't change any answers.
b. (For each item: Read the item. Call on a student to answer it. If the answer is wrong, say the correct answer. Refer to the Answer Key for the correct answers.)
c. Now use your marking pencil to fix up any items you got wrong. Remember, all mistakes must be fixed up before you hand in your independent work.

WRITING-SPELLING

(Present Writing-Spelling lesson 101 after completing Reading lesson 101. See Writing-Spelling Guide.)

LANGUAGE ARTS GUIDE

(Present Language Arts lesson 101 after completing Reading lesson 101. See Language Arts Guide.)

EXERCISE 1

VOCABULARY REVIEW

a. Here's the new vocabulary sentence: She commented about the still water.
 • Everybody, say the sentence. Get ready. (Signal.) *She commented about the still water.*
 • (Repeat until firm.)

b. Everybody, what word means **silent** or **peaceful?** (Signal.) *Still.*
 • What word means **quickly told about something?** (Signal.) *Commented.*

EXERCISE 2

READING WORDS

Column 1

a. **Find lesson 102 in your textbook.** ✓
 • Touch column 1. ✓
 • (Teacher reference:)

1. hinge	4. showers
2. unusual	5. towel
3. block	

b. Word 1 is **hinge.** What word? (Signal.) *Hinge.*
 • Spell **hinge.** Get ready. (Tap for each letter.) *H-I-N-G-E.*

c. Word 2 is **unusual.** What word? (Signal.) *Unusual.*
 • Spell **unusual.** Get ready. (Tap for each letter.) *U-N-U-S-U-A-L.*

d. Word 3. What word? (Signal.) *Block.*
 • Spell **block.** Get ready. (Tap for each letter.) *B-L-O-C-K.*
 • When you **block** in a football game, you push a player from the other team without using your hands to grab the player.
 • What do you do when you block in football? (Call on a student. Idea: *You push a player from the other team without using your hands.*)

e. Word 4. What word? (Signal.) *Showers.*
 • Spell **showers.** Get ready. (Tap for each letter.) *S-H-O-W-E-R-S.*

f. Word 5. What word? (Signal.) *Towel.*

g. Let's read those words again, the fast way.
 • Word 1. What word? (Signal.) *Hinge.*
 • (Repeat for words 2–5.)

h. (Repeat step g until firm.)

Column 2

i. Find column 2. ✓
 • (Teacher reference:)

1. count on	4. wildly
2. mean	5. experts
3. wild	

j. Number 1. What words? (Signal.) *Count on.*
 • When you can be **sure** of something, you can **count on** that thing. Here's another way of saying **He was sure that his horse would win: He counted on his horse winning.**

k. Your turn. What's another way of saying **He was sure that his horse would win?** (Signal.) *He counted on his horse winning.*

l. Word 2. What word? (Signal.) *Mean.*
 • When you do what you **mean** to do, you do what you **plan** to do. Here's another way of saying **She didn't plan to fall down: She didn't mean to fall down.**

m. Your turn. What's another way of saying **She didn't plan to fall down?** (Signal.) *She didn't mean to fall down.*
 • (Repeat step m until firm.)

n. What's another way of saying **He plans to say that?** (Signal.) *He means to say that.*

o. Word 3. What word? (Signal.) *Wild.*
 • (Repeat for words 4 and 5.)

p. Let's read those words again.
 • Number 1. What words? (Signal.) *Count on.*

q. Word 2. What word? (Signal.) *Mean.*
 • (Repeat for words 3–5.)

r. (Repeat steps p and q until firm.)

Column 3

s. Find column 3. ✓
• (Teacher reference:)

1. comment	3. teammates
2. mates	4. commenting

t. Word 1. What word? (Signal.)
Comment.
• (Repeat for words 2–4.)
u. (Repeat step t until firm.)

Individual Turns

(For columns 1–3: Call on individual students, each to read one to three words per turn.)

EXERCISE 3

STORY READING

a. Find part B in your textbook. ✓
• The error limit for this story is 14. Read carefully.
b. Everybody, touch the title. ✓
• (Call on a student to read the title.) [*Andrew Plays Harder.*]
• Everybody, what's the title? (Signal.) *Andrew Plays Harder.*
c. (Call on individual students to read the story, each student reading two or three sentences at a time. Ask questions marked **1**.)

• (Correct errors: Tell the word. Direct the student to reread the sentence.)
• (If the group makes more than 14 errors, direct the students to reread the story.)

d. (After the group has read the selection making no more than 14 errors, read the story to the students and ask questions marked **2**.)

Andrew Plays Harder

Andrew didn't mean to shout at Mean George. But Andrew was frightened.

2. Where were the men? (Call on a student. Idea: *In the locker room.*)
2. Why was Andrew frightened? (Call on a student. Idea: *Because he was losing his strength; because he wouldn't be able to help the Titans.*)

Andrew didn't want to go back to being plain old Andrew Dexter. He wanted to keep on being Handy Andy.

2. What's the difference between plain old Andrew Dexter and Handy Andy? (Call on a student. Ideas: *Everyone loved Handy Andy but hardly anybody loved plain old Andrew Dexter; Handy Andy was very strong, but Andrew Dexter wasn't.*)

Mean George said, "Hey man, you can count on me.

2. What does that mean, you can count on me? (Call on a student. Idea: *You can depend on me.*)

I'll give the Titans everything I got. But we want you out there with us. We need you."

2. Read what Mean George said just the way he said it to Andrew. (Call on a student. Student should read with a pleading tone of voice.)

"I'll do the best I can," Andrew said.
When Andrew had been as strong as an elephant, he hadn't tried to play as hard as he could have.

1. Why? (Call on a student. Idea: *Because he could've hurt the other players.*)

He didn't want to hurt the other players. So he ran just hard enough to get past the other players.
Now that Andrew's strength was fading, he tried harder.

2. Why did he have to try harder now? (Call on a student. Idea: *Because his strength was fading.*)

In the next game that Andrew played, he kicked the ball with all his strength. When his first kick was sailing through the air, the announcer said, "That's not much of a kick for Handy Andy, but it's still something to watch. It must have a hang-time of over six seconds. Not bad."

2. How does that kick compare with Andrew's best kicks? (Call on a student. Idea: *It wasn't as good as his best kicks.*)

During that game, Andrew was tackled for the first time. He tried to run through the other team instead of kicking the ball. Three players hit him at the same time. Andrew tried to keep his feet under him, but the players brought him down to the ground.

2. Everybody, had that ever happened to him before? (Signal.) *No.*
2. What did he usually do? (Call on a student. Idea: *Ran right through the other players.*)

Andrew was tackled three other times during that game.

1. Everybody, so how many times did he get tackled during that game? (Signal.) *Four.*

He was tackled four times, but he also scored four touchdowns. When Andrew got tackled, the other players on the Titans didn't yell at him. They said, "Good try, man. We'll do a better job of blocking for you."

2. How would they help Andrew by doing a better job of blocking? (Call on a student. Idea: *They would keep the other players away from Andrew so he could run.*)

"Thanks," Andrew said.
The game was close, but the Titans won it. The fans cheered for Andrew. They held up signs that said things like HANDY ANDY IS A DANDY, and WITH ANDY THE TITANS ARE NUMBER ONE. But when the game was over, Andrew Dexter sat on the bench in the locker room. He could hardly catch his breath.

2. What do you think was happening to Andrew? (Call on a student. Idea: *He was getting weaker.*)

His hands were tingling. So were his legs and feet. His body was losing power by the second.

2. What does that mean, by the second? (Call on a student. Idea: *Very quickly.*)

He wiped his sweaty face with a towel. His mind was racing.

1. Do you think he was daydreaming? (Call on a student. Idea: *No.*)
1. What was he thinking about? (Call on a student. Idea: *Losing his strength.*)

What would he do now? How long would it be before he lost all his strength? How could the Titans win the championship if he lost his strength? What would the fans do when he went out on the field and couldn't kick the ball any farther than any bank teller could? What would they say when he couldn't run any faster than any other man could run?
The fans would boo. They would throw things onto the field. Andrew could see them in his mind. "Boo," they would yell. "Get that bum off the field." Andrew could almost hear them. He buried his head in the towel.

2. Everybody, where was he when he was thinking all those things? (Signal.) *In the locker room.*
2. What was he imagining? (Call on a student. Idea: *What would happen when he lost all his strength.*)

He felt like crying.
"Good game, man."
Andrew didn't look up. He felt the bench bend down as somebody sat next to him.

1. Everybody, who is talking to Andrew? (Signal.) *Mean George.*
1. What clue do you have that it is Mean George? (Call on a student. Idea: *The bench bent down when he sat down.*)

> "We're going to do a better job next week," the voice said. It was Mean George. "We didn't do a good job of blocking for you today.

2. Everybody, was George blaming Andrew for being tackled? (Signal.) *No.*
2. Who was George blaming? (Call on a student. Ideas: *The team; the guys who were supposed to block for Andrew.*)

> But next week, not one of those guys is going to get near you. You'll run down the field like you're all alone."
>
> Andrew wiped his eyes and looked up. "Thanks, George," he said. "But I don't think I'll be able to play next week. I . . ."

2. Why did he stop talking? (Call on a student. Idea: *Because he was so upset.*)

> He shook his head and then buried it in the towel again.

2. How does he feel? (Call on a student. Ideas: *Very sad; worried.*)

> Andrew didn't want George to see the tears in his eyes.
>
> "What's this talk about not playing?" George asked, and slapped Andrew on the back. "Of course you're going to play. You're part of this team, right?"
>
> "Yeah," Andrew said, looking up.
>
> "Then you play on this team. I play and you play."
>
> Andrew smiled. "I'll do my best," Andrew said.
>
> "So will we," Mean George said.
>
> • • •

2. What do the dots in the story tell you? (Call on a student. Idea: *Part of the story is missing.*)

> There is a difference between players when they play to win and the same players when they are just playing. You could see that difference during the practices all week long.

2. What kind of differences would there be? (Call on individual students. Ideas: *The team would try harder; the team would run faster; the team would block better.*)

> The Titans ran their plays with a little more power, a little more speed, and with all the players trying harder—a lot harder.

1. Go back to the beginning of the story. Follow along while I read.
2. Read the rest of the story to yourself. Find out how much strength Andrew had. Raise your hand when you're done.

> Andrew watched the team and he was proud of them. They weren't blaming each other or blaming the coaches. They weren't arguing. They were trying hard and practicing as if they were champions.
>
> But Andrew didn't feel like a champion. His strength was no longer that of a quarter horse. It had faded to the strength of a Mongolian horse. Of course he was still much stronger than even the strongest man; however, his strength was fading.
>
> **MORE NEXT TIME**

2. (After all students have raised their hand:) How much strength did Andrew have now? (Call on a student. Idea: *The strength of a Mongolian horse.*)
2. How much strength did he have when he was the strongest? (Call on a student. Idea: *As strong as an African elephant.*)

EXERCISE 4

PAIRED PRACTICE

You're going to read aloud to your partner. Today the **A** members will read first. Then the **B** members will read from the star to the end of the story.
(Observe students and give feedback.)

End-of-Lesson Activities

Now finish your independent work for lesson 102. First do the worksheet. Raise your hand when you're finished.
(Observe students and give feedback.)

WORKCHECK

a. (Direct students to take out their marking pencils.)
- We're going to check your independent work. Remember, if you got an item wrong, make an **X** next to the item. Don't change any answers.
b. (For each item: Read the item. Call on a student to answer it. If the answer is wrong, say the correct answer. Refer to the Answer Key for the correct answers.)

c. Now use your marking pencil to fix up any items you got wrong. Remember, all mistakes must be fixed up before you hand in your independent work.

WRITING-SPELLING

(Present Writing-Spelling lesson 102 after completing Reading lesson 102. See Writing-Spelling Guide.)

LANGUAGE ARTS GUIDE

(Present Language Arts lesson 102 after completing Reading lesson 102. See Language Arts Guide.)

Lesson 103

EXERCISE 1

VOCABULARY REVIEW

a. You learned a sentence that tells what they had reasons for.
- Everybody, say that sentence. Get ready. (Signal.) *They had reasons for interrupting her talk.*
- (Repeat until firm.)

b. You learned a sentence that tells what he frequently did.
- Say that sentence. Get ready. (Signal.) *He frequently argued about the championship.*
- (Repeat until firm.)

c. Here's the last sentence you learned: She commented about the still water.
- Everybody, say that sentence. Get ready. (Signal.) *She commented about the still water.*
- (Repeat until firm.)

d. Everybody, what word means **quickly told about something?** (Signal.) *Commented.*
- What word means **silent** or **peaceful?** (Signal.) *Still.*

e. Once more. Say the sentence that tells what she commented about. Get ready. (Signal.) *She commented about the still water.*

EXERCISE 2

READING WORDS

Column 1

a. **Find lesson 103 in your textbook.** ✓
- Touch column 1. ✓
- (Teacher reference:)

1. breakfast	3. receive
2. television	4. ache

b. Word 1 is **breakfast.** What word? (Signal.) *Breakfast.*
- Spell **breakfast.** Get ready. (Tap for each letter.) *B-R-E-A-K-F-A-S-T.*
c. Word 2 is **television.** What word? (Signal.) *Television.*
- Spell **television.** Get ready. (Tap for each letter.) *T-E-L-E-V-I-S-I-O-N.*

d. Word 3 is **receive.** What word? (Signal.) *Receive.*
- Spell **receive.** Get ready. (Tap for each letter.) *R-E-C-E-I-V-E.*
- When somebody gives you something, you **receive** it. My turn. What do you do when somebody gives you five dollars? You **receive** five dollars.

e. Your turn. What do you do when somebody gives you five dollars? (Signal.) *Receive five dollars.*
- (Repeat step e until firm.)

f. What do you do when somebody throws you a football? (Signal.) *Receive a football.*

g. Word 4 is **ache.** What word? (Signal.) *Ache.*
- Spell **ache.** Get ready. (Tap for each letter.) *A-C-H-E.*

h. Let's read those words again, the fast way.
- Word 1. What word? (Signal.) *Breakfast.*
- (Repeat for words 2–4.)
i. (Repeat step h until firm.)

Column 2

j. Find column 2. ✓
- (Teacher reference:)

1. hinge	3. teammates
2. wildly	4. unusual

k. Word 1. What word? (Signal.) *Hinge.*
- (Repeat for words 2–4.)
l. (Repeat step k until firm.)

Individual Turns

(For columns 1 and 2: Call on individual students, each to read one to three words per turn.)

EXERCISE 3

STORY READING

a. Find part B in your textbook. ✓
- The error limit for this story is 14. Read carefully.
b. Everybody, touch the title. ✓
- (Call on a student to read the title.) *[The Titans Play Harder.]*

- Everybody, what's the title? (Signal.)
The Titans Play Harder.
c. (Call on individual students to read the story, each student reading two or three sentences at a time. Ask questions marked **1.**)

- (Correct errors: Tell the word. Direct the student to reread the sentence.)
- (If the group makes more than 14 errors, direct the students to reread the story.)

d. (After the group has read the selection making no more than 14 errors, read the story to the students and ask questions marked **2.**)

The Titans Play Harder

The Titans practiced hard all week. Andrew kicked the ball four times during the game on Sunday. But not one of his hang-times was six seconds.

2. Everybody, were they **more than six seconds** or **less than six seconds**? (Signal.) *Less than six seconds.*

The shortest hang-time was just under five seconds, and the longest hang-time was just under six seconds. Andrew carried the ball ten times during that game. He scored one touchdown.

2. How does **one** touchdown compare with his last game? (Call on a student. Idea: *Fewer touchdowns.*)

He tried to make his legs move as fast as they could. And that was very fast. He still had the strength of a small horse. With all that power in his legs, he could run faster than any man alive.

2. How fast was Andrew? (Call on a student. Idea: *Faster than any man alive.*)

He hadn't tried to use all his speed before, but he knew that he could be tackled. He ran as hard as he could so he could stay away from the players on the other team.

2. Why hadn't he used all his strength when he ran before? (Call on a student. Idea: *He didn't have to.*)
2. What was he trying to do now when he ran? (Call on a student. Idea: *Stay away from other players.*)

The Titans were one point behind with less than a minute to go.

2. Everybody, is this happening **near the beginning** of the game or **near the end?** (Signal.) *Near the end.*
2. How do you know? (Call on a student. Idea: *There was less than a minute to go.*)

The Titans had the ball. They were fifty yards from the goal line. They decided to try a field goal, with Andrew kicking the ball. The crowd was cheering wildly. If he made this field goal, the Titans would win and they would be in the championship game for the Professional Football League. If he missed, the Titans would lose the game and would not be in the championship game.

2. Everybody, who had the ball? (Signal.) *The Titans.*
2. Was the next play important? (Signal.) *Yes.*
2. Why? (Call on a student. Idea: *If the Titans won, they'd be in the championship game.*)

Andrew's heart was pounding. He kept reminding himself to think about kicking the ball and to think of nothing else. "Watch the ball. Keep your head down. Take two steps. Kick it just under the middle of the ball. Watch the ball. Keep your head down . . . "

2. What is all that talking? (Call on a student. Idea: *Andrew talking to himself.*)
2. What are some of the things he's telling himself? (Call on individual students. Idea: *Think; watch the ball; keep your head down; etc.*)

The ball was put in place. Andrew took two quick steps forward. He kept his head down. He kicked it, just below the middle of the ball.

2. Everybody, did he do the things he told himself to do? (Signal.) *Yes.*
2. So what do you think will happen? (Call on a student. Idea: *He will make the field goal.*)

For a moment he didn't look up. In the distance, he heard the sound of players' shoulder pads hitting other shoulder pads. He heard the whooping sound of the crowd—then a second of almost silence.

2. Why was everybody silent for a second? (Call on a student. Idea: *They were watching the ball.*)

And then he heard wild cheers.

1. Why was the crowd cheering? (Call on a student. Idea: *Because the kick was good.*)

Just as Andrew looked up, the ball sailed between the upright poles.

1. Everybody, was the kick good? (Signal.) *Yes.*
1. How do you know? (Call on a student. Idea: *Because the ball sailed between the poles.*)
1. Who remembers how far he kicked the ball for the field goal? (Call on a student.) *[50 yards.]*

The kick was good. The Titans had scored three more points and had won the game. In two weeks, they would be in the championship game.

2. Everybody, would Andrew be as strong in two weeks as he is now? (Signal.) *No.*

The locker room was wild. Reporters and TV cameras were everywhere.

2. Why was everyone so excited? (Call on a student. Idea: *Because the Titans had just won.*)

There were lights and owners and coaches and players and a lot of shouting: "We're number one!"
"Tell me," a voice said. There were lights in Andrew's eyes. On the other side of the lights was the outline of a TV camera.

1. The person saying "tell me" was a reporter.

"Tell me how it feels to be in the championship game."

2. Everybody, who was the reporter talking to? (Signal.) *Andrew.*
2. Look at the picture. Touch the TV camera. ✓
2. Touch the reporter. ✓
2. How do you know that the other players in the picture are happy? (Call on a student. Ideas: *They're jumping up and down; they're smiling;* etc.)

"I feel great," Andrew said. "We have a great team, and we're going to win the championship."
"You'll be playing the Wildcats. Many experts think that they are the strongest team in the league."

2. Who thinks that the Wildcats are the strongest team? (Call on a student. Idea: *Many experts.*)

Andrew said, "They're a good team, but we beat them once this year already. We're going to try to beat them again."
"That was a great game you played today," the announcer said. "A lot of people were commenting on your speed. We had never seen you run

that fast before. In fact, we didn't know you had so much speed."

Andrew didn't know what to say. "I had a lot of help today. My teammates did a great job of blocking for me."

The yelling and smiling and cheering went on for nearly an hour. Then the players took showers, got dressed, and left. The last player in the locker room was Andrew. He sat in front of his locker and said goodbye to each player. Then, when the locker room was empty, Andrew grabbed the handle of his locker and squeezed it as hard as he could.

1. He was trying to find out something by doing that. What was he trying to find out? (Call on a student. Idea: *How strong he was.*)

He couldn't make a dent in the steel handle.

2. What does that tell you about Andrew's strength? (Call on a student. Idea: *He's losing his strength.*)

"Two weeks," Andrew said to himself, and he felt frightened. "If only I could keep my strength for two weeks."

1. Why did Andrew want to be strong two weeks from now? (Call on a student. Idea: *To win the championship game.*)

Of course, Andrew wanted to be a star and wanted to have people love him and think he was great. But as he sat there in that still locker room, with only the sound of dripping showers, he wanted the championship for his teammates.

1. Go back to the beginning of the story. Follow along while I read.
2. Everybody, did he want the championship for himself? (Signal.) *No.*
2. Read the rest of the story to yourself. Find out why Andrew thought he wouldn't be able to help the team win the championship. Raise your hand when you're done.

Andrew imagined how the Titans would look if they could win the championship. He imagined how they would feel. They would feel proud. And Andrew wanted them to feel proud. But he was beginning to think that he wouldn't be able to help them. His hands and feet were tingling. In only three weeks, his strength had faded from that of an elephant to that of a small horse. What would happen in two more weeks?

MORE NEXT TIME

2. (After all students have raised their hand:) Why didn't Andrew think he'd be able to help the team win the championship? (Call on a student. Idea: *Because his strength was fading.*)

EXERCISE 4

PAIRED PRACTICE

You're going to read aloud to your partner. Today the **B** members will read first. Then the **A** members will read from the star to the end of the story.
(Observe students and give feedback.)

End-of-Lesson Activities

INDEPENDENT WORK

Now finish your independent work for lesson 103. First do the worksheet. Raise your hand when you're finished.
(Observe students and give feedback.)

WORKCHECK

a. (Direct students to take out their marking pencils.)
- We're going to check your independent work. Remember, if you got an item wrong, make an **X** next to the item. Don't change any answers.
b. (For each item: Read the item. Call on a student to answer it. If the answer is wrong, say the correct answer. Refer to the Answer Key for the correct answers.)
c. Now use your marking pencil to fix up any items you got wrong. Remember, all mistakes must be fixed up before you hand in your independent work.

WRITING-SPELLING

(Present Writing-Spelling lesson 103 after completing Reading lesson 103. See Writing-Spelling Guide.)

LANGUAGE ARTS GUIDE

(Present Language Arts lesson 103 after completing Reading lesson 103. See Language Arts Guide.)

EXERCISE 1

READING WORDS

Column 1

a. **Find lesson 104 in your textbook.** ✓
- Touch column 1. ✓
- (Teacher reference:)

1. **squeals**	4. **hinges**
2. **received**	5. **signaled**
3. **ached**	

- All these words have endings.
b. Word 1. What word? (Signal.) *Squeals.*
- (Repeat for words 2–5.)
c. (Repeat step b until firm.)

Column 2

d. Find column 2. ✓
- (Teacher reference:)

1. **shame**	4. **honest**
2. **shamed**	5. **television**
3. **ashamed**	6. **breakfast**

e. Word 1. What word? (Signal.) *Shame.*
- Word 2. What word? (Signal.) *Shamed.*
f. Word 3. What word? (Signal.) *Ashamed.*
- When you feel **ashamed,** you feel that you've done something bad. Here's another way of saying **She felt she had done something bad: She felt ashamed.**
g. Your turn. What's another way of saying **She felt she had done something bad?** (Signal.) *She felt ashamed.*
- (Repeat step g until firm.)
h. Word 4. What word? (Signal.) *Honest.*
- Another way of saying **I'm telling the truth** is: **Honest.** Here's another way of saying **I'm telling the truth; it's cold: Honest, it's cold.**
i. Your turn. What's another way of saying **I'm telling the truth; it's cold.** (Signal.) *Honest, it's cold.*
- (Repeat step i until firm.)
j. What's another way of saying **I'm telling the truth; you're pretty?** (Signal.) *Honest, you're pretty.*
- What's another way of saying **I'm telling the truth; I can't eat any more?** (Signal.) *Honest, I can't eat any more.*
k. Word 5. What word? (Signal.) *Television.*
- Word 6. What word? (Signal.) *Breakfast.*
l. Let's read those words again.
- Word 1. What word? (Signal.) *Shame.*
- (Repeat for words 2–6.)
m. (Repeat step l until firm.)

Column 3

n. Find column 3. ✓
- (Teacher reference:)

1. **let somebody down**	4. **signal**
2. **harm**	5. **grocery**
3. **rise**	6. **unusual**

o. Number 1. What words? (Signal.) *Let somebody down.*
- When you **let somebody down,** that person thinks you will help and you don't help.
- Everybody, what are you doing to people when they think you will help and you don't? (Signal.) *Letting them down.*
p. Word 2. What word? (Signal.) *Harm.*
- **Harm** is another word for **hurt.** Here's another way of saying **Smoking will hurt you: Smoking will harm you.**
q. Your turn. What's another way of saying **Smoking will hurt you?** (Signal.) *Smoking will harm you.*
- (Repeat step q until firm.)
r. What's another way of saying **The fire did not hurt the tree?** (Signal.) *The fire did not harm the tree.*
s. Word 3. What word? (Signal.) *Rise.*
- **Rise** is another word for **moves up.** Here's another way of saying **Heat moves up: Heat rises.**
t. Your turn. What's another way of saying **Heat moves up?** (Signal.) *Heat rises.*
- (Repeat step t until firm.)
u. What's another way of saying **The sun moves up in the east?** (Signal.) *The sun rises in the east.*
v. Word 4. What word? (Signal.) *Signal.*
- (Repeat for words 5 and 6.)

w. Let's read those words again.
- Number 1. What words? (Signal.) *Let somebody down.*
x. Word 2. What word? (Signal.) *Harm.*
- (Repeat for: **3. rise, 4. signal, 5. grocery, 6. unusual.**)
y. (Repeat steps w and x until firm.)

Individual Turns

(For columns 1–3: Call on individual students, each to read one to three words.)

EXERCISE 2

STORY READING

a. Find part B in your textbook. ✓
- The error limit for this story is 13. Read carefully.
b. Everybody, touch the title. ✓
- (Call on a student to read the title.) *[Andrew Leaves the Team.]*
- Everybody, what's the title? (Signal.) *Andrew Leaves the Team.*
c. (Call on individual students to read the story, each student reading two or three sentences at a time. Ask questions marked **1.**)

> - (Correct errors: Tell the word. Direct the student to reread the sentence.)
> - (If the group makes more than 13 errors, direct the students to reread the story.)

d. (After the group has read the selection making no more than 13 errors, read the story to the students and ask questions marked **2.**)

Andrew Leaves the Team

Andrew's super strength had faded completely.

1. Raise your hand if you think Andrew will be able to help the Titans.
2. Everybody, if his strength faded completely, was he stronger now than he was when he was a bank teller? (Signal.) *No.*

It was now a week before the championship. "Denny," he told the coach, "I can't play in the championship game."

1. How do you think Denny is going to feel about this? (Call on a student. Idea: *Not very good.*)

Denny was standing on the sideline with a whistle in his mouth when Andrew made this announcement. Denny almost swallowed the whistle.

2. Why? (Call on a student. Idea: *He was so surprised.*)

Denny coughed and stared at Andrew with big eyes. "You can't what?"
"I can't play," Andrew explained. "I couldn't do the team any good."

2. Why does he think he couldn't do the team any good? (Call on a student. Idea: *Because he isn't as strong as he used to be.*)

"Of course you can do us good. We need you. I mean, you've been the star of this team ever since you came to us. What's . . . "
Andrew shook his head. "I lost my strength," Andrew said. "I can't kick and I can't run. I won't do you any good."
"Maybe you need to rest for a couple of days," Denny said. "Why don't you take it easy for a few days. We've got time. Your strength will come back. You'll be just as good as you ever were."

2. Does Denny **know** that Andrew's strength will come back or is he just saying what he wants to believe? (Call on a student. Student preference.)

"No, Coach," Andrew said. "I'm through. I can't play." Andrew shook his head. He tried to say, "I want to thank you for letting me play with the Titans," but his voice wouldn't work.

1. Why wouldn't it work? (Call on a student. Idea: *Because he felt so sad.*)

His voice came out like a little squeak. He shook his head, looked down, took a deep breath, and said, "Good luck." Then he ran off the field to the locker room.

2. How does he feel? (Call on a student. Ideas: *Awful; sad; sorry.*)

Within a couple of minutes, most of the players were crowding around Andrew. "You can't leave us now," Mean George said. "You are a part of this team. We play, you play."

"I'd like to play," Andrew said, looking down. "But if I'm out there, I won't help you. I'll hurt you. I've got no strength. I'm . . . "

"Are you hurt?" one of the players asked.

"I can't explain," Andrew said. "But honest, I've got no more strength."

"Hey," George said to the other players. "Let Andy alone. Just get out of here. He'll be all right."

The other players left the locker room. Mean George slapped Andrew Dexter on the back. It hurt.

2. Everybody, who did it hurt? (Signal.) *Andrew.*
2. Would it have hurt Handy Andy? (Signal.) *No.*

"You just take it easy, Andy," he said. "Everything is going to be all right."

Outside the park four teenagers were waiting for Andrew. He signed their books. One of them said, "The Titans are going to kill the Wildcats next Sunday, right Andy?"

"They're going to play as hard as they can," Andrew said.

2. Everybody, did Andrew tell the truth? (Signal.) *Yes.*
2. Did he say that the Titans would **win?** (Signal.) *No.*

But when Sunday came around, Andrew decided not to go to the ball park. He felt ashamed.

1. Why was he ashamed? (Call on a student. Ideas: *Because he couldn't play anymore; he had no strength.*)

He didn't want to let the Titans down, but he knew that he couldn't help them.

2. Everybody, would he help them if he tried to play? (Signal.) *No.*

He had planned to watch the game on TV. He felt sick. He hadn't slept well the night before. He imagined the faces of the players and the coaches when he didn't show up.

2. How do you think those faces would look? (Call on a student. Idea: *Sad.*)

He imagined how they would feel after coming so close to winning the championship.

2. Everybody, did Andrew think they would **win** the championship or **just come close?** (Signal.) *Just come close.*

Andrew wanted to see them cheer and shout and hold up their fists as they yelled, "We're number one." But in his mind he could see them walking to the locker room after the game with their heads down.

2. What happened in that game? (Call on a student. Idea: *They lost.*)

He saw the tears on their faces. He saw the sadness in the faces of the crowd.

2. Everybody, did Andrew really see these things? (Signal.) *No.*

Andrew ate breakfast.

2. Everybody, where is Andrew? (Signal.) *At home.*

The phone rang three times but he didn't answer it. The doorbell rang and rang, but he didn't answer the door.

2. Who do you think was trying to find Andrew? (Call on a student. Ideas: *His teammates; Denny Brock.*)

He sat there trying to eat his eggs and toast. He wasn't hungry, and eating the toast was like eating paper. He couldn't seem to swallow.

At last he gave up and turned on his old television set. Nothing happened. He examined the set, but everything seemed to be all right. Then he thought that the wall plug might not be in right. He wiggled the plug from side to side. The electric cord that went from the plug to the television set was worn out.

1. Go back to the beginning of the story. Follow along while I read.
2. Everybody, look at the picture. What is Andrew doing in this picture? (Call on a student. Idea: *Putting the plug in the wall socket.*)
2. Everybody, touch the wall plug. ✓
2. Touch the cord that runs from the television to the wall. ✓
2. The part of that cord that is worn out is right next to Andrew's fingers.
2. Read the rest of the story to yourself. Find out what happened to Andrew when he wiggled the plug. Raise your hand when you're done.

When Andrew moved the plug from side to side, his finger touched the bare metal inside the electric cord. When his finger touched the bare metal, Andrew received a terrible electric shock. It knocked him over and almost knocked him out. His teeth ached because he had bitten down so hard from the shock. His arm felt as if somebody had hit it with a hammer. And his fingers tingled. And his feet tingled. And his legs tingled.
MORE NEXT TIME

2. (After all students have raised their hand:) What happened to Andrew when he wiggled the plug? (Call on a student. Idea: *He got a bad shock.*)

2. How did Andrew's fingers and feet feel? (Call on a student. Idea: *They tingled.*)
2. When did he first have tingling feelings? (Call on a student. Idea: *At Magnetic Research Company.*)
2. Who thinks Andrew will be able to help the Titans now? (Students should indicate "yes.")
2. Remember, this story about Andrew is make-believe. Don't play with electric sockets to try to be like Andrew.

EXERCISE 3

PAIRED PRACTICE

You're going to read aloud to your partner. Today the **A** members will read first. Then the **B** members will read from the star to the end of the story.
(Observe students and give feedback.)

End-of-Lesson Activities

INDEPENDENT WORK

Now finish your independent work for lesson 104. First do the worksheet. Raise your hand when you're finished.
(Observe students and give feedback.)

WORKCHECK

a. (Direct students to take out their marking pencils.)
• We're going to check your independent work. Remember, if you got an item wrong, make an **X** next to the item. Don't change any answers.
b. (For each item: Read the item. Call on a student to answer it. If the answer is wrong, say the correct answer. Refer to the Answer Key for the correct answers.)
c. Now use your marking pencil to fix up any items you got wrong. Remember, all mistakes must be fixed up before you hand in your independent work.

Note: For lesson 105, each student will need a copy of the thermometer chart for lessons 105–145.

WRITING-SPELLING

(Present Writing-Spelling lesson 104 after completing Reading lesson 104. See Writing-Spelling Guide.)

LANGUAGE ARTS GUIDE

(Present Language Arts lesson 104 after completing Reading lesson 104. See Language Arts Guide.)

Lesson 105

Materials: Each student will need their new thermometer chart for exercise 4.

READING WORDS

Column 1

a. **Find lesson 105 in your textbook.** ✓
- Touch column 1. ✓
- (Teacher reference:)

1. grocery	4. heavy
2. signaled	5. heavier
3. hinges	6. coast

b. Word 1. What word? (Signal.) *Grocery.*
- (Repeat for words 2–6.)
c. (Repeat step b until firm.)

Column 2

d. Find column 2. ✓
- (Teacher reference:)

1. remains	4. squeals
2. loss	5. rise
3. harm	6. groan

e. Word 1. What word? (Signal.)
Remains.
- Another way of saying **It stays the same** is: **It remains the same.** Here's another way of saying **The score stayed the same: The score remained the same.**
f. Your turn. What's another way of saying **The score stayed the same?** (Signal.)
The score remained the same.
- (Repeat step f until firm.)
g. What's another way of saying **The boys stayed in the same place?** (Signal.)
The boys remained in the same place.
h. Word 2. What word? (Signal.) *Loss.*
- When a ball carrier goes the **right** way in football, he makes a **gain.** When he gets tackled **before** he can make a gain, he makes a **loss.**
- Everybody, what does a ball carrier make if he gets tackled before he can make a gain? (Signal.) *A loss.*

i. Word 3. What word? (Signal.) *Harm.*
- (Repeat for words 4–6.)
j. Let's read those words again.
- Word 1. What word? (Signal.)
Remains.
- (Repeat for words 2–6.)
k. (Repeat step j until firm.)

Individual Turns

(For columns 1 and 2: Call on individual students, each to read one to three words per turn.)

STORY READING

a. Find part B in your textbook. ✓
- The error limit for this story is 14. Read carefully.
b. Everybody, touch the title. ✓
- (Call on a student to read the title.) *[The Championship Game.]*
- Everybody, what's the title? (Signal.) *The Championship Game.*
c. (Call on individual students to read the story, each student reading two or three sentences at a time. Ask questions marked 1.)

- (Correct errors: Tell the word. Direct the student to reread the sentence.)
- (If the group makes more than 14 errors, direct the students to reread the story.)

d. (After the group has read the selection making no more than 14 errors, read the story to the students and ask questions marked 2.)

The Championship Game

Andrew had just received a terrible electric shock.

2. How did he get that shock? (Call on a student. Idea: *His fingers touched the bare metal inside an electric cord.*)

His arm and his neck hurt. But he could tell by the tingling feeling in his feet and hands that he had changed.

1. How do you think he had changed? (Call on a student. Idea: *He got stronger.*)

He was strong again. But he couldn't tell how strong. Was he as strong as an elephant again, or as strong as a small horse? Andrew grabbed the doorknob and squeezed it as hard as he could. He did not dent it.

1. Everybody, was he as strong as an elephant? (Signal.) *No.*

Andrew pulled the door without turning the knob. He tore the door off the hinges.

1. How strong do you think he was? (Call on individual students. Ideas: *Very strong; as strong as a very strong man.*)

He was strong all right. He was about as strong as a super strong man.
Andy said to himself, "I might not be as strong as I was, but I'm strong enough to help the Titans." He grabbed his jacket and ran from the place he lived. There were many cars on the street. He thought, "I can probably run to the ball park as fast as I could go in a car."

2. A car goes faster than somebody can run, but what would slow a car down in a city? (Call on a student. Idea: *Traffic.*)

So Andy ran.
Nearly everybody in the city could recognize Andy. They had seen pictures of him on TV. There were pictures of him in the windows of grocery stores. People wore large buttons with Andy's picture on them. As Andy ran down the streets toward the ball park, kids of all ages ran along with him. There were big kids and little kids. At first, about twenty kids ran with him. Then the number continued to grow until hundreds of kids followed Andy on the way to the ball park.

2. Everybody, close your eyes and get a picture of that. Are they running fast? (Signal.) *Yes.*

2. How do you think they feel? (Call on a student. Ideas: *Excited, happy.*)

Crowds gathered along the streets. They cheered. "Andy's going to play," they shouted. Earlier that week, TV news stories had told that perhaps Andy would not play in the championship.

2. What had these stories told? (Call on a student. Idea: *That perhaps Andy wouldn't play in the championship.*)

The reporters had said that Andy was having some sort of problem and might not play. But when the people saw him running toward the ball park, they knew that he was going to play. "Hooray for Handy Andy," they yelled.
By the time Andy reached the ball park, he was exhausted.

2. Do you think he'll have enough strength to play? (Call on a student. Idea: *Yes.*)

He turned around and waved to the boys and girls who had been running with him. He caught his breath and yelled, "We're going to win." They cheered.
Andy ran to the locker room. All the members of the team were on the field. The game had started. Andy could hear the thunder of the crowd.

2. What does that mean, the thunder of the crowd? (Call on a student. Idea: *The crowd was cheering and making a lot of noise.*)

The old man who worked in the locker room said to Andy, "It looks serious. The Wildcats have already scored a touchdown."

2. Everybody, which team was ahead? (Signal.) *The Wildcats.*

Andy struggled into his uniform. He ran out of the locker room and into the ball park. As soon as the fans saw him, they let out a great roar. Andy's muscles were sore from running. He was out of breath. But he was very glad to be on the field.

He told himself, "I'm fast and I'm strong. I'll just use my speed and my strength as well as I can."

The coach signaled Andy to kick a field goal. The announcer's voice came over the loudspeakers. "Now playing for the Titans, Handy Andy Dexter."

1. Let's hear you make that announcement just the way the announcer said it. (Call on a student. Student should read the announcement in an excited voice.)

The crowd went wild. Fans jumped up and down and beat each other on the back. They squealed and shouted and whistled until they almost lost their voices.

Andrew huddled with the other players. The sound of the crowd was so loud that he could hardly hear what they said. Mean George smiled and said, "When I play, you play, right?"

"Right," Andy said.

1. Andrew is part of the team again.

Andy went back as if he was going to kick the ball.

1. Do you think he'll kick? (Call on a student. Student preference.)
2. Everybody, who's ahead in this game? (Signal.) *The Wildcats.*

The ball came to him and he started to run. He didn't fool anybody on the Wildcat team. They charged at him and caught him before he could gain anything.

2. Everybody, did he get any closer to the goal line? (Signal.) *No.*
2. What happened? (Call on a student. Idea: *The Wildcats charged and caught him.*)

First, two Wildcats hit him. Then a third charged into him, helmet first. That was Smiling Sam. His helmet drove right into Andy's ribs.

2. Everybody, show me where Smiling Sam's helmet would hit you if you were Andy. ✓
2. How do you think that felt? (Call on a student. Idea: *It hurt.*)

Andy went down and the crowd groaned. Smiling Sam smiled.

2. Everybody, what kind of smile was that? (Signal.) *A mean smile.*

Then Smiling Sam said, "Hey, little man, you're not going anywhere today except down."

1. Say that the way Smiling Sam said it. (Call on a student. Student should read in a mean voice.)

Andy hurt. The Wildcats now had the ball. They moved down the field and scored. They were ahead 14 to 0.

1. Go back to the beginning of the story. Follow along while I read.
2. Everybody, how many times had the Wildcats scored in this game? (Signal.) *Two.*
2. Read the rest of the story to yourself. Find out how the Titans planned to score a touchdown. Raise your hand when you're done.

The Titans received the ball and moved up the field. But the Wildcats stopped them. Andy came out to kick the ball. The fans began to clap and stamp their feet.

Andy went into the huddle. "They think I'm going to kick the ball or run with it," Andy said. "I think we can fool them if I throw the ball. I don't think the Wildcats will be ready for a pass."

"Let's try a pass," the other Titans said.

Andy dropped back as if he was going to kick. The ball came to him. The Wildcats charged toward him. Andy dropped the ball.
MORE NEXT TIME

2. (After all students have raised their hand:) I'll name some events. You tell me whether each event happened in the part you read to yourself.

2. The Titans scored a touchdown after they received the ball. Everybody, did that happen? (Signal.) *No.*

2. Mean George had a plan for fooling the Titans. Did that happen? (Signal.) *No.*

2. The fans clapped and stamped their feet when Smiling Sam left the field. Did that happen? (Signal.) *No.*

2. Andrew dropped the ball. Did that happen? (Signal.) *Yes.*

2. What plan did the Titans have to score a touchdown? (Call on a student. Idea: *Andrew would throw the ball.*)

2. Why did Andrew think that plan would fool the Wildcats? (Call on a student. Idea: *Because the Wildcats think Andrew will kick the ball or run with it; because the Wildcats won't be ready for a pass.*)

2. What happened at the end of the story that makes you think their plan may not work? (Call on a student. Idea: *Andrew dropped the ball.*)

> *Note:* There is a reading checkout in this lesson; therefore, there is no paired practice.

EXERCISE 3
READING CHECKOUTS

a. Today is a reading-checkout day. While you're doing your independent work, I'm going to call on you one at a time to read part of the story from lesson 104. When I call you to come and do your checkout, bring your new thermometer chart.

• Remember, you pass the checkout by reading the passage in less than a minute without making more than 2 mistakes. And when you pass the checkout, you'll color the space for lesson 105 on your new thermometer chart.

b. (Call on individual students to read the portion of story 104 marked with ❀.)

• (Time the student. Note words that are missed and total number of words read.)

• (Teacher reference:)

❀ **Andrew's super strength had faded completely. It was now a week before the championship. "Denny," he told the coach, "I can't play in the championship game."**

Denny was standing on the sideline with a whistle in his mouth when Andrew made this announcement. Denny almost swallowed the whistle. Denny coughed [50] and stared at Andrew with big eyes. "You can't what?"

"I can't play," Andrew explained. "I couldn't do the team any good."

"Of course you [75] can do us good. We need you. I mean, you've been the star of this team ever since you came to us. What's . . ."

Andrew shook ❀ [100] his head.

• (If the student reads the passage in one minute or less and makes no more than 2 errors, direct the student to color in the space for lesson 105 on the new thermometer chart.)

• (If the student makes any mistakes, point to each word that was misread and identify it.)

• (If the student does not meet the time-error criterion for the passage, direct the student to practice reading the story with the assigned partner.)

End-of-Lesson Activities

INDEPENDENT WORK

Now finish your independent work for lesson 105. Raise your hand when you're finished. (Observe students and give feedback.)

WORKCHECK

a. (Direct students to take out their marking pencils.)

• We're going to check your independent work. Remember, if you got an item wrong, make an **X** next to the item. Don't change any answers.

b. (For each item: Read the item. Call on a student to answer it. If the answer is wrong, say the correct answer. Refer to the Answer Key for the correct answers.)

c. Now use your marking pencil to fix up any items you got wrong. Remember, all mistakes must be fixed up before you hand in your independent work.

WRITING-SPELLING

(Present Writing-Spelling lesson 105 after completing Reading lesson 105. See Writing-Spelling Guide.)

LANGUAGE ARTS GUIDE

(Present Language Arts lesson 105 after completing Reading lesson 105. See Language Arts Guide.)

Lessons 106–110 • Planning Page

	Lesson 106	Lesson 107	Lesson 108	Lesson 109	Lesson 110
Lesson Events	Reading Words Story Reading Paired Practice Guide Words Independent Work Workcheck Writing-Spelling	**Vocabulary Sentence** Reading Words Vocabulary Review Comprehension Passage Story Reading Paired Practice Guide Words Independent Work Workcheck Writing-Spelling	Vocabulary Review Reading Words Comprehension Passage Story Reading Paired Practice Guide Words Independent Work Workcheck Writing-Spelling	Vocabulary Review Reading Words Review Passage Story Reading Paired Practice Dictionary Skills Independent Work Workcheck Writing-Spelling	Fact Game Reading Checkouts Test Marking the Test Test Remedies Literature Lesson
Vocabulary Sentence		#26: Their <u>amazing</u> <u>effort</u> surprised the <u>neighbors</u>.	#26: Their <u>amazing</u> <u>effort</u> surprised the <u>neighbors</u>.	sentence #24 sentence #25 sentence #26	
Reading Words: Word Types	modeled words words with endings mixed words	modeled words compound words words with endings mixed words	multi-syllable words words that begin with **w**	words about numbers words with endings mixed words	
New Vocabulary	treasures shallow before long spices	confusion rich sunken ship	relative		
Comprehension Passages		*Places You Have Learned About*	*Words That Talk*		
Story	*The End of the Game*	*Looking for Treasures*	*Hohoboho*	*The Words That Sat in the Back Rows*	
Skill Items	Guide Words	Guide Words	Guide Words Compare	Vocabulary Sentence Deductions	Test: Guide words; Vocabulary Sentences #25, 26
Special Materials	*Materials for project	Globe		Children's dictionaries (same edition for all students)	Thermometer charts, dice, Fact Game 110, Fact Game Answer Key, scorecard sheets, **materials for literature project
Special Projects/ Activities	Project after lesson 106				

* Pictures of and information sources for football.

** Literature anthology; blackline master 11A, 11B; lined paper; ruler; red marker.

Lesson 106

EXERCISE 1

READING WORDS

Column 1
a. **Find lesson 106 in your textbook.** ✓
- Touch column 1. ✓
- (Teacher reference:)

1. treasure	3. decision
2. difficult	4. shallow

b. Word 1 is **treasure.** What word? (Signal.) *Treasure.*
- Spell **treasure.** Get ready. (Tap for each letter.) *T-R-E-A-S-U-R-E.*
- **Treasures** are things that are worth a lot of money. Everybody, what do we call things that are worth a lot of money? (Signal.) *Treasures.*
c. Word 2 is **difficult.** What word? (Signal.) *Difficult.*
- Spell **difficult.** Get ready. (Tap for each letter.) *D-I-F-F-I-C-U-L-T.*
d. Word 3. What word? (Signal.) *Decision.*
- Spell **decision.** Get ready. (Tap for each letter.) *D-E-C-I-S-I-O-N.*
e. Word 4. What word? (Signal.) *Shallow.*
- Spell **shallow.** Get ready. (Tap for each letter.) *S-H-A-L-L-O-W.*
- **Shallow** is the opposite of **deep.** Everybody, what's the opposite of **a deep river?** (Signal.) *A shallow river.*
- What's the opposite of **a deep well?** (Signal.) *A shallow well.*
f. Let's read those words again, the fast way.
- Word 1. What word? (Signal.) *Treasure.*
- (Repeat for words 2–4.)
g. (Repeat step f until firm.)

Column 2
h. Find column 2. ✓
- (Teacher reference:)

1. <u>eighty</u>	4. <u>sunken</u>
2. <u>guarded</u>	5. <u>diver</u>
3. <u>remains</u>	

- All of these words have endings.
i. Word 1. What's the underlined part? (Signal.) *eight.*
- What's the whole word? (Signal.) *Eighty.*
j. Word 2. What's the underlined part? (Signal.) *guard.*
- What's the whole word? (Signal.) *Guarded.*
k. Word 3. What's the underlined part? (Signal.) *remain.*
- What's the whole word? (Signal.) *Remains.*
l. Word 4. What's the underlined part? (Signal.) *sunk.*
- What's the whole word? (Signal.) *Sunken.*
m. Word 5. What's the underlined part? (Signal.) *dive.*
- What's the whole word? (Signal.) *Diver.*
n. Let's read those words again, the fast way.
- Word 1. What word? (Signal.) *Eighty.*
- (Repeat for words 2–5.)
o. (Repeat step n until firm.)

Column 3
p. Find column 3. ✓
- (Teacher reference:)

1. **before long**	4. **motioned**
2. **careful**	5. **bouncing**
3. **carefully**	

q. Number 1. What words? (Signal.) *Before long.*
- If something happens **very soon,** we say it happens **before long.** Here's another way of saying **It will rain soon: It will rain before long.**
r. Your turn. What's another way of saying **It will rain soon?** (Signal.) *It will rain before long.*
- (Repeat step r until firm.)
s. What's another way of saying **She will eat soon?** (Signal.) *She will eat before long.*
t. Word 2. What word? (Signal.) *Careful.*
- (Repeat for words 3–5.)

u. Let's read those words again.
- Number 1. What words? (Signal.)
  Before long.
v. Word 2. What word? (Signal.) *Careful.*
- (Repeat for: **3. carefully, 4. motioned, 5. bouncing.**)
w. (Repeat steps u and v until firm.)

Column 4

x. Find column 4. ✓
- (Teacher reference:)

1. **spices**	4. **ashamed**
2. **loss**	5. **groan**
3. **receive**	

y. Word 1. What word? (Signal.) *Spices.*
- **Spices** are things that you add to food to give it a special flavor. Pepper is a spice. Who can name other spices? (Call on individual students. Ideas: *Cinnamon, cloves, oregano,* etc.)
z. Word 2. What word? (Signal.) *Loss.*
- (Repeat for words 3–5.)
a. Let's read those words again.
- Word 1. What word? (Signal.) *Spices.*
- (Repeat for words 2–5.)
b. (Repeat step a until firm.)

Individual Turns

(For columns 1–4: Call on individual students, each to read one to three words per turn.)

EXERCISE 2

STORY READING

a. Find part B in your textbook. ✓
- The error limit for this story is 16. Read carefully.
b. Everybody, touch the title. ✓
- (Call on a student to read the title.) *[The End of the Game.]*
- Everybody, what's the title? (Signal.) *The End of the Game.*
c. (Call on individual students to read the story, each student reading two or three sentences at a time. Ask questions marked **1.**)

- (Correct errors: Tell the word. Direct the student to reread the sentence.)
- (If the group makes more than 16 errors, direct the students to reread the story.)

d. (After the group has read the selection making no more than 16 errors, read the story to the students and ask questions marked **2.**)

The End of the Game

The ball was on the ground, bouncing around in front of Andy.

2. What had just happened? (Call on a student. Idea: *Andrew had dropped the ball.*)

The Wildcats were charging toward him. There was Smiling Sam, with his helmet down and yelling at Andy, "I got you now."
   Andy made himself think. "Use your speed," he told himself. He picked up the ball and then began to run back. The Wildcats couldn't catch him because he was faster than they were. He ran back farther and farther. Then he stopped. For a moment, the crowd was silent.

1. Why was the crowd silent? (Call on a student. Idea: *They didn't know what he was going to do.*)

Andy looked down the field, stepped forward, and passed the ball. It was a beautiful pass.
   The ball sailed through the air, all the way down the field. The fans were standing. The Wildcats stopped and turned around to watch the ball.
   All the Titans except one turned around to watch the ball. That Titan ran. He ran toward the goal. And as he ran, he looked over his shoulder. The ball looked as if it was going to go too far.
   But the player made a leap, caught the ball, and slid over the goal line. Touchdown. Andy had just thrown an eighty-yard pass. The Wildcat players were shaking their heads. Andy was smiling. But Smiling Sam wasn't. "You got lucky," he told Andy, and made a mean face.

2. Everybody, look at the picture.
2. Touch Andy. ✓
2. Touch the player who is going to catch the ball. ✓
2. Show me how that player is looking over his shoulder. ✓
2. What are the other players watching? (Signal.) *The ball.*
2. I'll read that part again. Close your eyes and get a picture of what's happening.

All the Titans except one turned around to watch the ball. That Titan ran. He ran toward the goal. And as he ran, he looked over his shoulder. The ball looked as if it was going to go too far.

But the player made a leap, caught the ball, and slid over the goal line. Touchdown. Andy had just thrown an eighty-yard pass. The Wildcat players were shaking their heads. Andy was smiling. But Smiling Sam wasn't. "You got lucky," he told Andy, and made a mean face.

The Wildcats did not score another touchdown. The Titan players played like champions. They stopped the Wildcats again and again. Late in the game, the Titans scored a field goal. They now had 10 points. The Wildcats had 14 points.

2. Everybody, who is ahead? (Signal.) *The Wildcats.*

But time was running out.

2. What does that mean? (Call on a student. Idea: *The game is going to be over soon.*)

The Wildcats held the ball and moved slowly down the field. They tried to kick a field goal but a Titan player blocked the kick. The score remained at 14 to 10.

2. Everybody, if the score remained at 14 to 10, did the score change? (Signal.) *No.*
2. Why didn't it change when the Wildcats tried to kick a field goal? (Call on a student. Ideas: *A Titan blocked the kick; they didn't make it.*)

But now there was less than two minutes left in the game. "Let me go in and try to pass again," Andy said to the coach.

Denny looked at Andy. "Okay, it's your game. Go and win it."

2. Everybody, does Denny think that Andy can win the game? (Signal.) *Yes.*
2. What did he say to let you know he feels that way? (Call on a student. Idea: *He told Andrew to go and win the game.*)

Andy ran onto the field. He ran into the huddle. "Let's try another pass," Andy said. Andy dropped back as if he was going to kick the ball. The ball came to him, and he looked for a Titan player to catch the ball. All the players were being guarded by Wildcats.

2. How many Titans were free to catch the ball? (Call on a student. Idea: *None.*)
2. Why weren't any of them free? (Call on a student. Idea: *The Wildcats were guarding them.*)

Andy had to try to run with the ball. "I got you now," a mean voice said.

1. Everybody, whose voice is that? (Signal.) *Smiling Sam's.*

CRACK—the sound of a helmet driving into Andy's shoulder pad. He went down for a loss of nearly ten yards. The crowd groaned.

2. What happened on that play? (Call on a student. Idea: *Andrew got tackled by Sam and lost 10 yards.*)

One of the coaches motioned for the team to try a running play.

2. What's the team going to do on the next play? (Call on a student. Idea: *Try to run with the ball.*)

The Titans lined up quickly. Less than a minute remained in the game. The ball went to one of the players who tried to run wide.

1. When you run wide, you run to one side first.

The Wildcats were waiting. CRACK.

2. What made that "crack" sound? (Call on a student. Idea: *The player got tackled.*)

Another loss. The clock continued to move.
   Denny motioned from the sideline. He wanted the team to try another pass. Andy went back. He received the ball. At almost the same time, three Wildcats hit him. Another loss.

2. Everybody, did the Titans gain on that play? (Signal.) *No.*
2. What happened? (Call on a student. Idea: *They had another loss.*)

The team huddled for the last time. "This is it," Mean George said. "Let's make it a good one."

2. What does he mean by that? (Call on a student. Idea: *This is their last chance to win the game.*)

Andy went back. The crowd was not yelling and whooping anymore. In fact, lots of fans were leaving the stands.

1. Why? (Call on a student. Ideas: *They thought the Titans had lost; they thought the game was over.*)

The fans thought that the Titans had no chance.

2. What does that mean, they had no chance? (Call on a student. Idea: *They couldn't win.*)

The ball came to Andy. He ran back and stopped as if he was going to throw the ball. The Wildcats did not charge after him. They were waiting for the pass. So Andy made a decision: Run. And he ran.
   Andy put every bit of strength he had into every step. He ran toward the sideline. He outran every player except one.

2. Everybody, how many players were left for Andrew to get by? (Signal.) *One.*

Smiling Sam was charging toward him. "This is it," Andy told himself. He dropped his shoulder and met Sam's charge. Andy drove with his feet as hard as he could. CRACK.

1. What do you think happened? (Call on a student. Student preference.)
1. If Andrew is tackled, how many more plays will the Titans be able to run? (Call on a student. Idea: *None.*)

The people in the stands were standing. Those fans who had started to leave were coming back. They groaned as the football players hit.

2. Which players were those? (Call on a student. Idea: *Smiling Sam and Andy.*)

The fans saw Smiling Sam fly back. Andy managed to keep running, but he had been slowed down. Two Wildcat players were near him. He dodged one and ran over the other.

2. What do you do when you dodge a player? (Call on a student. Idea: *You run around him.*)
2. Everybody, how many did he dodge? (Signal.) *One.*
2. What did he do with the other player? (Call on a student. Idea: *Ran over him.*)

There was one more Wildcat that Andy had to outrun. Andy gave the run everything he had. And he did it. The crowd went wild. The Titans went wild. With only about 10 seconds left in the game, Andy had scored the winning touchdown!

2. How much time was left when Andrew scored the winning touchdown? (Call on a student. Idea: *About 10 seconds.*)

2. Everybody, close your eyes and get a picture of what happened. I'll read that part again.

> Andy put every bit of strength he had into every step. He ran toward the sideline. He outran every player except one. Smiling Sam was charging toward him. "This is it," Andy told himself. He dropped his shoulder and met Sam's charge. Andy drove with his feet as hard as he could. CRACK.
>
> The people in the stands were standing. Those fans who had started to leave were coming back. They groaned as the football players hit. The fans saw Smiling Sam fly back. Andy managed to keep running, but he had been slowed down. Two Wildcat players were near him. He dodged one and ran over the other. There was one more Wildcat that Andy had to outrun. Andy gave the run everything he had. And he did it. The crowd went wild. The Titans went wild. With only about 10 seconds left in the game, Andy had scored the winning touchdown!

2. Open your eyes. There are three dots after the last sentence I read. What does that mean? (Call on a student. Idea: *Part of the story is missing.*)

• • •

Andy quit playing for the Titans after the championship game.

2. Everybody, when did he quit? (Signal.) *After the championship game.*

And he never played football again. He lost his super strength. But the Titans gave him a job working with the coaches.

1. Go back to the beginning of the story. Follow along while I read.

2. What did he now do for a job? (Call on a student. Idea: *Worked with the coaches for the Titans.*)

2. Read the rest of the story to yourself. Find out what Andrew liked about his new life, even though he didn't have super strength. Raise your hand when you're done.

Andy didn't mind losing his strength because he had lived the greatest dream that anybody could have lived. And after that year, he didn't daydream as much. Once in a while he would daydream. But he kept his mind on his job because he really liked his job.

One more thing about Andy: If he goes for a walk, he doesn't walk alone. Before long, a group of kids walks with him. And when they go home, they tell their friends, "Today I was with the greatest football player in the world—Handy Andy."
THE END

2. (After all students have raised their hand:) Name something that Andrew liked about his new life. (Call on individual students. Ideas: *He liked his new job; kids walk with him; people remember him.*)

2. Why didn't Andrew daydream as much? (Call on a student. Ideas: *Because he liked his job; he kept his mind on his job.*)

2. Let me read that part to you. Imagine how Andrew felt.

> Andy didn't mind losing his strength because he had lived the greatest dream that anybody could have lived. And after that year, he didn't daydream as much. Once in a while he would daydream. But he kept his mind on his job because he really liked his job.
>
> One more thing about Andy: If he goes for a walk, he doesn't walk alone. Before long, a group of kids walks with him. And when they go home, they tell their friends, "Today I was with the greatest football player in the world—Handy Andy."
> **THE END**

PAIRED PRACTICE

You're going to read aloud to your partner. Today the **B** members will read first. Then the **A** members will read from the star to the end of the story.
(Observe students and give feedback.)

End-of-Lesson Activities

INDEPENDENT WORK

Now finish your independent work for lesson 106. First do the worksheet. Raise your hand when you're finished.
(Observe students and give feedback.)

WORKCHECK

a. (Direct students to take out their marking pencils.)

• We're going to check your independent work. Remember, if you got an item wrong, make an **X** next to the item. Don't change any answers.

b. (For each item: Read the item. Call on a student to answer it. If the answer is wrong, say the correct answer. Refer to the Answer Key for the correct answers.)

c. Now use your marking pencil to fix up any items you got wrong. Remember, all mistakes must be fixed up before you hand in your independent work.

Note: You will need a globe for lesson 107.

WRITING-SPELLING

(Present Writing-Spelling lesson 106 after completing Reading lesson 106. See Writing-Spelling Guide.)

LANGUAGE ARTS GUIDE

(Present Language Arts lesson 106 after completing Reading lesson 106. See Language Arts Guide.)

Special Project

Note: After completing lesson 106, do this special project with the students. You may do the project during another part of the school day.

Purpose: To make a display about football.

a. (For this class project, divide the class into four groups.)

Group 1 will locate pictures and information about the equipment that a football player wears.

Group 2 will locate pictures and information about the way players train and how injuries are treated.

Group 3 could identify a coach or expert who could talk to the class about the problems and joys of being a coach. Group 3 would also make up a list of questions to ask the speaker.

Group 4 could locate pictures and information about the playing field and football records (largest stadium, longest game, highest score, etc.)

b. (Students may make posters with the pictures and information they have gathered. They may also make a presentation to the rest of the class or to another class.)

Materials: You will need a globe for exercise 4.

READING WORDS

Column 1

a. Find lesson 107 in your textbook. ✓
* Touch column 1. ✓
* (Teacher reference:)

1. confusion	4. telephone
2. effort	5. Hohoboho
3. neighbor	

b. Word 1 is **confusion.** What word? (Signal.) *Confusion.*
* Spell **confusion.** Get ready. (Tap for each letter.) *C-O-N-F-U-S-I-O-N.*
* When things are very strange and mixed up, we say things are **thrown into confusion.** If somebody dropped dollar bills all over the playground, the playground would be thrown into confusion. If a tiger ran through this room, this room would be thrown into confusion.

c. Your turn. If a tiger ran through this room, what would happen to the room? (Signal.) *The room would be thrown into confusion.*
* (Repeat step c until firm.)

d. If an elephant walked into the school, what would happen to the school? (Signal.) *The school would be thrown into confusion.*

e. Word 2 is **effort.** What word? (Signal.) *Effort.*
* Spell **effort.** Get ready. (Tap for each letter.) *E-F-F-O-R-T.*

f. Word 3 is **neighbor.** What word? (Signal.) *Neighbor.*
* Spell **neighbor.** Get ready. (Tap for each letter.) *N-E-I-G-H-B-O-R.*

g. Word 4 is **telephone.** What word? (Signal.) *Telephone.*
* Spell **telephone.** Get ready. (Tap for each letter.) *T-E-L-E-P-H-O-N-E.*

h. Word 5 is **Hohoboho.** What word? (Signal.) *Hohoboho.*
* Hohoboho is the name of a make-believe place you're going to read about.

VOCABULARY

a. **Find page 342 in your textbook.** ✓
* Touch sentence 26. ✓
* This is a new vocabulary sentence. It says: Their amazing effort surprised the neighbors.
Everybody, read that sentence. Get ready. (Signal.) *Their amazing effort surprised the neighbors.*
* Close your eyes and say the sentence. Get ready. (Signal.) *Their amazing effort surprised the neighbors.*
* (Repeat until firm.)

b. Something that is **amazing** is very hard to believe. An amazing story is a story that is hard to believe. Everybody, what do we call an **experience** that is hard to believe? (Signal.) *An amazing experience.*
* What do we call a **fact** that is hard to believe? (Signal.) *An amazing fact.*

c. Something that takes a lot of strength takes a lot of **effort.**
* What's another way of saying **It didn't take much strength?** (Signal.) *It didn't take much effort.*
* What's another way of saying **That kind of work takes a lot of strength?** (Signal.) *That kind of work takes a lot of effort.*

d. **Neighbors** are people who live near you or sit near you. What do we call people who live near you? (Signal.) *Neighbors.*

e. Listen to the sentence again: Their amazing effort surprised the neighbors. Everybody, say the sentence. Get ready. (Signal.) *Their amazing effort surprised the neighbors.*

f. Everybody, what word tells about how much strength it needed? (Signal.) *Effort.*
* What word means that something is hard to believe? (Signal.) *Amazing.*
* What word names people who live near you? (Signal.) *Neighbors.*
* (Repeat step f until firm.)

i. Let's read those words again, the fast way.
- Word 1. What word? (Signal.) *Confusion.*
- (Repeat for: **2. effort, 3. neighbor, 4. telephone, 5. Hohoboho.**)

j. (Repeat step i until firm.)

Column 2

k. Find column 2. ✓
- (Teacher reference:)

1. <u>half</u>way	3. <u>earth</u>quake
2. <u>some</u>body	4. <u>flash</u>light

- All these words are compound words. The first part of each word is underlined.

l. Word 1. What's the underlined part? (Signal.) *half.*
- What's the whole word? (Signal.) *Halfway.*

m. Word 2. What's the underlined part? (Signal.) *some.*
- What's the whole word? (Signal.) *Somebody.*

n. Word 3. What's the underlined part? (Signal.) *earth.*
- What's the whole word? (Signal.) *Earthquake.*

o. Word 4. What's the underlined part? (Signal.) *flash.*
- What's the whole word? (Signal.) *Flashlight.*

p. Let's read those words again, the fast way.
- Word 1. What word? (Signal.) *Halfway.*
- (Repeat for words 2–4.)

q. (Repeat step p until firm.)

Column 3

r. Find column 3. ✓
- (Teacher reference:)

1. strangest	4. carefully
2. hardly	5. diving
3. divers	6. lucky

- All these words have endings.

s. Word 1. What word? (Signal.) *Strangest.*
- (Repeat for words 2–6.)

t. (Repeat step s until firm.)

Column 4

u. Find column 4. ✓
- (Teacher reference:)

1. sunken ship	4. shallow
2. treasures	5. difficult
3. electric	6. mummy

v. Number 1. What words? (Signal.) *Sunken ship.*
- A **sunken ship** is a ship at the bottom of the ocean. Everybody, what do we call a ship at the bottom of the ocean? (Signal.) *A sunken ship.*

w. Word 2. What word? (Signal.) *Treasures.*
- (Repeat for words 3–6.)

x. Let's read those words again.
- Number 1. What words? (Signal.) *Sunken ship.*

y. Word 2. What word? (Signal.) *Treasures.*
- (Repeat for words 3–6.)

z. (Repeat steps x and y until firm.)

Column 5

a. Find column 5. ✓
- (Teacher reference:)

1. rich	4. noisy
2. spices	5. noisier
3. noise	

b. Word 1. What word? (Signal.) *Rich.*
- If you have lots and lots of money, you are **rich.** Everybody, what do we call somebody who has lots and lots of money? (Signal.) *Rich.*

c. What's another way of saying **That man has lots and lots of money?** (Signal.) *That man is rich.*
- (Repeat step c until firm.)

d. Word 2. What word? (Signal.) *Spices.*
- (Repeat for words 3–5.)

e. Let's read those words again.
- Word 1. What word? (Signal.) *Rich.*
- (Repeat for words 2–5.)

f. (Repeat step e until firm.)

Column 6

g. Find column 6. ✓

• (Teacher reference:)

1. trace	4. worst
2. cabin	5. hooray
3. sharks	

h. Word 1. What word? (Signal.) *Trace.*
  • (Repeat for: **2. cabin, 3. sharks, 4. worst, 5. hooray.**)
i. (Repeat step h until firm.)

Individual Turns

(For columns 1–6: Call on individual students, each to read one to three words.)

EXERCISE 3

VOCABULARY REVIEW

a. Here's the new vocabulary sentence: Their amazing effort surprised the neighbors.
  • Everybody, say the sentence. Get ready. (Signal.) *Their amazing effort surprised the neighbors.*
  • (Repeat until firm.)
b. Everybody, what word names people who live near you? (Signal.) *Neighbors.*
  • What word tells about how much strength it needed? (Signal.) *Effort.*
  • What word means that something is hard to believe? (Signal.) *Amazing.*

EXERCISE 4

COMPREHENSION PASSAGE

Note: You will need a globe for step d.

a. Find part B in your textbook. ✓
  • You're going to read a story about looking for treasures. First you'll read the information passage. It reviews some facts you have learned.
b. Everybody, touch the title. ✓
  • (Call on a student to read the title.) *[Places You Have Learned About.]*
  • Everybody, what's the title? (Signal.) *Places You Have Learned About.*
c. (Call on individual students to read the passage, each student reading two or three sentences at a time. Ask the specified questions as the students read.)

Places You Have Learned About

In today's story, you're going to read about different places in the world. Make sure that you understand the facts you have learned about the world.
Touch A on map 1.

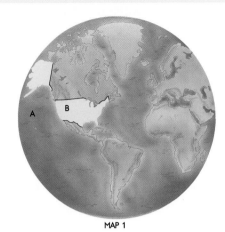

MAP 1

• Everybody, do it. ✓

What ocean is that?

• Everybody, name it. Get ready. (Signal.) *Pacific Ocean.*

Touch B.

• Everybody, do it. ✓

What country is that?

• Everybody, name it. Get ready. (Signal.) *United States.*

Name two cities in that country.

• Do it. (Call on a student. Ideas: *New York City, San Francisco, Chicago,* etc.)

Look at map 2. What is the name of country F?

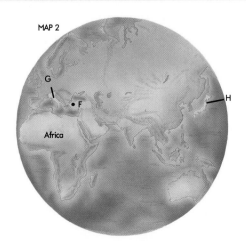

MAP 2

- Everybody, tell me the answer. Get ready. (Signal.) *Turkey.*

What happened there about 3 thousand years ago?

- What happened? (Call on a student. Idea: *The war between Greece and Troy.*)

What's the name of country G?

- Everybody, tell me the answer. Get ready. (Signal.) *Italy.*

What's the name of country H?

- Everybody, tell me the answer. Get ready. (Signal.) *Japan.*

Name two girls who went to that country.

- Do it. (Call on a student. Idea: *Linda and Kathy.*)

See if you can find these places on a globe of the world.
  - **The United States**
  - **Italy**
  - **Turkey**
  - **Japan**
  - **The Pacific Ocean**

d. I'll show you a globe. You see how many of the places you can find. (Call on individual students to find all of the places.)

EXERCISE 5

STORY READING

a. Find part C in your textbook. ✓
  - The error limit for this story is 13. Read carefully.
b. Everybody, touch the title. ✓
  - (Call on a student to read the title.) *[Looking for Treasures.]*
  - Everybody, what's the title? (Signal.) *Looking for Treasures.*
c. (Call on individual students to read the story, each student reading two or three sentences at a time. Ask questions marked **1.**)

- (Correct errors: Tell the word. Direct the student to reread the sentence.)
- (If the group makes more than 13 errors, direct the students to reread the story.)

d. (After the group has read the selection making no more than 13 errors, read the story to the students and ask questions marked **2.**)

Looking for Treasures

Things have changed a lot in the last two hundred years.

1. Everybody, what year is it now? (Signal.) (Accept appropriate response.)
1. What year was it 200 years ago? (Signal.) (Accept appropriate response.)

Two hundred years ago, people traveled from place to place by foot, by horse, or by water.

2. What are the three ways that people used? (Call on a student. Idea: *By foot, by horse, by water.*)
2. How do you go places by foot? (Call on a student. Idea: *You walk.*)
2. Two hundred years ago they had to row the boats or use sails. No boats had engines.
2. If you traveled by horse, you wouldn't always ride the horse. The horse might pull a wagon.

Two hundred years ago it took a long, long time to go from one place to another. With a good horse, you could travel 30 miles a day.

2. Everybody, how far could you travel in a day with a good horse? (Signal.) *30 miles.*

At that speed, it would take you about three months to go from New York to San Francisco.

2. Everybody, how long would it take to make that trip? (Signal.) *Three months.*
2. How far is it from New York to San Francisco? (Signal.) *25 hundred miles.*

If you fly a jet plane today, it takes far less time to make the same trip.

2. Everybody, how long does it take to go from New York to San Francisco in a jet? (Signal.) *Six hours.*

Ships went across the ocean two hundred years ago, but the ships were not ocean liners like the ones that Linda and Kathy were on.

The ships of two hundred years ago were sailing ships. They had large sails that caught the wind.

2. Everybody, touch the stern of the sailing ship. ✓
2. Now touch the arrow that shows the direction of the wind. ✓
2. The wind hits the sails. Point your finger to show which way the wind hits the sails. ✓
2. Point your finger to show which way the ship is moving. ✓

The faster ships went 6 miles per hour when a good wind was blowing.

2. Everybody, would they **always** go 6 miles per hour? (Signal.) *No.*
2. Why not? (Call on a student. Idea: *Because there wasn't always a good wind.*)

But the trip from San Francisco to Japan took over 30 days. That is a much longer time than the trip would take in an ocean liner.

2. Everybody, how long did the trip take on a sailing ship? (Signal.) *Over thirty days.*
2. Would it take **more time** or **less time** in a modern ocean liner? (Signal.) *Less time.*

The ships of two hundred years ago didn't have refrigerators or electric lights.

2. Why not? (Call on a student. Idea: *They weren't invented yet.*)

Rats and insects would often get into the food and ruin it.

Today, the trip from San Francisco to Japan takes only about 5 days, because the ships of today do not use sails. They have large engines. They can move 40 miles per hour.

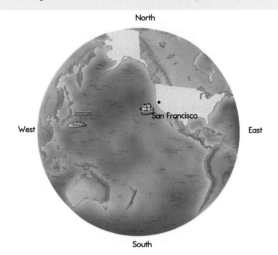

2. Why do the ships of today move faster? (Call on a student. Idea: *They use engines instead of sails.*)
2. Everybody, how long does the trip from San Francisco to Japan take in a modern ship? (Signal.) *Five days.*
2. Touch the map. It shows two ships that started from San Francisco at the same time. Everybody, in which direction did they go? (Signal.) *West.*
2. One of the ships is already in Japan. Which ship? (Call on a student. Idea: *The ocean liner.*)
2. How far did the old-time sailing ship get in the same amount of time? (Call on a student. Idea: *Not very far.*)

Two hundred years ago, not many ships went between Japan and San Francisco because the trip took so long. But many ships sailed around Italy and Turkey. Ships carried spices, cloth, and things made of gold and silver.

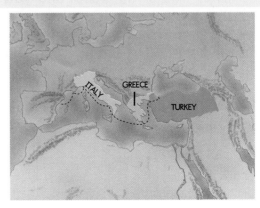

2. Everybody, touch the map of Italy and Turkey on the next page. ✓
2. The arrows show some of the routes that the ships used to take. Everybody, trace the route from Italy to Greece. ✓
2. Many ships have taken that route.

Sometimes, ships with great treasures would get caught in a storm. The sails would be torn from the ship. Waves would smash over the ship and it would sink. There are many sunken ships in the oceans around Italy and Turkey.

Divers have found some ships that were carrying great treasures. Can you imagine what it would be like to find such a ship? You dive for days and days in the blue water, looking for signs of a sunken ship, but you find nothing. The boat that you dive from moves slowly through the sea, trying to trace the path that the sunken ship took when it was on its way to Italy. Parts of the ocean are deep and parts are shallow. You hope that the ship is found in the shallow parts of the ocean, because it is very difficult to dive in the deep parts. Some parts are so deep that you could not go to the bottom without a very special diving outfit.

1. Everybody, where would you want to find the ship, **in deep water** or **in shallow water?** (Signal.) *In shallow water.*
1. Why? (Call on a student. Idea: *It's safer and easier to dive in shallow water.*)

Day after day, you dive. Then one day, you see something in the shallow water. It looks like part of an old ship. You swim closer and you see that it is an old ship. You go inside it very carefully. You watch out for sharks and strange fish with long teeth.

1. It's probably very scary going inside an old sunken ship.

It's dark inside the sunken ship. You swim to the captain's cabin. Then you see the treasure—boxes with locks on them. Inside are gold coins—piles of them. You are rich.

But not many divers who look for sunken ships are as lucky as you are.

2. Everybody, do many divers who look for sunken treasures find them? (Signal.) *No.*

Things have changed a lot in the past two hundred years. The trip from New York to Italy would have taken 40 days by sailing ship two hundred years ago.

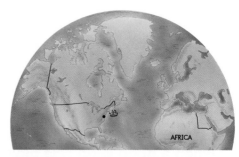

2. Everybody, how long would the trip have taken 200 years ago? (Signal.) *40 days.*
2. Touch the map on the next page. ✓
2. Start at New York and go to Italy. ✓
2. In which direction are you going? (Signal.) *East.*

But today, we can go to the airport in New York, get on a jet, and be in Italy 7 hours later.

2. Everybody, how long does the trip from New York to Italy take today? (Signal.) *Seven hours.*
2. The map shows how far the sailing ship got in the same time it took the jet to go all the way to Italy. How far did the sailing ship go? (Call on a student. Idea: *Just a tiny distance; it's hardly left New York.*)

We can call on the phone from New York and tell somebody in Italy that we will be there at 3 o'clock. We can order diving equipment by phone. When we get off the plane in Italy, we can take a cab to the harbor. We can then rent a boat and begin our search for sunken treasure.

THE END

1. Go back to the beginning of the story. Follow along while I read.
2. What's a harbor? (Call on a student. Idea: *A place where ships land.*)
2. Why are we going to the harbor? (Call on a student. Idea: *To find a boat.*)
2. Why do we want a boat? (Call on a student. Idea: *To search for sunken treasure.*)

EXERCISE 6

PAIRED PRACTICE

You're going to read aloud to your partner. Today the **A** members will read first. Then the **B** members will read from the star to the end of the story.
(Observe students and give feedback.)

End-of-Lesson Activities

INDEPENDENT WORK

Now finish your independent work for lesson 107. First do the worksheet. Raise your hand when you're finished.
(Observe students and give feedback.)

WORKCHECK

a. (Direct students to take out their marking pencils.)
- We're going to check your independent work. Remember, if you got an item wrong, make an **X** next to the item. Don't change any answers.
b. (For each item: Read the item. Call on a student to answer it. If the answer is wrong, say the correct answer. Refer to the Answer Key for the correct answers.)
c. Now use your marking pencil to fix up any items you got wrong. Remember, all mistakes must be fixed up before you hand in your independent work.

WRITING-SPELLING

(Present Writing-Spelling lesson 107 after completing Reading lesson 107. See Writing-Spelling Guide.)

LANGUAGE ARTS GUIDE

(Present Language Arts lesson 107 after completing Reading lesson 107. See Language Arts Guide.)

Lesson 108

EXERCISE 1

VOCABULARY REVIEW

a. Here's the new vocabulary sentence: Their amazing effort surprised the neighbors.
  • Everybody, say the sentence. Get ready. (Signal.) *Their amazing effort surprised the neighbors.*
  • (Repeat until firm.)

b. Everybody, what word means that something is hard to believe? (Signal.) *Amazing.*
  • What word tells about how much strength it needed? (Signal.) *Effort.*
  • What word names people who live near you? (Signal.) *Neighbors.*

EXERCISE 2

READING WORDS

Column 1

a. **Find lesson 108 in your textbook.** ✓
  • Touch column 1. ✓
  • (Teacher reference:)

1. relative	4. neighbors
2. Hohoboho	5. strangest
3. confusion	6. telephone

b. Word 1 is **relative.** What word? (Signal.) *Relative.*
  • Your relatives are people in your family. Everybody, what's another word for people in your family? (Signal.) *Relatives.*

c. Word 2. What word? (Signal.) *Hohoboho.*
  • (Repeat for words 3–6.)

d. Let's read those words again.
  • Word 1. What word? (Signal.) *Relative.*
  • (Repeat for words 2–6.)

e. (Repeat step d until firm.)

Column 2

f. Find column 2. ✓
  • (Teacher reference:)

1. worst	3. wander
2. wonder	4. world

  • All these words begin with the letter **W.**

g. Word 1. What word? (Signal.) *Worst.*
  • Spell **worst.** Get ready. (Tap for each letter.) *W-O-R-S-T.*

h. Word 2. What word? (Signal.) *Wonder.*
  • Spell **wonder.** Get ready. (Tap for each letter.) *W-O-N-D-E-R.*

i. Word 3. What word? (Signal.) *Wander.*
  • Spell **wander.** Get ready. (Tap for each letter.) *W-A-N-D-E-R.*

j. Word 4. What word? (Signal.) *World.*
  • Spell **world.** Get ready. (Tap for each letter.) *W-O-R-L-D.*

k. Let's read those words again, the fast way.
  • Word 1. What word? (Signal.) *Worst.*
  • (Repeat for words 2–4.)

l. (Repeat step k until firm.)

Column 3

m. Find column 3. ✓
  • (Teacher reference:)

1. noisier	4. happiest
2. rather	5. effort
3. happy	6. hooray

n. Word 1. What word? (Signal.) *Noisier.*
  • (Repeat for words 2–6.)

o. (Repeat step n until firm.)

Individual Turns

(For columns 1–3: Call on individual students, each to read one to three words per turn.)

EXERCISE 3

COMPREHENSION PASSAGE

a. Find part B in your textbook. ✓
  • You're going to read a story about a make-believe place. First you'll read the information passage. It gives some information about talking words.

b. Everybody, touch the title. ✓
  • (Call on a student to read the title.) *[Words That Talk.]*
  • Everybody, what's the title? (Signal.) *Words That Talk.*

c. (Call on individual students to read the passage, each student reading two or three sentences at a time. Ask the specified questions as the students read.)

Words That Talk

You're going to read a story about words that talk. The picture shows some of those words. The words are saying things to each other.

- Everybody, look at the picture. Name the words that are talking in the picture. (Call on a student.) *[Hot, cold, worry, calm.]*

What is the word <u>hot</u> saying?

- What's the answer? (Call on a student.) *[I hate cold.]*

What is <u>cold</u> saying?

- What's the answer? (Call on a student.) *[Stay away from me.]*

Who is <u>cold</u> talking to?

- Everybody, what's the answer? (Signal.) *Hot.*
- Why wouldn't **cold** want **hot** to be close? (Call on a student. Idea: ***Hot** would make **cold** hotter.*)

What is <u>worry</u> saying?

- What's the answer? (Call on a student.) *[I think I'm too close to hot and cold.]*
- Everybody, does it look like **worry** is too close to hot or cold? (Signal.) *No.*
- I think **worry** is just worrying over nothing.

Who is saying, "Everybody, take it easy"?

- Everybody, what's the answer? (Signal.) *Calm.*

<u>Calm</u> is trying to keep things calm.

- What's **calm** trying to do? (Call on a student. Idea: *Keep things calm.*)

EXERCISE 4

STORY READING

a. Find part C in your textbook. ✓
- The error limit for this story is 11. Read carefully.
b. Everybody, touch the title. ✓
- (Call on a student to read the title.) *[Hohoboho.]*
- What is this story going to tell about? (Call on a student. Idea: *Hohoboho.*)
- Do you think there is such a place as Hohoboho? (Call on a student. Student preference.)
c. (Call on individual students to read the story, each student reading two or three sentences at a time. Ask questions marked **1**.)

- (Correct errors: Tell the word. Direct the student to reread the sentence.)
- (If the group makes more than 11 errors, direct the students to reread the story.)

d. (After the group has read the selection making no more than 11 errors, read the story to the students and ask questions marked **2**.)

Hohoboho

This is a story about a sad word that lived in a make-believe place called Hohoboho.

2. Everybody, is there really a Hohoboho? (Signal.) *No.*

The words in Hohoboho were not like the words in our world. And the people in Hohoboho were not like the people in our world. These people talked, but they didn't do anything else.

2. How were the people different from the people in our world? (Call on a student. Idea: *They didn't do anything but talk.*)

The people didn't read. They didn't play baseball. They didn't eat. They didn't even sing. All they did was talk.

2. Everybody, what's the only thing they did? (Signal.) *Talk.*

Here's the strangest part about Hohoboho. Every time a person said a word, that word felt happy.

2. What happened every time a person said a word? (Call on a student. Idea: *That word felt happy.*)

Words that were said a lot were very, very, happy.
Words that were said quite a bit were happy part of the time.

2. Everybody, which words were happiest? (Signal.) *Words that were said a lot.*
2. Which words were happy part of the time? (Call on a student. Idea: *Words that were said quite a bit.*)

Words that were said only once in a while were sort of sad.
The rest of the words were very sad.
How often did people say words that were very sad?

2. What's the answer? (Call on a student. Idea: *Almost never.*)

The word in our story was hardly ever said. So you know how that word felt.

2. Everybody, if it was hardly ever said, was it said very often? (Signal.) *No.*
2. So how would it feel? (Signal.) *Sad.*

All words in Hohoboho stayed in a strange place called the word bank.

2. Everybody, where did they stay? (Signal.) *In the word bank.*

There were over one hundred rows in the word bank.

Here are the rules about where the words sat in the word bank: <u>The words that people said more often sat near the front of the word bank. The words that people didn't say very much sat near the back of the word bank.</u>

2. Where were the words that people said a lot? (Call on a student. Idea: *Near the front of the word bank.*)
2. Where were the words that people didn't say very often? (Call on a student. Idea: *Near the back of the word bank.*)

The happiest words sat in the front rows of the word bank.

2. When did words feel happy? (Call on a student. Idea: *When somebody said them.*)
2. Everybody, which words were said more often, the ones near the front of the word bank or the ones near the back of the word bank? (Signal.) *The ones near the front.*
2. So which words were happier, the ones near the front or the ones near the back? (Signal.) *The ones near the front.*

Every time somebody said a word, that word would jump up and yell, "I'm the best," or "Hooray for me." Here are some of the words that sat in the best seats of the word bank: <u>me, am, what, who, is, we, I, not.</u> These are words people say all the time. They say the word <u>me</u> and the word <u>you</u>. They say the word <u>here</u> and the word <u>there</u>. They say the word <u>have</u> and the word <u>had.</u> Name some other words that people say a lot.

2. Say some of the words that you say all the time. (Call on a student. Ideas: *When, why, because, want,* etc.)

Words that were sort of happy sat in the middle rows of the word bank.

2. Why weren't those words as happy as the words in the best seats? (Call on a student. Idea: *Because they weren't said as often.*)

These words were said quite a bit but not as often as words like you and how. Here are some words that sat in the middle: should, other, telephone, rather.

2. Name some other words that sat in the middle. (Call on individual students. Ideas: *Always, hungry,* etc.)

These words didn't yell and shout all day long. But they were a lot noisier than the words in the back.

2. Why were they noisier than the words in back? (Call on a student. Idea: *Because they were said more often.*)

Every now and then one of the words in the middle of the word bank would jump up and say, "That's me."

2. When would a word do this? (Call on a student. Idea: *When somebody said the word.*)

**With all the yelling and shouting, the word bank was very loud.
Which part of the bank was the loudest?**

2. Everybody, what's the answer? (Signal.) *The front.*

Which part was sort of loud?

2. Everybody, what's the answer? (Signal.) *The middle.*

Which part was pretty quiet?

2. Everybody, what's the answer? (Signal.) *The back.*

The back of the bank was so quiet that a whole day might pass without one sound from the back of the bank.

2. Why wouldn't there be any sound from the back of the bank? (Call on a student. Ideas: *Because the words in the back were very sad; because nobody said them.*)

The words that sat near the back of the word bank were words that you wouldn't say very often. Here are some words that sat near the back: confusion, fifteenth, mummy. Name some other words that sat near the back of the word bank.

2. Name some. (Call on individual students. Ideas: *Wobble, discover, umbrella,* etc.)

**You'll never guess which words sat in the very last rows of the word bank.
MORE NEXT TIME**

1. Go back to the beginning of the story. Follow along while I read.

EXERCISE 5

PAIRED PRACTICE

You're going to read aloud to your partner. Today the **B** members will read first. Then the **A** members will read from the star to the end of the story.
(Observe students and give feedback.)

End-of-Lesson Activities

INDEPENDENT WORK

Now finish your independent work for lesson 108. First do the worksheet. Raise your hand when you're finished.
(Observe students and give feedback.)

WORKCHECK

a. (Direct students to take out their marking pencils.)
- We're going to check your independent work. Remember, if you got an item wrong, make an **X** next to the item. Don't change any answers.
b. (For each item: Read the item. Call on a student to answer it. If the answer is wrong, say the correct answer. Refer to the Answer Key for the correct answers.)
c. Now use your marking pencil to fix up any items you got wrong. Remember, all mistakes must be fixed up before you hand in your independent work.

WRITING-SPELLING

(Present Writing-Spelling lesson 108 after completing Reading lesson 108. See Writing-Spelling Guide.)

LANGUAGE ARTS GUIDE

(Present Language Arts lesson 108 after completing Reading lesson 108. See Language Arts Guide.)

Materials: Each student will need the same edition of a children's dictionary for exercise 6. Preview exercise 6 before presenting to ensure that the page numbers in the exercise work for the dictionary you're using.

EXERCISE 1

VOCABULARY REVIEW

a. You learned a sentence that tells what he frequently did.
- Everybody, say that sentence. Get ready. (Signal.) *He frequently argued about the championship.*
- (Repeat until firm.)

b. You learned a sentence that tells what she commented about.
- Say that sentence. Get ready. (Signal.) *She commented about the still water.*
- (Repeat until firm.)

c. Here's the last sentence you learned: Their amazing effort surprised the neighbors.
- Everybody, say that sentence. Get ready. (Signal.) *Their amazing effort surprised the neighbors.*
- (Repeat until firm.)

d. Everybody, what word tells about how much strength it needed? (Signal.) *Effort.*
- What word names people who live near you? (Signal.) *Neighbors.*
- What word means that something is hard to believe? (Signal.) *Amazing.*

e. Once more. Say the sentence that tells what surprised the neighbors. Get ready. (Signal.) *Their amazing effort surprised the neighbors.*

EXERCISE 2

READING WORDS

Column 1

a. **Find lesson 109 in your textbook.** ✓
- Touch column 1. ✓

- (Teacher reference:)

1. seven	4. ninth
2. nine	5. seventh
3. fifteen	6. fifteenth

- All these words tell about numbers.
b. Word 1. What word? (Signal.) *Seven.*
- (Repeat for words 2–6.)
c. (Repeat step b until firm.)

Column 2

d. Find column 2. ✓
- (Teacher reference:)

1. <u>six</u>th	3. <u>relative</u>s
2. <u>whoop</u>ing	4. <u>bound</u>ing

- All these words have endings.
e. Word 1. What's the underlined part? (Signal.) *six.*
- What's the whole word? (Signal.) *Sixth.*
f. Word 2. What's the underlined part? (Signal.) *whoop.*
- What's the whole word? (Signal.) *Whooping.*
g. Word 3. What's the underlined part? (Signal.) *relative.*
- What's the whole word? (Signal.) *Relatives.*
h. Word 4. What's the underlined part? (Signal.) *bound.*
- What's the whole word? (Signal.) *Bounding.*
i. Let's read those words again, the fast way.
- Word 1. What word? (Signal.) *Sixth.*
- (Repeat for words 2–4.)
j. (Repeat step i until firm.)

Column 3

k. Find column 3. ✓
- (Teacher reference:)

1. Thursday	4. Friday
2. confusion	5. cargo
3. prow	

l. Word 1. What word? (Signal.)
Thursday.
- (Repeat for: **2. confusion, 3. prow, 4. Friday, 5. cargo.**)

m. (Repeat step l until firm.)

Individual Turns

(For columns 1–3: Call on individual students, each to read one to three words.)

EXERCISE 3

REVIEW PASSAGE

a. Find part B in your textbook. ✓
- I'll read this story with you today and help you with the answers. In lesson 111 you'll do this story by yourselves.

b. I'll read each sentence and say the word **blank** for any words that are missing. Then I'll read the sentence again. You say what goes in the blank. Follow along as I read. Don't write anything.

c. Liz liked cool weather. It was the middle of the summer, and she wanted to go to a city in California that was cool in the summer. So she went to the city of **blank.** Get ready to tell me the name. She went to the city of: (Signal.) *San Francisco.*

d. Liz knew that the temperature of an object tells how **blank** that object is. Get ready to tell me the words. The temperature of an object tells how: (Signal.) *Hot or cold that object is.*

e. When she left New York City, the air on the ground was 30 degrees. When the plane went higher and higher, did the air outside the plane get **hotter** or **colder?** Get ready to tell me the word. The air outside the plane got: (Signal.) *Colder.*

f. The plane flew much faster than a car can go. How fast did the plane fly? Everybody, what's the answer? (Signal.) *500 miles per hour.*

g. When the plane went from New York City to San Francisco, it was going in which direction? What's the answer? (Signal.) *West.*

h. The plane was facing the wind, so the name of the wind was a **blank.** Get ready to tell me the words. That wind was a: (Signal.) *West wind.*

i. Did the plane go **faster** or **slower** than a plane going in the opposite direction? Everybody, what's the answer? (Signal.) *Slower.*

j. The air that rushed from the jet engines was going to the east so the jet engines moved toward the **blank.** Get ready to tell me the word. The jet engines moved toward the: (Signal.) *West.*

k. The jet engines were attached to parts of the plane. Those parts were the **blank.** Get ready to tell me the word. Those parts were the: (Signal.) *Wings.*

l. As Liz flew along, she wanted to get a good look at things on the ground below. So she looked through something that makes things look very big. She looked through **blank.** Get ready to tell me the word. She looked through: (Signal.) *Binoculars.*

m. She saw the city that is between Chicago and Salt Lake City. What city was that? Everybody, what's the answer? (Signal.) *Denver.*

n. In San Francisco, Liz saw a lot of animals at a zoo. She knew how much some of the animals weigh.

o. Everybody, look at the picture and get ready to tell me how much each animal weighs.
- (Teacher reference:)

- How much does animal A weigh? (Signal.) *About 100 pounds.*
- How much does animal B weigh? (Signal.) *About 100 pounds.*
- How many third-graders weigh as much as animal C? (Signal.) *Thirty.*

p. (Repeat items c–o that were not firm.)

EXERCISE 4

STORY READING

a. Find part C in your textbook. ✓
- The error limit for this story is 11. Read carefully.

b. Everybody, touch the title. ✓
- (Call on a student to read the title.) *[The Words That Sat in the Back Rows.]*

- What is this story going to tell about? (Call on a student. Idea: *Words that sit in the back.*)

c. (Call on individual students to read the story, each student reading two or three sentences at a time. Ask questions marked **1.**)

- (Correct errors: Tell the word. Direct the student to reread the sentence.)
- (If the group makes more than 11 errors, direct the students to reread the story.)

d. (After the group has read the selection making no more than 11 errors, read the story to the students and ask questions marked **2.**)

The Words That Sat in the Back Rows

The words that sat in the back of the word bank didn't have much fun.

2. Why not? (Call on a student. Idea: *Because nobody said them very much.*)

They tried not to listen to the other words yelling and cheering, but they couldn't help it. They wanted to be said more often. Every now and then one of the words in front would turn around and say something like, "Look at those words in the back of the bank. They aren't any good at all."
One word that sat in the very last row of the word bank was the word <u>run.</u>

2. If that word sat in the last row, what do you know about how often that word was said? (Call on a student. Idea: *It wasn't said very often.*)

If we had a word bank in our world, the word <u>run</u> would not sit in the back row.

2. Why not? (Call on a student. Idea: *Because we use the word <u>run</u> a lot.*)

The word <u>run</u> would be said very often because people run and talk about running. But you must remember that the people in Hohoboho did not do anything. So they didn't talk much about doing

things. They didn't talk about running or jumping or walking. You know other things they didn't talk about very much.

2. Name some. (Call on individual students. Ideas: *Skiing, skating, skipping,* etc.)

So the word <u>run</u> sat in the last row. The word <u>run</u> sat behind words like <u>speedometer</u> and <u>temperature</u>. The word <u>run</u> sat behind words like <u>maggots</u>, <u>enough</u>, <u>binoculars</u>, and <u>direction</u>. <u>Run</u> sat next to its relatives. One relative was the word <u>runner</u>. Another relative was the word <u>ran.</u> You know some of the other relatives of <u>run</u>.

2. Name some. (Call on individual students. Ideas: *Running, runs,* etc.)

Next to the <u>run</u> family sat the <u>walk</u> family. You know some of the relatives of <u>walk</u> that were in that family.

2. Name some. (Call on individual students. Ideas: *Walking, walked, walker.*)

And next to that family was the <u>jump</u> family, and then the <u>ride</u> family, and the <u>eat</u> family.

2. Name some relatives of the **eat** family. (Call on individual students. Ideas: *Ate, eaten, eater, eats, eating.*)

Every once in a while, one of the words from the back row would try to sit closer to the front of the word bank.

2. Why would the word do that? (Call on a student. Idea: *So it would have more fun.*)

Look at the picture. Two words are sitting in the wrong seats.

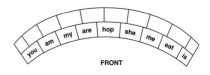

2. Everybody, look at the picture and figure out the words that shouldn't be near the front of the bank. Remember, those are words that tell about doing things. Which words are out of place? (Signal.) *Hop and eat.*

> **This trick didn't work because the other words always caught the words from the back row. "Hey, you can't move up here," they would say. "Go back to the last row where you belong." So the sad words would sit and wait and hope.**

2. What did they hope for? (Call on a student. Idea: *That somebody would say their names.*)

> **Once in a while, somebody would say their names and they would feel good, very good. They tried to remember how good they felt. Sometimes, they would talk about it. The word <u>runner</u> liked to say, "I remember one day when my name was said four times. Four times in one day."**

1. How do you think the other sad words felt when **runner** talked this way? (Call on a student. Idea: *Jealous.*)

> **The other sad words got tired of hearing this story. They would say, "Oh, be quiet. You just got lucky. You usually don't have your name said once a month."**
>
> **"Yeah," one of the other sad words would say. "You don't get said any more often than the rest of us."**
>
> **"It will happen again," <u>runner</u> would reply. "You'll see. One of these days, they're going to start saying my name all the time. I'll bet I get to move up five rows. You'll see."**
>
> **"Oh, be quiet."**

2. Who said that? (Call on a student. Ideas: *The other sad words; the words in the back.*)

> **Then the sad words would sit back and feel sad. Long day after long day, they would sit and try not to listen to those words in the front of the bank whooping and howling.**
> **MORE NEXT TIME**

1. Go back to the beginning of the story. Follow along while I read.
2. Why were the words in the front whooping and howling? (Call on a student. Ideas: *Because they were said a lot; they were happy.*)

EXERCISE 5

PAIRED PRACTICE

You're going to read aloud to your partner. Today the **A** members will read first. Then the **B** members will read from the star to the end of the story.
(Observe students and give feedback.)

End-of-Lesson Activities

INDEPENDENT WORK

Now finish your independent work for lesson 109. First do the worksheet. Raise your hand when you're finished.
(Observe students and give feedback.)

WORKCHECK

a. (Direct students to take out their marking pencils.)
• We're going to check your independent work. Remember, if you got an item wrong, make an **X** next to the item. Don't change any answers.
b. (For each item: Read the item. Call on a student to answer it. If the answer is wrong, say the correct answer. Refer to the Answer Key for the correct answers.)
c. Now use your marking pencil to fix up any items you got wrong. Remember, all mistakes must be fixed up before you hand in your independent work.

Note: Before presenting lesson 110, you will need to:
- Reproduce blackline masters for the Fact Game;
- Preview Literature lesson 11, secure materials and reproduce blackline masters. (See the Literature Guide.)

WRITING-SPELLING

(Present Writing-Spelling lesson 109 after completing Reading lesson 109. See Writing-Spelling Guide.)

LANGUAGE ARTS GUIDE

(Present Language Arts lesson 109 after completing Reading lesson 109. See Language Arts Guide.)

Lesson 110

Test 11

Materials for Lesson 110
Fact Game

For each team (4 or 5 students):
- pair of number cubes (or dice)
- copy of Fact Game 110

For each student:
- their copy of the scorecard sheet

For each monitor:
- a pencil
- Fact Game 110 answer key (at end of textbook C)

Reading Checkout

Each student needs their thermometer chart.

Literature Lesson 11

See Literature Guide for the materials you will need.

EXERCISE 1
FACT GAME

a. You're going to play the game that uses the facts you have learned. Remember the rules. The player rolls the number cubes, figures out the number of the question, reads that question out loud, and answers it. The monitor tells the player if the answer is right or wrong. If it's wrong, the monitor tells the right answer. If it's right, the monitor gives the player one point. Don't argue with the monitor. The number cubes go to the left and the next player has a turn. You'll play the game for 10 minutes.

b. (Divide students into groups of four or five. Assign monitors. Direct the monitors to write the correct answers for items 12a and 12b on their lined paper. Circulate as students play the game. Comment on groups that are playing well.)

c. (At the end of 10 minutes, have all students who earned more than 10 points stand up.)

- (Tell the monitor of each game that ran smoothly:) Your group did a good job.

EXERCISE 2
READING CHECKOUTS

a. Today is a test day and a reading-checkout day. While you're writing answers, I'm going to call on you one at a time to read part of the story we read in lesson 109. When I call on you to come and do your checkout, bring your thermometer chart.

- Remember, you pass the checkout by reading the passage in less than a minute without making more than 2 mistakes. And when you pass the checkout, you color the space for lesson 110 on your thermometer chart.

b. (Call on individual students to read the portion of story 109 marked with ●.)

- (Time the student. Note words that are missed and number of words read.)
- (Teacher reference:)

● **This trick didn't work because the other words always caught the words from the back row. "Hey, you can't move up here," they would say. "Go back to the last row where you belong." So the sad words would sit and wait and hope. Once in a while, somebody would [50] say their names and they would feel good, very good. They tried to remember how good they felt. Sometimes, they would talk about it. The [75] word <u>runner</u> liked to say, "I remember one day when my name was said four times. Four times in one day."**

The other sad words ● [100] got tired of hearing this story.

- (If the student reads the passage in one minute or less and makes no more than 2 errors, direct the student to color in the space for lesson 110 on the thermometer chart.)

- (If the student makes any mistakes, point to each word that was misread and identify it.)

- (If the student does not meet the rate-error criterion for the passage, direct the student to practice reading the story with the assigned partner.)

EXERCISE 3

TEST

a. **Find page 70 in your textbook.** ✓
- This is a test. You'll work items you've done before.
b. Work carefully. Raise your hand when you've completed all the items. (Observe students but do not give feedback on errors.)

EXERCISE 4

MARKING THE TEST

a. (Check students' work before beginning lesson 111. Refer to the Answer Key for the correct answers.)
b. (Record all test 11 results on the Test Summary Sheet and the Group Summary Sheet. Reproducible Summary Sheets are at the back of the Teacher's Guide.)

EXERCISE 5

TEST REMEDIES

- (Provide any necessary remedies for test 11 before presenting lesson 111. Test remedies are discussed in the Teacher's Guide.)

Test 110 Firming Table

Test Item	Introduced in lesson	Test Item	Introduced in lesson	Test Item	Introduced in lesson
1	107	7	107	13	101
2	107	8	109	14	107
3	107	9	109	15	106
4	107	10	101	16	106
5	107	11	107	17	106
6	107	12	107	18	106

LITERATURE

(Present Literature lesson 11 after completing Reading lesson 110. See Literature Guide.)

LANGUAGE ARTS GUIDE

(Present Language Arts lesson 110 after completing Reading lesson 110. See Language Arts Guide.)

Lessons 111–115 · Planning Page

	Lesson 111	Lesson 112	Lesson 113	Lesson 114	Lesson 115
Lesson Events	**Vocabulary Sentence** Reading Words Vocabulary Review Comprehension Passage Story Reading Paired Practice Dictionary Skills Independent Work Workcheck Writing-Spelling	Vocabulary Review Reading Words Story Reading Paired Practice Dictionary Skills Independent Work Workcheck Writing-Spelling	Vocabulary Review Reading Words Comprehension Passage Globe Story Reading Paired Practice Independent Work Workcheck Writing-Spelling	Reading Words Comprehension Passage Story Reading Paired Practice Independent Work Workcheck Writing-Spelling	**Vocabulary Sentence** Reading Words Vocabulary Review Comprehension Passage Story Reading Reading Checkouts Independent Work Workcheck Writing-Spelling
Vocabulary Sentence	#27: Police officers checked the ship's cargo.	#27: Police officers checked the ship's cargo.	sentence #25 sentence #26 sentence #27		#28: The champions performed perfectly.
Reading Words: Word Types	modeled words mixed words	modeled words words with endings multi-syllable words mixed words	words with endings mixed words	modeled words mixed words multi-syllable words	**e-a** words multi-syllable words mixed words
New Vocabulary		double Australia	finest triple	koala ruin India lookout pouch warn	peacock screech
Comprehension Passages	*Facts About Canada*		*Facts About Australia*	*Facts About Kangaroos*	*Facts About Peacocks*
Story	*The Big Change in Hohoboho*	*Run Gets Moved*	*Toby the Kangaroo*	*A Job for Toby*	*The Kangaroo Hunters*
Skill Items	Vocabulary Sentences	Compare	Vocabulary Sentence	Compare Vocabulary Sentences	Vocabulary Compare
Special Materials	Children's dictionaries (same edition for all students)	Children's dictionaries (same edition for all students)	Globe; writing materials for activity		Thermometer charts
Special Projects/ Activities			Activity after lesson 113		

Materials: Each student will need the same edition of a children's dictionary for exercise 7. Preview exercise 7 before presenting to ensure that the words in the exercise work for the dictionary you're using.

EXERCISE 1

VOCABULARY

a. **Find page 342 in your textbook.** ✓
  • Touch sentence 27.
  • This is a new vocabulary sentence. It says: Police officers checked the ship's cargo. Everybody, read that sentence. Get ready. (Signal.) *Police officers checked the ship's cargo.*
  • Close your eyes and say the sentence. Get ready. (Signal.) *Police officers checked the ship's cargo.*
  • (Repeat until firm.)
b. The sentence says that **police officers** checked the ship's cargo. Police officers are cops. Everybody, what's another way of saying **The cop was tired?** (Signal.) *The police officer was tired.*
c. Police officers checked the ship's **cargo**. **Cargo** is what ships carry from one place to another. The cargo can be anything from automobiles to grain or paper. Everybody, what do we call the things that a ship carries? (Signal.) *Cargo.*
d. Listen to the sentence again: Police officers checked the ship's cargo. Everybody, say the sentence. Get ready. (Signal.) *Police officers checked the ship's cargo.*
e. What word refers to the things that a ship carries? (Signal.) *Cargo.*
  • What words mean **cops?** (Signal.) *Police officers.*

EXERCISE 2

READING WORDS

Column 1

a. Find lesson 111 in your textbook. ✓
  • Touch column 1. ✓

• (Teacher reference:)

1. officer	3. Friday
2. police	4. cargo

b. Word 1 is **officer.** What word? (Signal.) *Officer.*
  • Spell **officer.** Get ready. (Tap for each letter.) *O-F-F-I-C-E-R.*
c. Word 2 is **police.** What word? (Signal.) *Police.*
  • Spell **police.** Get ready. (Tap for each letter.) *P-O-L-I-C-E.*
d. Word 3. What word? (Signal.) *Friday.*
  • Spell **Friday.** Get ready. (Tap for each letter.) *F-R-I-D-A-Y.*
e. Word 4. What word? (Signal.) *Cargo.*
  • Spell **cargo.** Get ready. (Tap for each letter.) *C-A-R-G-O.*
f. Let's read those words again, the fast way.
  • Word 1. What word? (Signal.) *Officer.*
  • (Repeat for words 2–4.)
g. (Repeat step f until firm.)

Column 2

h. Find column 2. ✓
  • (Teacher reference:)

1. happy	3. happier
2. fifteenth	4. sixth

i. Word 1. What word? (Signal.) *Happy.*
  • (Repeat for words 2–4.)
j. (Repeat step i until firm.)

Column 3

k. Find column 3. ✓
  • (Teacher reference:)

1. squeeze	4. seventh
2. tumble	5. stumbled
3. stumble	

l. Word 1. What word? (Signal.) *Squeeze.*
  • (Repeat for: **2. tumble, 3. stumble, 4. seventh, 5. stumbled.**)
m. (Repeat step l until firm.)

Column 4

n. Find column 4. ✓
  • (Teacher reference:)

1. ninth	4. Thursday
2. begin	5. confusion
3. beginner	

o. Word 1. What word? (Signal.) *Ninth.*
  • (Repeat for words 2–5.)
p. (Repeat step o until firm.)

Individual Turns

(For columns 1–4: Call on individual students, each to read one to three words per turn.)

EXERCISE 3

VOCABULARY REVIEW

a. Here's the new vocabulary sentence: Police officers checked the ship's cargo.
  • Everybody, say that sentence. Get ready. (Signal.) *Police officers checked the ship's cargo.*
  • (Repeat until firm.)
b. What word refers to the things that a ship carries? (Signal.) *Cargo.*
  • What words mean **cops?** (Signal.) *Police officers.*

EXERCISE 4

COMPREHENSION PASSAGE

a. Find part B in your textbook. ✓
  • You're going to read the next story about Hohoboho. First you'll read the information passage. It tells some facts about the country that is just north of the United States.
b. Everybody, touch the title. ✓
  • (Call on a student to read the title.) *[Facts About Canada.]*
  • Everybody, what's the title? (Signal.) *Facts About Canada.*
c. (Call on individual students to read the passage, each student reading two or three sentences at a time.)

Facts About Canada

You have learned about the United States. The United States is not a city and not a state. What is it?

• Everybody, what's the answer? (Signal.) *A country.*

The United States is one of the largest countries in the world, but the country that is just north of the United States is much larger. That country is Canada.

• Everybody, is the United States **bigger** or **smaller** than most of the other countries in the world? (Signal.) *Bigger.*
• What's the name of the country to the north of the United States? (Signal.) *Canada.*
• Is Canada **bigger** or **smaller** than the United States? (Signal.) *Bigger.*

Alaska touches the west side of Canada. The rest of the United States touches the south side of Canada.

• Everybody, touch Canada on the map on the next page. ✓
• Touch the line between Canada and Alaska. ✓
• Which side of Canada touches Alaska? (Signal.) *West.*
• Touch the line between Canada and the United States. ✓
• Which side of Canada touches the United States? (Signal.) *South.*

EXERCISE 5

STORY READING

a. Find part C in your textbook. ✓
  • The error limit for this story is 11. Read carefully.
b. Everybody, touch the title. ✓
  • (Call on a student to read the title.) *[The Big Change in Hohoboho.]*
  • What's going to happen in this story? (Call on a student. Idea: *There will be a big change in Hohoboho.*)

c. (Call on individual students to read the story, each student reading two or three sentences at a time. Ask questions marked **1.**)

> • (Correct errors: Tell the word. Direct the student to reread the sentence.)
> • (If the group makes more than 11 errors, direct the students to reread the story.)

d. (After the group has read the selection making no more than 11 errors, read the story to the students and ask questions marked **2.**)

The Big Change in Hohoboho

Every Friday, words in the word bank were moved. Sometimes the people in Hohoboho started to say a word more often. On Friday, that word would be moved closer to the front of the word bank.

2. Why would it be moved closer to the front of the word bank? (Call on a student. Idea: *Because it was being said more often.*)
2. Everybody, on which day would the word be moved? (Signal.) *Friday.*

The opposite also happened.

1. Everybody, when the opposite happened, where would the word be moved? (Signal.) *Toward the back.*
1. Why? (Call on a student. Idea: *Because it wasn't being said as much.*)

If a word was not said as often as it had been said, it was moved toward the back of the word bank.

2. Why would it be moved closer to the back? (Call on a student. Idea: *Because that's where words sat when they weren't said very often.*)
2. How do you think words felt when they were moved toward the back of the word bank? (Call on a student. Ideas: *Sad, upset.*)

A lot of words would be moved around every Friday, but they were usually moved only one or two rows. The word eraser was usually in the sixth row, but every now and then it

would move up as far as the fourth row or as far back as the ninth row.
When eraser was in the ninth row, it felt quite sad.

2. Why? (Call on a student. Idea: *Because it wasn't being said much.*)
2. Everybody, in which row would **eraser** feel happier, the fourth row or the sixth row? (Signal.) *The fourth row.*

But the words in the very back row would give anything to be able to sit in the ninth row.

1. Why? (Call on a student. Idea: *Because the words in the ninth row were said more often.*)

The ninth row was near the front of the bank. In fact, it was so close to the front of the bank that run couldn't even see it.

2. Everybody, where was **run** sitting? (Signal.) *In the back row.*

Anyhow, words got moved around every Friday, and the words that moved up cheered and shouted. The words that got moved toward the back didn't act the same way.

1. How did they act? (Call on a student. Idea: *They moped; they frowned; etc.*)
1. Why? (Call on a student. Idea: *Because they were being said less often.*)

The word that got moved the most rows was summer. Summer once went from the fifteenth row to the seventh row.

2. Everybody, what row did it start out in? (Signal.) *Fifteenth.*

2. What row did it end up in? (Signal.)
   Seventh.
2. Is it going toward the **front** of the word bank or the **back** of the word bank? (Signal.) *Front.*
2. The picture shows **summer** moving to its new seat. What row is it going to? (Signal.) *Seventh.*
2. How does it feel? (Call on a student. Idea: *Happy.*)

Summer **didn't stay in the seventh row very long. The move to the seventh row happened during the summer when the weather got very hot. People talked a lot about summer. Then the weather cooled down, and summer got moved back to the fifteenth row.**

2. Why did **summer** move up in the first place? (Call on a student. Idea: *Because it was being said more often.*)
2. Everybody, did **summer** stay there very long? (Signal.) *No.*
2. What happened to the weather to make **summer** move back to the fifteenth row? (Call on a student. Idea: *It cooled down.*)

As you know, words were always moved on Friday. But one Thursday, a big change took place, and the entire word bank was thrown into confusion.

2. Everybody, on what day did this big change take place? (Signal.) *Thursday.*
2. And what happened to the entire word bank? (Signal.) *It was thrown into confusion.*
2. What does that mean, it was thrown into confusion? (Call on a student. Idea: *It got all mixed up.*)

Here's what happened. The people in Hohoboho began to <u>do</u> things.

2. What was the only thing the people in Hohoboho did **before** the big change? (Call on a student. Idea: *Talk.*)

The people began to swim and walk and eat and run. They began to look at things, kick things, and sit on things. They began to wonder, and sing, and dance.

1. Name some other things the people started to do for the first time. Call on individual students. Ideas: *Hop, roller skate, fly, jump, read,* etc.)
1. Everybody, do you think they talked about the new things they were doing? (Signal.) *Yes.*
1. Would that make a big change in the word bank? (Signal.) *Yes.*

The people talked about the things they did.

2. Tell me some words they used now that they didn't use very much before. (Call on individual students. Ideas: *Swim, dance, kick,* etc.)

So the whooping and hollering in the word bank now came from a different part of the bank.

2. Everybody, if the people were talking about things like swimming and running, which part of the word bank would do a lot of cheering and shouting? (Signal.) *The back.*

"Let's dance," the people in Hohoboho would say, and a great cry went out from one of the rows.

2. Which row? (Call on a student. Idea: *The back row.*)

"That's me," a word shouted.

2. Everybody, which word? (Signal.) *Dance.*

"Dancing is fun," another person would say, and one of the relatives of <u>dance</u> would jump up. "That's me. People are talking about me."

2. Everybody, which relative of **dance** said that? (Signal.) *Dancing.*

Things were crazy in the word bank. The words in the front of the bank turned around and looked and listened. They couldn't believe what was happening. There was still some shouting and yelling from the front of the word bank, but there was much more noise from the back of

the bank. The words in the back were so happy that they were jumping and howling and bounding all over the place.

"Twenty times," the word <u>hop</u> said. "They said my name twenty times and the day isn't even over yet."

2. How did **hop** feel about this? (Call on a student. Ideas: *Excited, happy,* etc.)

"That's nothing," run said, "I'm already up to 56."

2. What does **run** mean by that? (Call on a student. Idea: *His name has been said 56 times.*)

Two words in the front row, <u>we</u> and <u>us</u>, were talking. <u>We</u> said, "Tomorrow is Friday. What do you think will happen to those words in the back row?"

"I don't know," <u>us</u> said. "We'll have to wait and see."

MORE NEXT TIME

1. Go back to the beginning of the story. Follow along while I read.
2. What do you think will happen? (Call on a student. Idea: *The words in the back will move up to the front.*)

EXERCISE 6
PAIRED PRACTICE

You're going to read aloud to your partner. Today the **B** members will read first. Then the **A** members will read from the star to the end of the story.
(Observe students and give feedback.)

End-of-Lesson Activities

INDEPENDENT WORK

Now finish your independent work for lesson 111. First do the worksheet. Raise your hand when you're finished.
(Observe students and give feedback.)

WORKCHECK

a. (Direct students to take out their marking pencils.)
• We're going to check your independent work. Remember, if you got an item wrong, make an **X** next to the item. Don't change any answers.
b. (For each item: Read the item. Call on a student to answer it. If the answer is wrong, say the correct answer. Refer to the Answer Key for the correct answers.)
c. Now use your marking pencil to fix up any items you got wrong. Remember, all mistakes must be fixed up before you hand in your independent work.

WRITING-SPELLING

(Present Writing-Spelling lesson 111 after completing Reading lesson 111. See Writing-Spelling Guide.)

LANGUAGE ARTS GUIDE

(Present Language Arts lesson 111 after completing Reading lesson 111. See Language Arts Guide.)

Lesson 112

Materials: Each student will need the same edition of a children's dictionary for exercise 5. Preview exercise 5 before presenting to ensure that the words in the exercise work for the dictionary you're using.

EXERCISE 1
VOCABULARY REVIEW

a. Here's the new vocabulary sentence:
   Police officers checked the ship's cargo.
   • Everybody, say that sentence. Get ready. (Signal.) *Police officers checked the ship's cargo.*
   • (Repeat until firm.)
b. What words mean **cops?** (Signal.) *Police officers.*
   • What word refers to the things that a ship carries? (Signal.) *Cargo.*

EXERCISE 2
READING WORDS

Column 1

a. **Find lesson 112 in your textbook.** ✓
   • Touch column 1. ✓
   • (Teacher reference:)

1. **double**	3. **kangaroo**
2. **Australia**	4. **squeezed**

b. Word 1 is **double.** What word? (Signal.) *Double.*
   • Spell **double.** Get ready. (Tap for each letter.) *D-O-U-B-L-E.*
   • **Double** means two times as much. If you double how much you eat, you eat two times as much.
c. Word 2 is **Australia.** What word? (Signal.) *Australia.*
   • Spell **Australia.** Get ready. (Tap for each letter.) *A-U-S-T-R-A-L-I-A.*
   • **Australia** is the name of a country you'll be reading about.
d. Word 3 is **kangaroo.** What word? (Signal.) *Kangaroo.*
   • Spell **kangaroo.** Get ready. (Tap for each letter.) *K-A-N-G-A-R-O-O.*

e. Word 4 is **squeezed.** What word? (Signal.) *Squeezed.*
   • Spell **squeezed.** Get ready. (Tap for each letter.) *S-Q-U-E-E-Z-E-D.*
f. Let's read those words again, the fast way.
   • Word 1. What word? (Signal.) *Double.*
   • (Repeat for words 2–4.)
g. (Repeat step f until firm.)

Column 2

h. Find column 2. ✓
   • (Teacher reference:)

1. **stumbled**	4. **breathed**
2. **beginner**	5. **dusty**
3. **finest**	6. **stomping**

   • All these words have endings.
i. Word 1. What's the underlined part? (Signal.) *stumble.*
   • What's the whole word? (Signal.) *Stumbled.*
j. Word 2. What's the underlined part? (Signal.) *begin.*
   • What's the whole word? (Signal.) *Beginner.*
k. Word 3. What's the underlined part? (Signal.) *fine.*
   • What's the whole word? (Signal.) *Finest.*
l. Word 4. What's the underlined part? (Signal.) *breathe.*
   • What's the whole word? (Signal.) *Breathed.*
m. Word 5. What's the underlined part? (Signal.) *dust.*
   • What's the whole word? (Signal.) *Dusty.*
n. Word 6. What's the underlined part? (Signal.) *stomp.*
   • What's the whole word? (Signal.) *Stomping.*
o. Let's read those words again, the fast way.
   • Word 1. What word? (Signal.) *Stumbled.*
   • (Repeat for words 2–6.)
p. (Repeat step o until firm.)

Column 3

q. Find column 3. ✓
- (Teacher reference:)

1.	complete	4.	easy
2.	notice	5.	easier
3.	happier	6.	officer

r. Word 1. What word? (Signal.) *Complete.*
- (Repeat for words 2–6.)

s. (Repeat step r until firm.)

Column 4

t. Find column 4. ✓
- (Teacher reference:)

1.	cloud	4.	drunk
2.	Toby	5.	silent
3.	police	6.	joey

u. Word 1. What word? (Signal.) *Cloud.*
- (Repeat for words 2–6.)

v. (Repeat step u until firm.)

Individual Turns

(For columns 1–4: Call on individual students, each to read one to three words per turn.)

EXERCISE 3

STORY READING

a. Find part B in your textbook. ✓
- The error limit for this story is 13. Read carefully.

b. Everybody, touch the title. ✓
- (Call on a student to read the title.) *[Run Gets Moved.]*
- What's going to happen in this story? (Call on a student. Idea: **Run** will get moved.)

c. (Call on individual students to read the story, each student reading two or three sentences at a time. Ask questions marked **1.**)

- (Correct errors: Tell the word. Direct the student to reread the sentence.)
- (If the group makes more than 13 errors, direct the students to reread the story.)

d. (After the group has read the selection making no more than 13 errors, read the story to the students and ask questions marked **2.**)

Run Gets Moved

It was the day that the words in the word bank got moved.

1. Everybody, what day was that? (Signal.) *Friday.*
1. What day comes before Friday? (Signal.) *Thursday.*
1. Why was the word bank thrown into confusion on Thursday? (Call on a student. Idea: *People started to say the words in the back rows more often.*)
1. So what will happen on this Friday? (Call on a student. Idea: *The words in the back will move toward the front.*)

Here's how the words got moved every week. A voice would make the announcements about which words were to move. For example, the voice would say, "Telephone moves to row six." How would the voice announce that me has to sit in row three?

2. Tell me. (Call on a student. Idea: **Me** *moves to row three.*)

If a word was named in an announcement, the word would have to go to a new seat. The word would have to keep that seat until the voice announced that the word was to move again.

2. Everybody, when would the next announcements be made? (Signal.) *Next Friday.*
2. So how long would the word have to keep that seat? (Call on a student. Idea: *At least a week.*)

The announcements in the word bank were made at 9:00 in the morning on Fridays. The announcements were usually over by 9:30.

2. Everybody, when did they start? (Signal.) *9:00.*
2. When did they usually finish? (Signal.) *9:30.*
2. So how long did they usually take? (Call on a student. Idea: *30 minutes.*)

But on the Friday after the big change, all the words knew that things would be different. They knew that a lot of announcements would be made.

2. Why would there be a lot of announcements? (Call on a student. Ideas: *Because words in the back were being said more often; a lot of words were going to move.*)
2. Everybody, would the announcements take longer on this Friday? (Signal.) *Yes.*

The words like <u>me</u> and <u>are</u> were interested in what would happen to those words in the back row. <u>Me</u> and <u>are</u> were so interested that they did not do much yelling and shouting when the people in Hohoboho said their names.

1. Why didn't **me** and **are** do much yelling and shouting? (Call on a student. Idea: *Because they were more interested in what would happen to words in the back row.*)
1. Do you think they were worried about where the words in the back row would sit? (Call on a student. Student preference.)

The words in the back row had been so happy that they were tired of yelling and shouting and feeling good.

1. Why did they get happy in the first place? (Call on a student. Idea: *Because people were saying their names a lot.*)

<u>Run</u> said to <u>walk</u>, "I don't really care if they move me or not. I feel great." "Me, too," the other word said.

2. Everybody, what word said, "Me, too"? (Signal.) *Walk.*

At 9:00 the announcements began, and they were not finished until late at night.

2. Why did they take so long? (Call on a student. Idea: *Because so many changes had to be made.*)

Nearly every word in the word bank was moved. Sometimes whole rows of words were moved. And some words moved more than 100 rows.

2. What kind of words do you think moved that much? (Call on a student. Idea: *Action words.*)

The most amazing announcement of the day came about 10:30 in the morning after two or three hundred words had been moved. Here was that announcement: "The words <u>run</u> and <u>walk</u> will move from row 110 to row 1."

2. Everybody, in which row had they been sitting? (Signal.) *110.*
2. Which row did they move to? (Signal.) *One.*
2. What does that mean about how often these words were said? (Call on a student. Idea: *It means they were said very often.*)

For a moment the word bank was silent. Some words turned to their neighbors and said, "Did that announcement say that <u>run</u> and <u>walk</u> will move to row 1?"
<u>Run</u> looked over at <u>walk</u>. They just stared at each other.

2. How did they feel when they were staring at each other? (Call on a student. Ideas: *Excited, surprised,* etc.)

Then they stood up and started to walk to the front row. Suddenly the words in the back row began to clap for them. Then they began to cheer.
"That's my relative," the word <u>walking</u> said. "That word used to sit right next to me."
There are only so many seats in each row. Two new words were moved to row one.

2. Everybody, which words? (Signal.) *Run and walk.*

So you know what had to happen to two words that were already in row one.

2. What had to happen? (Call on a student. Idea: *They had to be moved.*)

> **The word <u>were</u> and the word <u>only</u> moved to row two. They were very mad.**
>
> **<u>Run</u> sat in the seat that <u>were</u> had used. <u>Run</u> was next to some relatives of <u>were</u> who were still in the first row. One word was <u>are</u>.**

2. Everybody, which relative of **were** was still in the front row? (Signal.) *Are.*

> **<u>Are</u> turned to <u>run</u> and said, "They'll probably move you back next week."**
>
> **<u>Run</u> laughed and said, "I don't care. I'll remember this forever. This is great."**
>
> **By the end of that Friday, <u>run</u> could turn around and talk to some of its relatives that were in row two.**

1. Name some relatives of **run.** (Call on individual students. Ideas: *Runner, ran, running,* etc.)

> **The words <u>running</u>, <u>runs</u>, and <u>ran</u> were in row 2. <u>Runner</u> was in row five, but runner was very happy. "I never thought I would even see this part of the word bank," <u>runner</u> said.**

2. Everybody, who was said more often, **running** or **runner?** (Signal.) *Running.*
2. How do you know? (Call on a student. Idea: *Because it was closer to the front.*)
2. Everybody, which member of the **run** family was said most often? (Signal.) *Run.*

> **When the next Friday came around, the words like <u>run</u> and <u>walk</u> and <u>jump</u> and the others kept their seats near the front of the word bank. In fact, they're still there. And <u>run</u> is no longer sad. In fact, run is happy all day and all night. <u>Run</u> yells and shouts and says, "That's me. I'm number one." And the other words that had been in the last row are happier than they ever thought they would be.**
>
> **THE END**

1. Go back to the beginning of the story. Follow along while I read.

2. Why were they happy? (Call on a student. Ideas: *Because they were being said a lot; because they're not in the back row anymore.*)

EXERCISE 4

PAIRED PRACTICE

You're going to read aloud to your partner. Today the **A** members will read first. Then the **B** members will read from the star to the end of the story.
(Observe students and give feedback.)

End-of-Lesson Activities

INDEPENDENT WORK

Now finish your independent work for lesson 112. First do the worksheet. Raise your hand when you're finished.
(Observe students and give feedback.)

WORKCHECK

a. (Direct students to take out their marking pencils.)
• We're going to check your independent work. Remember, if you got an item wrong, make an **X** next to the item. Don't change any answers.
b. (For each item: Read the item. Call on a student to answer it. If the answer is wrong, say the correct answer. Refer to the Answer Key for the correct answers.)
c. Now use your marking pencil to fix up any items you got wrong. Remember, all mistakes must be fixed up before you hand in your independent work.

> *Note:* You will need a globe for lesson 113.

WRITING-SPELLING

(Present Writing-Spelling lesson 112 after completing Reading lesson 112. See Writing-Spelling Guide.)

LANGUAGE ARTS GUIDE

(Present Language Arts lesson 112 after completing Reading lesson 112. See Language Arts Guide.)

Lesson 113

Materials: You will need a globe for exercise 4.

EXERCISE 1
VOCABULARY REVIEW

a. You learned a sentence that tells what she commented about.
- Everybody, say that sentence. Get ready. (Signal.) *She commented about the still water.*
- (Repeat until firm.)

b. You learned a sentence that tells what surprised the neighbors.
- Say that sentence. Get ready. (Signal.) *Their amazing effort surprised the neighbors.*
- (Repeat until firm.)

c. Here's the last sentence you learned: Police officers checked the ship's cargo.
- Everybody, say that sentence. Get ready. (Signal.) *Police officers checked the ship's cargo.*
- (Repeat until firm.)

d. What words mean **cops?** (Signal.) *Police officers.*
- What word refers to the things that a ship carries? (Signal.) *Cargo.*

e. Once more. Say the sentence that tells what the police officers checked. Get ready. (Signal.) *Police officers checked the ship's cargo.*

EXERCISE 2
READING WORDS

Column 1

a. **Find lesson 113 in your textbook.** ✓
- Touch column 1. ✓
- (Teacher reference:)

1. finest	4. ashamed
2. breathed	5. dancing
3. dusty	6. soundly

- All these words have endings.

b. Word 1. What word? (Signal.) *Finest.*

- Something that is the finest is the most expensive or the best. They had the finest table. That means their table was very special.

c. Word 2. What word? (Signal.) *Breathed.*
- (Repeat for words 3–6.)

d. Let's read those words again.
- Word 1. What word? (Signal.) *Finest.*
- (Repeat for words 2–6.)

Column 2

e. Find column 2. ✓
- (Teacher reference:)

1. triple	4. double
2. Australia	5. Toby
3. cloud	6. refers

f. Word 1. What word? (Signal.) *Triple.*
- **Triple** means **three times as much.** If you triple how many books you read, you read three times as many books.

g. Word 2. What word? (Signal.) *Australia.*
- (Repeat for words 3–6.)

h. Let's read those words again.
- Word 1. What word? (Signal.) *Triple.*
- (Repeat for words 2–6.)

Column 3

i. Find column 3. ✓
- (Teacher reference:)

1. kangaroo	4. drunk
2. joey	5. stomping
3. herd	6. carries

j. Word 1. What word? (Signal.) *Kangaroo.*
- (Repeat for words 2–6.)

k. Let's read those words again.
- Word 1. What word? (Signal.) *Kangaroo.*
- (Repeat for words 2–6.)

Individual Turns

(For columns 1–3: Call on individual students, each to read one to three words per turn.)

COMPREHENSION PASSAGE

a. Find part B in your textbook. ✓
- You're going to read a story about a kangaroo. First you'll read the information passage. It gives some facts about Australia.

b. Everybody, touch the title. ✓
- (Call on a student to read the title.) *[Facts About Australia.]*
- Everybody, what's the title? (Signal.) *Facts About Australia.*

c. (Call on individual students to read the passage, each student reading two or three sentences at a time.)

Facts About Australia

The story that you will read today begins in Australia.

- Everybody, where does it begin? (Signal.) *Australia.*

The map shows that the United States and Canada are on one side of the world. Australia is on the other side of the world.

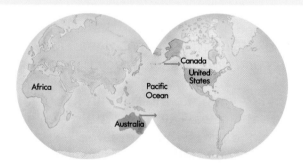

- Everybody, touch the side of the world that has the United States and Canada on it. ✓
- Touch the side of the world that has Australia on it. ✓

Touch the United States.

- Everybody, do it. ✓

Touch Canada.

- Everybody, do it. ✓

Touch Australia.

- Everybody, do it. ✓

Touch the United States again.

- Everybody, do it. ✓

Now go west from the United States.

- Everybody, do it. ✓

What's the name of the ocean you go through when you go west from the United States?

- Everybody, what's the answer? (Signal.) *Pacific Ocean.*

The ocean that is west of the United States is the same ocean that is east of Australia.

- Everybody, touch the arrow that is leaving Australia. ✓
- In which direction is that arrow pointing? (Signal.) *East.*
- Now touch the arrow that is touching Canada. ✓
- In which direction is that arrow pointing? (Signal.) *East.*

Many animals that live in Australia do not live in any other place in the world.

- Listen to that fact again: Many animals that live in Australia do not live in any other place in the world.

You can find some of these animals in zoos, but the only place you can find them living as wild animals is Australia.
Below are some animals that live in Australia.

- I'll read the names of the animals in the picture. You touch the pictures.
- Platypus. ✓
- Kangaroo. ✓

- Koala. ✓
- Your turn to read the names. Tell me the name of the first animal. Get ready. (Signal.) *Platypus.*
- Next animal. Get ready. (Signal.) *Kangaroo.*
- Next animal. Get ready. (Signal.) *Koala.*
- (Repeat student identification of animals until firm.)

EXERCISE 4

GLOBE

a. I'll show the path from Australia to Canada. (Present a globe. Face the same direction the students are facing. Touch Australia on the globe. Start moving your finger north and east across the Pacific. Continue moving north and east until you reach Canada.)
b. Touch Australia. (Call on a student.) ✓
- Now go north and east to Canada. (As the student's finger moves north and east, ask:) In which directions are you going? *[North and east.]*
- (Repeat step b with other students.)
c. (Call on a student.)
- Touch the United States.
- Go south and west from the United States until you reach Australia. (As the student's finger moves south and west, ask:) In which directions are you going? *[South and west.]*
- (Repeat step c with other students.)

EXERCISE 5

STORY READING

a. Find part C in your textbook. ✓
- The error limit for group reading is 10. Read carefully.
b. Everybody, touch the title. ✓
- (Call on a student to read the title.) *[Toby the Kangaroo.]*
- Everybody, what's the title? (Signal.) *Toby the Kangaroo.*
c. (Call on individual students to read the story, each student reading two or three sentences at a time. Ask questions marked **1.**)

- (Correct errors: Tell the word. Direct the student to reread the sentence.)
- (If the group makes more than 10 errors, direct the students to reread the story.)

d. (After the group has read the selection making no more than 10 errors, read the story to the students and ask questions marked **2.**)

Toby the Kangaroo

1. Everybody, what kind of animal is Toby? (Signal.) *A kangaroo.*

This story starts in Australia, where Toby lived. Toby was a kangaroo. Like other kangaroos, he was part of a mob. A mob is a herd of kangaroos. There were over 50 kangaroos in Toby's mob.

2. Everybody, listen to the fact again: A mob is a herd of kangaroos. What do we call a herd of kangaroos? (Signal.) *A mob.*
2. How many kangaroos were in Toby's mob? (Signal.) *Over 50.*

Toby's mob was not the biggest mob in Australia and it was not the smallest, but it was like the other mobs in one way: It moved around from place to place.

2. What did Toby's mob do that other mobs did? (Call on a student. Idea: *Moved around from place to place.*)

Every year, the mob would move in a great circle. The mob would stay in a place for a while, until the kangaroos had eaten the grass or drunk the water holes dry.

1. Everybody, what kind of food do kangaroos eat? (Signal.) *Grass.*
1. So after they've eaten all the grass, what do they have to do? (Call on a student. Ideas: *Find more grass; move on.*)
1. And what do they have to do when they run out of water to drink? (Call on a student. Ideas: *Find more water; move on.*)

Then the mob would hop, hop, hop to the next place where there was grass and water.

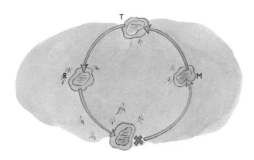

2. Everybody, touch the map. It shows how Toby's mob moved every year. The **X** is where it starts out. Touch the **X**. ✓
2. Follow the arrow to the first place it stops.
2. What's the letter of that place? (Signal.) *M.*
2. Follow the next arrow around to the next letter. What letter? (Signal.) *T.*
2. Keep following the arrows all the way around until you get back to the **X**. ✓
2. That's the path that Toby's mob took every year.

> **Those 50 kangaroos hop, hop, hopped on ground that was dry and dusty.**

1. If you stamp around on dry, dusty ground, you're going to make dust. Can you imagine the cloud of dust that 50 hopping kangaroos would make?

> **Those kangaroos made a cloud of dust that you could see for many miles. When the ground was very, very dry, the leader of the mob would be the first to hop along. Just behind the leader would be other kangaroos that were important in the mob. The kangaroos that were right behind the leader were more important than the kangaroos that came after them.**

2. Everybody, who is the most important kangaroo in the mob? (Signal.) *The leader.*
2. Where is the leader when the mob moves? (Call on a student. Idea: *In front.*)

2. Which kangaroos come just behind the leader? (Call on a student. Idea: *Other important kangaroos.*)
2. Everybody, touch the leader in the picture. ✓
2. Touch a kangaroo that is not a leader but that is important to the mob. ✓
2. Touch a kangaroo that is not very important to the mob. ✓

> **The leader did not have to breathe any dust. The important kangaroos that came right after the leader had to breathe a little bit of dust. The kangaroos that were not very important to the mob came last, right in the middle of the dust.**

1. How much dust did the leader breathe? (Call on a student. Idea: *None.*)
1. How much dust did the important kangaroos breathe? (Call on a student. Idea: *A little bit.*)
1. If a kangaroo is not very important, how far back is that kangaroo? (Call on a student. Idea: *Very far back.*)
1. So if a kangaroo is not very important, how much dust does that kangaroo breathe? (Call on a student. Idea: *A lot.*)

> **Toby was the last kangaroo in the whole mob.**

2. If Toby was the last kangaroo in the whole mob, you know how important he was to the mob. How important? (Call on a student. Idea: *Not very.*)
2. And how much fun do you think he had when the mob moved from place to place? (Call on a student. Ideas: *Not very much; none.*)
2. Why? (Call on a student. Idea: *Because he had to breathe lots of dust.*)

> **Toby breathed lots and lots of dust. When the leader said that the mob was going to move to another place, some of the kangaroos would cheer.**

2. Which ones do you think would cheer? (Call on a student. Idea: *The ones near the front of the mob.*)

> **Toby did not cheer. He would say things like, "Oh, bad, double bad, and big bad."**

1. Who can say that the way Toby would say it? (Call on a student. Student should speak in a grumbling tone of voice.)

> If you looked at Toby, you might wonder why he was the very last kangaroo. He was a fine-looking kangaroo. He was strong. And he had the finest tail of any kangaroo in the mob. He was nearly as big as the biggest kangaroo in the mob, but Toby was just a boy kangaroo.

1. Everybody, was Toby full-grown? (Signal.) *No.*
1. How big was he? (Call on a student. Idea: *Nearly as big as the biggest kangaroos in the mob.*)
1. What do you know about his tail? (Call on a student. Idea: *It was the finest in the mob.*)
• He seems like a fine kangaroo. I wonder why he was not important in the mob.

> The other kangaroos looked at Toby and said, "He is a fine-looking kangaroo. Too bad he's a joey."

2. Everybody, what do they call him? (Signal.) *A joey.*

> A kangaroo does not like to be called a joey. A joey is a baby kangaroo. So when you call a big boy kangaroo a joey, you are calling him a big baby.

2. Everybody, what's a joey? (Signal.) *A baby kangaroo.*

> Toby sure didn't like to be called a joey, but Toby was a big baby. He didn't work. He was always saying things like, "Bad, double bad, big bad." The only two things he liked to do were eat and sleep.

2. Everybody, did he like to work? (Signal.) *No.*

> He could eat faster than anything you've ever seen eat. And he could sleep so soundly that he wouldn't wake up if the mob was singing and dancing and stomping all around him.

1. Go back to the beginning of the story. Follow along while I read.
2. Read the rest of the story to yourself. Find out what Toby will do later in this story. Raise your hand when you're done.

> So Toby had to stay near the back of the mob as he hopped along and breathed dust. He kept mumbling, "Oh, double and triple bad." When the mob stopped for a rest, Toby had to listen to the other kangaroos call him a joey. Even Toby's mother was ashamed of him. She liked him, but she wished that he would grow up and stop being a joey. She did not know that very soon Toby would save the mob from kangaroo hunters.
> **MORE NEXT TIME**

2. (After all students have raised their hand:) What is Toby going to do later in this story? (Call on a student. Idea: *Save the mob from kangaroo hunters.*)
2. Everybody, does his mother know that he'll do that? (Signal.) *No.*
2. How does she feel about him now? (Call on a student. Ideas: *Sort of ashamed; likes him; wishes he'd grow up.*)

EXERCISE 6

PAIRED PRACTICE

You're going to read aloud to your partner. Today the **B** members will read first. Then the **A** members will read from the star to the end of the story.
(Observe students and give feedback.)

End-of-Lesson Activities

INDEPENDENT WORK

Now finish your independent work for lesson 113. Raise your hand when you're finished. (Observe students and give feedback.)

WORKCHECK

a. (Direct students to take out their marking pencils.)
• We're going to check your independent work. Remember, if you got an item wrong, make an **X** next to the item.

b. (For each item: Read the item. Call on a student to answer it. If the answer is wrong, say the correct answer. Refer to the Answer Key for the correct answers.)

c. Now use your marking pencil to fix up any items you got wrong. Remember, all mistakes must be fixed up before you hand in your work.

WRITING-SPELLING

(Present Writing-Spelling lesson 113 after completing Reading lesson 113. See Writing-Spelling Guide.)

ACTIVITY

(Present Activity 32 after completing Reading lesson 113. See Activities Across the Curriculum.)

LANGUAGE ARTS GUIDE

(Present Language Arts lesson 113 after completing Reading lesson 113. See Language Arts Guide.)

Lesson 114

READING WORDS

Column 1

a. **Find lesson 114 in your textbook.** ✓
- Touch column 1. ✓
- (Teacher reference:)

1. koala	4. tough
2. ruin	5. suit
3. India	

b. Word 1 is **koala.** What word? (Signal.) *Koala.*
- Spell **koala.** Get ready. (Tap for each letter.) *K-O-A-L-A.*
- A koala is an animal that looks like a teddy bear and lives in Australia.

c. Word 2 is **ruin.** What word? (Signal.) *Ruin.*
- Spell **ruin.** Get ready. (Tap for each letter.) *R-U-I-N.*
- When you ruin something, you destroy it or do something to it so it won't work. Everybody, what's another word for **destroy?** (Signal.) *Ruin.*

d. Word 3 is **India.** What word? (Signal.) *India.*
- Spell **India.** Get ready. (Tap for each letter.) *I-N-D-I-A.*
- India is a large country on the other side of the world. It is just south of China.

e. Word 4 is **tough.** What word? (Signal.) *Tough.*
- Spell **tough.** Get ready. (Tap for each letter.) *T-O-U-G-H.*

f. Word 5 is **suit.** What word? (Signal.) *Suit.*

g. Let's read those words again, the fast way.
- Word 1. What word? (Signal.) *Koala.*
- (Repeat for words 2–5.)

h. (Repeat step g until firm.)

Column 2

i. Find column 2. ✓

- (Teacher reference:)

1. lookout	4. perfect
2. pouch	5. perfectly
3. warn	

j. Word 1. What word? (Signal.) *Lookout.*
- A lookout is a person who looks in all directions to see if trouble is near. Everybody, what do we call a person who looks to see if trouble is near? (Signal.) *Lookout.*

k. Word 2. What word? (Signal.) *Pouch.*
- A pouch is a small bag that holds things. Everybody, what do we call a small bag? (Signal.) *Pouch.*
- A mother kangaroo has a pouch on her belly where the baby kangaroo stays for a long time.

l. Word 3. What word? (Signal.) *Warn.*
- When you warn people, you let them know that trouble is near. Everybody, what are you doing when you tell somebody that trouble is near? (Signal.) *Warning.*

m. Word 4. What word? (Signal.) *Perfect.*

n. Word 5. What word? (Signal.) *Perfectly.*

o. Let's read those words again.
- Word 1. What word? (Signal.) *Lookout.*
- (Repeat for words 2–5.)

p. (Repeat step o until firm.)

Column 3

q. Find column 3. ✓
- (Teacher reference:)

1. perform	3. forgotten
2. honey	4. performed

r. Word 1. What word? (Signal.) *Perform.*
- (Repeat for words 2–4.)

s. (Repeat step r until firm.)

Individual Turns

(For columns 1–3: Call on individual students, each to read one to three words per turn.)

COMPREHENSION PASSAGE

a. Find part B in your textbook. ✓
- You're going to read the next story about Toby. First you'll read the information passage. It gives some facts about kangaroos.

b. Everybody, touch the title. ✓
- (Call on a student to read the title.) *[Facts About Kangaroos.]*
- Everybody, what's the title? (Signal.) *Facts About Kangaroos.*

c. (Call on individual students to read the passage, each student reading two or three sentences at a time.)

> **Facts About Kangaroos**
>
> **Here are facts about kangaroos:**
> • **There are many different kinds of kangaroos.**

- Everybody, say that fact. Get ready. (Signal.) *There are many different kinds of kangaroos.*
- (Repeat until firm.)

> **Some kangaroos are as big as a man. Other full-grown kangaroos are not much bigger than a rabbit.**

- Show me the size of a kangaroo that is not much bigger than a rabbit. ✓

> **When a kangaroo is born, it is only three centimeters long.**

3 centimeters

PICTURE 1

- Everybody, listen to that fact again: When a kangaroo is born, it is only three centimeters long.
- Say that fact. Get ready. (Signal.) *When a kangaroo is born, it is only three centimeters long.*
- (Repeat until firm.)
- Show me how long three centimeters is. ✓
- Picture 1 shows how big a newborn kangaroo is. Use your fingers to measure that kangaroo. ✓
- That's the real size of a newborn kangaroo.

> **The baby kangaroo lives in its mother's pouch for half a year.**

- Everybody, listen to that fact again: The baby kangaroo lives in its mother's pouch for half a year.
- Say that fact. Get ready. (Signal.) *The baby kangaroo lives in its mother's pouch for half a year.*
- (Repeat until firm.)
- Where does the baby kangaroo live at first? (Signal.) *In its mother's pouch.*
- How long does the baby kangaroo live in its mother's pouch? (Signal.) *Half a year.*
- Touch the baby kangaroo in picture 2. ✓
- Everybody, is that a newborn kangaroo? (Signal.) *No.*
- How do you know? (Call on a student. Ideas: *Because it's much bigger; it looks older.*)

> **Kangaroos have strong back legs and strong tails.**

- Everybody, touch the back leg of the mother kangaroo in picture 2. ✓
- Touch the tail. ✓
- You can see that the back legs and the tail are very strong. Their back legs are very strong because kangaroos use their back legs to hop around.

> **In one jump, bigger kangaroos can jump over 10 feet.**

- Everybody, how far can a big kangaroo go in one jump? (Signal.) *Over 10 feet.*

> **If a big kangaroo hit you with its tail, it would knock you down.**

STORY READING

a. Find part C in your textbook. ✓
- The error limit for group reading is 10. Read carefully.

b. Everybody, touch the title. ✓

- (Call on a student to read the title.)
  [*A Job for Toby.*]
- Everybody, what's the title? (Signal.)
  A Job for Toby.
c. (Call on individual students to read the story, each student reading two or three sentences at a time. Ask questions marked **1.**)

> - (Correct errors: Tell the word. Direct the student to reread the sentence.)
> - (If the group makes more than 10 errors, direct the students to reread the story.)

d. (After the group has read the selection making no more than 10 errors, read the story to the students and ask questions marked **2.**)

A Job for Toby

Toby was called a joey. Toby had to hop along through the dust at the back of the mob. And there were only two things that Toby really liked to do.

1. What were the other kangaroos saying about Toby when they called him a joey? (Call on a student. Idea: *That he acted like a big baby.*)
1. What kind of kangaroos were near the front of the mob? (Call on a student. Idea: *Important ones.*)
1. Why was Toby at the back? (Call on a student. Idea: *Because he wasn't very important.*)
1. What were the two things that Toby liked to do? (Call on a student. Idea: *Eat and sleep.*)

Just after the sun came up one day, the leader of the mob hopped over to where Toby was sleeping. The leader hit the ground with his tail. He hit it so hard that it made a thump you could hear two miles away.

2. Everybody, how far away could you hear that thump? (Signal.) *2 miles.*
2. Was that very loud? (Signal.) *Yes.*

Although Toby could sleep through nearly anything, he woke up. The leader looked at him and said, "The time has come for you to stop being a joey. Today you are going to be a lookout."

1. Everybody, what does the leader want Toby to be? (Signal.) *A lookout.*

Then the leader asked, "Do you know what a lookout does?"

1. What would a lookout do? (Call on a student. Idea: *Watch for trouble.*)

Toby said, "A lookout looks out for trouble." Toby was a little frightened. This was the first time the leader had spoken to him.
The leader said, "And what does a lookout do if there is trouble?"
Toby blinked. Then he said, "Smack your foot on the ground so that it makes a big noise."
"You are right," the leader said.

2. How was Toby to warn the others about trouble? (Call on a student. Idea: *Smack his foot on the ground so that it made a big noise.*)

Then the leader continued, "Go to the top of that hill and look out for a couple of hours. Then the mob will start moving."

2. Everybody, how long will Toby look out from the hill? (Signal.) *A couple of hours.*
2. How long is a couple of hours? (Call on a student. Idea: *About two hours.*)
2. What will happen after a couple of hours have passed? (Call on a student. Idea: *The mob will start moving.*)

Toby looked at the hill the leader pointed to. It was a very big hill. Toby was thinking about how hard it was going to be to climb to the top of that hill. But he didn't say anything, except, "Okay."

2. Why do you think he didn't say anything like, "Oh double bad?" (Call on a student. Ideas: *Because he was afraid of the leader; because he didn't want the leader to think he was a baby.*)

As Toby started up the hill, his mother hopped up to him. "Be careful, honey," she said. "Remember what happened to your father."

"Oh, bad and big bad," Toby mumbled. He had almost forgotten about his father.

Years ago, when Toby was just a tiny kangaroo in his mother's pouch, Toby's father was a lookout. But he fell asleep and hunters caught him. Nobody in the mob ever saw his father again. But some of the kangaroos heard that he had been taken from Australia to another country, far across the Pacific Ocean. He was supposed to be in some kind of circus in that country.

2. What was his father supposed to be doing when he fell asleep? (Call on a student. Idea: *Looking out for trouble.*)
2. Everybody, who caught him? (Signal.) *Hunters.*
2. Where did some kangaroos say his father went? (Call on a student. Ideas: *To another country far away; to a circus across the Pacific Ocean.*)

Toby remembered his father. His father had the longest tail that any kangaroo ever had. And Toby's father had three large white spots on the top of his tail. Toby would never forget such a fine tail.

2. How was his father's tail different from those of other kangaroos? (Call on a student. Ideas: *It was the longest; it had three large white spots on top.*)

So Toby continued up the hill.

1. We're back to the day when Toby is going up the hill to be a lookout.

He was getting so tired that he could hardly mumble, "Double, double bad." Finally, he reached the top, where he caught his breath.

2. What does that mean, he caught his breath? (Call on a student. Idea: *He stopped and rested.*)

The sun was bright. The air was clear. There was no dust. When Toby sat down, he didn't mean to fall asleep, but he did.

2. What did Toby do after he sat down? (Call on a student. Idea: *Fell asleep.*)
• That's the same thing his father did.

Toby really wanted to be a good lookout. He wanted to show the other kangaroos that he was not a big, lazy joey. But with the bright sun shining down, and that soft grass under him, he just rolled over, closed his eyes, and . . . zzzzzzzzz . . . zzzzzzzzz . . . . He was snoring away.

1. Go back to the beginning of the story. Follow along while I read.
2. Read the rest of the story to yourself. Find out what Toby saw when he woke up. Raise your hand when you're done.

For a while, he was having a nice dream. Then he heard a voice in his dream. The voice said, "Don't wake that lookout. He'll warn the others." Suddenly, Toby realized that the voice was not part of a dream. He opened his eyes and looked around. Five hunters were sneaking past him on their way down the hill to the mob.
MORE NEXT TIME

2. (After all the students have raised their hand:) Everybody, who was sneaking past Toby when he woke up? (Signal.) *Hunters.*
2. How many hunters were there? (Signal.) *Five.*
2. At first, Toby thought he was having a dream. What did he hear a voice say in his dream? (Call on a student. Idea: *Don't wake the lookout. He'll warn the others.*)
2. Everybody, were those hunters after Toby? (Signal.) *No.*
2. Who were they after? (Call on a student. Idea: *The mob.*)
2. Why didn't they want to wake Toby? (Call on a student. Idea: *Because they didn't want Toby to warn the mob that hunters were coming.*)

PAIRED PRACTICE

You're going to read aloud to your partner. Today the **A** members will read first. Then the **B** members will read from the star to the end of the story.

(Observe students and give feedback.)

End-of-Lesson Activities

INDEPENDENT WORK

Now finish your independent work for lesson 114. Raise your hand when you're finished.

(Observe students and give feedback.)

WORKCHECK

a. (Direct students to take out their marking pencils.)

- We're going to check your independent work items. Remember, if you got an item wrong, make an **X** next to the item.

b. (For each item: Read the item. Call on a student to answer it. If the answer is wrong, say the correct answer. Refer to the Answer Key for the correct answers.)

c. Now use your marking pencil to fix up any items you got wrong. Remember, all mistakes must be fixed up before you hand in your work.

WRITING-SPELLING

(Present Writing-Spelling lesson 114 after completing Reading lesson 114. See Writing-Spelling Guide.)

LANGUAGE ARTS GUIDE

(Present Language Arts lesson 114 after completing Reading lesson 114. See Language Arts Guide.)

Materials: Each student will need their thermometer chart for exercise 6.

EXERCISE 1

VOCABULARY

a. **Find page 342 in your textbook.** ✓
- Touch sentence 28.
- This is a new vocabulary sentence. It says: The champions performed perfectly.
 Everybody, read that sentence. Get ready. (Signal.) *The champions performed perfectly.*
- Close your eyes and say the sentence. Get ready. (Signal.) *The champions performed perfectly.*
- (Repeat until firm.)

b. The sentence says the champions **performed perfectly.** When you **perform,** you put on a show. If you perform well, you put on a good show. If you perform **perfectly,** you don't make any mistakes.

c. Listen to the sentence again: The champions performed perfectly. Everybody, say the sentence. Get ready. (Signal.) *The champions performed perfectly.*

d. What word means **put on a show?** (Signal.) *Performed.*
- What word means **without any mistakes?** (Signal.) *Perfectly.*
- What word means they won the championship? (Signal.) *Champions.*
- (Repeat step d until firm.)

EXERCISE 2

READING WORDS

Column 1

a. Find lesson 115 in your textbook. ✓
- Touch column 1. ✓
- (Teacher reference:)

1. **feather**	3. **heading**
2. **spread**	

- All these words have the combination **E-A.** That combination makes the sound ĕ in these words.
b. Word 1. What word? (Signal.) *Feather.*
- Spell **feather.** Get ready. (Tap for each letter.) *F-E-A-T-H-E-R.*
c. Word 2. What word? (Signal.) *Spread.*
- Spell **spread.** Get ready. (Tap for each letter.) *S-P-R-E-A-D.*
d. Word 3. What word? (Signal.) *Heading.*
- Spell **heading.** Get ready. (Tap for each letter.) *H-E-A-D-I-N-G.*
e. Let's read those words again, the fast way.
- Word 1. What word? (Signal.) *Feather.*
- (Repeat for words 2–3.)
f. (Repeat step e until firm.)

Column 2

g. Find column 2. ✓
- (Teacher reference:)

1. **pea**cock	4. **signal**ed
2. **color**ful	5. **tack**led
3. **sail**ors	

- All these words have more than one syllable. The first part of each word is underlined.
h. Word 1. What's the underlined part? (Signal.) *pea.*
- What's the whole word? (Signal.) *Peacock.*
- A peacock is a very large bird with beautiful feathers.
i. Word 2. What's the underlined part? (Signal.) *color.*
- What's the whole word? (Signal.) *Colorful.*
j. Word 3. What's the underlined part? (Signal.) *sail.*
- What's the whole word? (Signal.) *Sailors.*
k. Word 4. What's the underlined part? (Signal.) *sig.*
- What's the whole word? (Signal.) *Signaled.*
l. Word 5. What's the underlined part? (Signal.) *tack.*
- What's the whole word? (Signal.) *Tackled.*

m. Let's read those words again, the fast way.
- Word 1. What word? (Signal.) *Peacock.*
- (Repeat for: **2. colorful, 3. sailors, 4. signaled, 5. tackled.**)
n. (Repeat step m until firm.)

Column 3

o. Find column 3. ✓
- (Teacher reference:)

1. **screeches**	4. **tough**
2. **dark-colored**	5. **performed**
3. **ruin**	

p. Word 1. What word? (Signal.) *Screeches.*
- A screech is a high, sharp sound. Some birds screech.
q. Word 2. What word? (Signal.) *Dark-colored.*
- (Repeat for words 3–5.)
r. Let's read those words again.
- Word 1. What word? (Signal.) *Screeches.*
- (Repeat for words 2–5.)
s. (Repeat step r until firm.)

Column 4

t. Find column 4. ✓
- (Teacher reference:)

1. **Mabel**	4. **argued**
2. **koalas**	5. **perfectly**
3. **suit**	

u. Word 1. What word? (Signal.) *Mabel.*
- That's the name of a woman you'll read about.
v. Word 2. What word? (Signal.) *Koalas.*
- (Repeat for words 3–5.)
w. Let's read those words again.
- Word 1. What word? (Signal.) *Mabel.*
- (Repeat for words 2–5.)
x. (Repeat step w until firm.)

Individual Turns

(For columns 1–4: Call on individual students, each to read one to three words)

EXERCISE 3

VOCABULARY REVIEW

a. Here's the new vocabulary sentence: The champions performed perfectly.

- Everybody, say that sentence. Get ready. (Signal.) *The champions performed perfectly.*
- (Repeat until firm.)
b. What word means **without any mistakes?** (Signal.) *Perfectly.*
- What word means **put on a show?** (Signal.) *Performed.*

EXERCISE 4

COMPREHENSION PASSAGE

a. Find part B in your textbook. ✓
- You're going to read the next story about Toby. First you'll read the information passage. It gives some facts about peacocks.
b. Everybody, touch the title. ✓
- (Call on a student to read the title.) *[Facts About Peacocks.]*
- Everybody, what's the title? (Signal.) *Facts About Peacocks.*
- What will this passage tell about? (Signal.) *Peacocks.*
c. (Call on individual students to read the passage, each student reading two or three sentences at a time.)

Facts About Peacocks

You will read about a peacock in the next lesson. Here are facts about peacocks:
A peacock is a large bird.

- Everybody, say that fact. Get ready. (Signal.) *A peacock is a large bird.*
- (Repeat until firm.)

A full-grown peacock is two meters long from its head to the end of its tail.

- Everybody, how long is a peacock from its head to the end of its tail? (Signal.) *Two meters long.*
- Show me one meter long. ✓
- So that is a very long bird.

The feathers of the male peacock are more colorful than the feathers of any other bird.

- Everybody, is a male peacock a "man" or a "woman"? (Signal.) *A man.*

- A male peacock has blue feathers, green feathers, and golden feathers. The male peacock looks like a rainbow of colors.

When the male peacock shows off, it spreads out its tail feathers.

- The peacock is so long because its tail is very long. When the male shows off, it spreads its tail out so it looks like a fan.
- Touch the tail of the peacock in the picture. ✓
- That's how the male looks when it is showing off. The rest of the time, the tail is not spread out like that.

The peacock is not a wild bird of Australia.

- Everybody, is the peacock wild in Australia? (Signal.) *No.*
- It doesn't live in Australia. It lives in a country called India.

The peacock has a very unpleasant voice. The peacock does not sing. It screeches.

- The peacock looks as if it should have a beautiful voice, but its voice is ugly.

EXERCISE 5

STORY READING

a. Find part C in your textbook. ✓
- The error limit for group reading is 11. Read carefully.
b. Everybody, touch the title. ✓
- (Call on a student to read the title.) *[The Kangaroo Hunters.]*
- Everybody, what's the title? (Signal.) *The Kangaroo Hunters.*
c. (Call on individual students to read the story, each student reading two or three sentences at a time. Ask questions marked 1.)

> - (Correct errors: Tell the word. Direct the student to reread the sentence.)
> - (If the group makes more than 11 errors, direct the students to reread the story.)

d. (After the group has read the selection making no more than 11 errors, read the story to the students and ask questions marked 2.)

The Kangaroo Hunters

Toby woke up and saw five kangaroo hunters. The leader was named Mabel. She was tough and nobody argued with her, not even the captain.

2. Everybody, how many hunters were trying to sneak past Toby? (Signal.) *Five.*
2. We know about two of them. Everybody, who was the leader? (Signal.) *Mabel.*
2. Who was the second hunter? (Signal.) *The captain.*

The captain was the captain of a ship that was waiting about ten miles from Toby and the mob. The captain's sailor suit was too big for him and he kept pulling his pants up. The other three hunters were sailors from the ship.

2. Everybody, about how far away was the captain's ship? (Signal.) *10 miles.*
2. Two of the five hunters were Mabel and the captain. Who were the last three hunters? (Call on a student. Idea: *Sailors from the ship.*)

Mabel ran a large circus in Canada. She was on a trip around the world to get animals—lots of them. She came to Australia to get kangaroos and koalas. She didn't plan to use all the animals that she caught. She planned to sell many of them to zoos or other circuses. She would keep the best animals.

2. Which animals was she after in Australia? (Call on a student.) *Kangaroos and koalas.*
2. Everybody, what was she going to do with the best animals? (Signal.) *Keep them.*
2. What was she going to do with the rest of the animals she caught? (Call on a student. Idea: *Sell them to zoos or circuses.*)

When Mabel saw the mob down at the bottom of the hill, she knew that she was close to some very good animals. She sat down in the tall grass next to the captain. She whispered, "There's a big, dark kangaroo down there. We must get her."

"Yeah," the captain said in a loud voice.

"Be quiet," Mabel whispered. "If you wake up that lookout, you'll ruin everything."

2. Everybody, what lookout is she worried about? (Signal.) *Toby.*

"Oh, yeah," the captain said in a whisper and turned around to see if Toby was still sleeping. He seemed to be sleeping, but he wasn't. He was listening to everything Mabel and the captain were saying. He was pretending to be asleep because he didn't know what else to do. He didn't want to slam his foot against the ground because he was afraid that the hunters might shoot him. He didn't want to be shot.

2. Everybody, was Toby asleep? (Signal.) *No.*
2. Why didn't he warn the mob? (Call on a student. Idea: *Because he didn't want to get shot.*)

"Come on," Mabel said as she put her binoculars away. "Let's sneak down this hill and get behind the mob. We should be able to catch at least five kangaroos before they know we're around. Let's just make sure that we get that big, dark-colored one."

2. Which kangaroo are they most interested in? (Call on a student. Idea: *The big, dark-colored one.*)
2. How do they plan to get that kangaroo? (Call on a student. Idea: *By sneaking down the hill.*)

"Yeah, let's go," the captain said, and signaled his men to follow Mabel down the hill.

2. Everybody, show me how he would do that. ✓

So there was Toby, pretending to be asleep as the hunters started to sneak down the hill. Below him was the mob. As Toby watched the hunters move down the hill, he said to himself, "Oh, great big bad. I can't let those hunters take kangaroos from my mob."

What do you think he'll do? (Call on a student. Ideas: *Warn them; smack his foot on the ground.*)

Toby sat up. He lifted his foot into the air and he brought it down with a terrible smack. The sound echoed through the hills. For a moment, every kangaroo in the mob stood still, without moving and without breathing. Again, Toby signaled— smack.

1. What do you think the kangaroos will do? (Call on a student. Idea: *Get away.*)

This time, the kangaroos moved. And did they ever move fast. They all took off in the same direction at full speed.

2. How fast were they going? (Call on a student. Ideas: *As fast as they could; at full speed.*)

They made a cloud of dust that you could see all the way back at the captain's ship.

2. Raise your hand if you can remember about how far away that ship was. (Call on a student.) How far? *[10 miles.]*

"Run, jump, get away from those hunters," Toby shouted as he smacked his foot against the ground again.

Mabel stood up, turned around, and looked at Toby. Then she shouted, "Well, there is <u>one</u> kangaroo that is not going to get away."

1. Say that the way Mabel said it. Say the underlined word very loudly. (Call on a student. Student should say **one** louder than the other words.)

1. Everybody, which kangaroo was she talking about? (Signal.) *Toby.*

> "Yeah, that's <u>right</u>," the captain hollered in a mean voice. The captain and Mabel were looking right at Toby.

1. Go back to the beginning of the story. Follow along while I read.
2. Read the rest of the story to yourself. Find out what happened to Toby. Raise your hand when you're finished.

> "Oh, triple bad," Toby said to himself and started to hop down the other side of the hill. He went fast, but one of the sailors went faster than Toby went. By the time Toby reached the bottom of the hill, that sailor was right behind him. With a great leap, Toby tried to get away. With a greater leap, the sailor tackled Toby.
> "We <u>got</u> him," Mabel yelled.
> "Yeah," the captain said.
> **MORE NEXT TIME**

2. (After all students have raised their hand:) What happened to Toby? (Call on a student. Ideas: *He got tackled; he got caught.*)
2. Where was he when he finally got caught? (Call on a student. Idea: *At the bottom of the hill.*)
2. Who caught him? (Call on a student. Idea: *One of the sailors.*)
2. Everybody, did Toby save the mob? (Signal.) *Yes.*

EXERCISE 6

> ***Note:*** There is a reading checkout in this lesson; therefore, there is no paired practice.

READING CHECKOUTS

a. Today is a reading-checkout day. While you're doing your independent work, I'm going to call on you one at a time to read part of the story from lesson 114. When I call you to come and do your checkout, bring your thermometer chart.

- Remember, you pass the checkout by reading the passage in less than a minute without making more than 2 mistakes. And when you pass the checkout, you'll color the space for lesson 115 on your thermometer chart.
b. (Call on individual students to read the portion of story 114 marked with ❀.)
- (Time the student. Note words that are missed and total number of words read.)
- (Teacher reference:)

> ❀ Toby looked at the hill the leader pointed to. It was a very big hill. Toby was thinking about how hard it was going to be to climb to the top of that hill. But he didn't say anything, except, "Okay."
> As Toby started up the hill, his mother hopped [50] up to him. "Be careful, honey," she said. "Remember what happened to your father."
> "Oh, bad and big bad," Toby mumbled. He had almost forgotten [75] about his father.
> Years ago, when Toby was just a tiny kangaroo in his mother's pouch, Toby's father was a lookout. But he fell asleep [100] ❀ and hunters caught him.

- (If the student reads the passage in one minute or less and makes no more than 2 errors, direct the student to color in the space for lesson 115 on the thermometer chart.)
- (If the student makes any mistakes, point to each word that was misread and identify it.)
- (If the student does not meet the time-error criterion for the passage, direct the student to practice reading the story with the assigned partner.)

End-of-Lesson Activities

INDEPENDENT WORK

Now finish your independent work for lesson 115. Raise your hand when you're finished. (Observe students and give feedback.)

a. (Direct students to take out their marking pencils.)

• We're going to check your workbook and textbook items. Remember, if you got an item wrong, make an **X** next to the item.

b. (For each item: Read the item. Call on a student to answer it. If the answer is wrong, say the correct answer. Refer to the Answer Key for the correct answers.)

c. Now use your marking pencil to fix up any items you got wrong. Remember, all mistakes must be fixed up before you hand in your work.

> **Note:** You will need a clock with a second hand for Reading lesson 116.

WRITING-SPELLING

(Present Writing-Spelling lesson 115 after completing Reading lesson 115. See Writing-Spelling Guide.)

LANGUAGE ARTS GUIDE

(Present Language Arts lesson 115 after completing Reading lesson 115. See Language Arts Guide.)

Lessons 116–120 · Planning Page

	Lesson 116	**Lesson 117**	**Lesson 118**	**Lesson 119**	**Lesson 120**
Lesson Events	Vocabulary Review Reading Words Comprehension Passages Story Reading Paired Practice Independent Work Workcheck Writing-Spelling	Vocabulary Review Reading Words Story Reading Paired Practice Sequencing Independent Work Workcheck Writing-Spelling	**Vocabulary Sentence** Reading Words Vocabulary Review Comprehension Passage Story Reading Paired Practice Sequencing Independent Work Workcheck Writing-Spelling	Vocabulary Review Reading Words Comprehension Passage Story Reading Paired Practice Independent Work Workcheck Writing-Spelling	Fact Game Reading Checkouts Test Marking the Test Test Remedies Literature Lesson
Vocabulary Sentence	#28: The <u>champions</u> <u>performed</u> <u>perfectly</u>.	sentence #26 sentence #27 sentence #28	#29: She paid the <u>correct</u> <u>amount</u>.	#29: She paid the <u>correct</u> <u>amount</u>.	
Reading Words: Word Types	modeled words	modeled words multi-syllable words words with endings mixed words	modeled words multi-syllable words compound words mixed words	multi-syllable words mixed words	
New Vocabulary	preserve strutted ramp	certain recognize	illegal scolding roadside worthless sped graph	shabby rip-off	
Comprehension Passages	1) *Facts About Minutes* 2) *Facts About Ships*		*More Facts About Canada*	*Facts About a Circus*	
Story	*Toby on the Ship*	*The End of the Trip*	*The Ship Arrives in Canada*	*Toby's New Job*	
Skill Items	Deductions Compare	Vocabulary Sentence Sequencing	Vocabulary Sentences Sequencing	Sequencing	Test: Sequencing; Vocabulary Sentences #27, 28
Special Materials	Clock with second hand; writing materials for activity	Writing materials for activity	Writing materials for activity	Drawing materials (including large paper) for activity	Thermometer charts, dice, Fact Game 120, Fact Game Answer Key, scorecard sheets, *materials for literature project.
Special Projects/ Activities	Activity after lesson 116	Activity after lesson 117	Activity after lesson 118	Activity after lesson 119	

* Literature anthology; blackline masters 12A, 12B; lined paper; drawing materials (paper, crayons, markers, etc.).

Lesson 116

Materials: You will need a clock with a second hand for exercise 3, passage B.

EXERCISE 1

VOCABULARY REVIEW

a. Here's the new vocabulary sentence: The champions performed perfectly.
 • Everybody, say that sentence. Get ready. (Signal.) *The champions performed perfectly.*
 • (Repeat until firm.)
b. What word means **put on a show?** (Signal.) *Performed.*
 • What word means **without any mistakes?** (Signal.) *Perfectly.*

EXERCISE 2

READING WORDS

a. **Find lesson 116 in your textbook.** ✓
 • Touch word 1. ✓
 • (Teacher reference:)

1. **preserve**	4. **India**
2. **strutted**	5. **rainbow**
3. **ramp**	6. **aren't**

b. Word 1 is **preserve.** What word? (Signal.) *Preserve.*
 • Spell **preserve.** Get ready. (Tap for each letter.) *P-R-E-S-E-R-V-E.*
 • When you preserve something, you save it or protect it. An animal preserve is a place that protects animals. The animals run free on the animal preserve, and no hunting is allowed.
c. Word 2. What word? (Signal.) *Strutted.*
 • Spell **strutted.** Get ready. (Tap for each letter.) *S-T-R-U-T-T-E-D.*
 • Strutting is a kind of show-off walking. You act very proud. Everybody, what do we call show-off walking? (Signal.) *Strutting.*
d. Word 3. What word? (Signal.) *Ramp.*
 • Spell **ramp.** Get ready. (Tap for each letter.) *R-A-M-P.*

 • A ramp is a walkway that goes uphill. Everybody, what do we call a walkway that goes uphill? (Signal.) *Ramp.*
e. Word 4. What word? (Signal.) *India.*
 • Spell **India.** Get ready. (Tap for each letter.) *I-N-D-I-A.*
f. Word 5. What word? (Signal.) *Rainbow.*
g. Word 6. What word? (Signal.) *Aren't.*
h. Let's read those words again, the fast way.
 • Word 1. What word? (Signal.) *Preserve.*
 • (Repeat for words 2–6.)
i. (Repeat step h until firm.)

Individual Turns

(Call on individual students, each to read one to three words per turn.)

EXERCISE 3

COMPREHENSION PASSAGES

Passage B

a. Find part B in your textbook. ✓
 • You're going to read the next story about Toby. First you'll read two information passages. The first one gives some facts about time.
b. Everybody, touch the title. ✓
 • (Call on a student to read the title.) [*Facts About Minutes.*]
 • Everybody, what will this passage tell about? (Signal.) *Minutes.*
c. (Call on individual students to read the passage, each student reading two or three sentences at a time.)

> **Facts About Minutes**
>
> Today's story tells that Toby's eyes got used to the dark after a few minutes went by.
> Here are facts about minutes:
> There are 60 seconds in a minute.

 • Everybody, say that fact. Get ready. (Signal.) *There are 60 seconds in a minute.*
 • (Repeat until firm.)

- How many seconds are in one minute? (Signal.) *60.*

If you count slowly to 60, one minute will go by.

- I'll count seconds. One . . . two . . . three . . . four . . . five. Everybody, how many seconds did I count? (Signal.) *Five.*
- How many seconds would I have to count for one minute? (Signal.) *60.*

Some clocks have a hand that moves fast. When that hand goes all the way around the clock, one minute goes by.

- Everybody, when that hand goes all the way around the clock, how much time goes by? (Signal.) *One minute.*
- (Present a clock with a second hand.) We'll watch one minute. The hand that moves fast will have to go around the clock one time. We'll mark where it starts and then see how long a minute is. (Mark a starting point on the clock. Indicate when one minute has passed.)
- Remember the fact: There are 60 seconds in a minute. Everybody, say the fact about seconds in a minute. (Signal.) *There are 60 seconds in a minute.*

Passage C

d. Find part C in your textbook. ✓
- The next information passage gives some facts about ships.
e. Everybody, touch the title. ✓
- (Call on a student to read the title.) *[Facts About Ships.]*
- Everybody, what's the title? (Signal.) *Facts About Ships.*
f. (Call on individual students to read the passage, each student reading two or three sentences at a time.)

Facts About Ships

In today's story, you will read about a ship. The picture shows the parts of a ship.

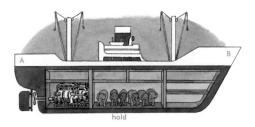

- Everybody, what's the name of the front of the ship? (Signal.) *The bow.*
- What letter shows the bow? (Signal.) *B.*
- Touch the bow in the picture. ✓
- What's the name of the back of the ship? (Signal.) *The stern.*
- What letter shows the stern? (Signal.) *A.*
- Touch the stern in the picture. ✓
- What's the name for the floors? (Signal.) *Decks.*
- Touch a deck in the picture. ✓
- What are the walls called? (Signal.) *Bulkheads.*
- Touch a bulkhead in the picture. ✓

Ships carry things from place to place. Ships may carry grain or cars or machines. These things are called the <u>cargo</u>.

- Everybody, what do we call the things that a ship carries? (Signal.) *Cargo.*

A ship that carries grain has a cargo of grain.

- Everybody, what does a ship that is carrying grain have? (Signal.) *A cargo of grain.*
- What does a ship that is carrying **cars** have? (Signal.) *A cargo of cars.*
- What does a ship that is carrying **machines** have? (Signal.) *A cargo of machines.*
- Touch the cargo in the picture. ✓
- What kind of cargo does this ship have? (Signal.) *Elephants.*

The cargo is carried in a part of the ship called the <u>hold</u>. The hold is at the bottom of the ship.

- Everybody, what part of the ship carries the cargo? (Signal.) *The hold.*
- Everybody, touch the hold in the picture. It's that big room that is full of elephants. ✓

STORY READING

a. Find part D in your textbook. ✓
- The error limit for group reading is 12. Read carefully.

b. Everybody, touch the title. ✓
- (Call on a student to read the title.) *[Toby on the Ship.]*
- Everybody, what's the title? (Signal.) *Toby on the Ship.*
- Everybody, about how far away is the captain's ship from Toby? (Signal.) *10 miles.*

c. (Call on individual students to read the story, each student reading two or three sentences at a time. Ask questions marked **1**.)

- (Correct errors: Tell the word. Direct the student to reread the sentence.)
- (If the group makes more than 12 errors, direct the students to reread the story.)

d. (After the group has read the selection making no more than 12 errors, read the story to the students and ask questions marked **2**.)

Toby on the Ship

Toby was in a cage, hanging from a long pole.

1. Part of the story is missing. Where was Toby when we left him? (Call on a student. Ideas: *On a hill; being tackled by a sailor.*)
1. Where is he now? (Call on a student. Idea: *In a cage.*)
1. So what must have happened in the part of the story that is missing? (Call on a student. Idea: *He was put in a cage.*)

Two sailors were carrying the pole— one at each end. Toby bounced up and down as the sailors walked. Next to them, the captain moved along, pulling up his pants every few steps.

2. Why is he doing that? (Call on a student. Idea: *Because his sailor suit pants are too big for him.*)

Mabel led the group. "Come on," she would holler from time to time. "Let's get moving."

"Yeah, get moving," the captain would say.

2. What would Mabel holler? (Call on a student.) *[Come on, let's get moving.]*
2. How often did she say that? (Call on a student. Idea: *From time to time.*)
2. Everybody, touch Toby in the picture. ✓
2. What is he in? (Signal.) *A cage.*
2. Who is carrying him? (Signal.) *Two sailors.*
2. Who is leading the group? (Signal.) *Mabel.*
2. What is the captain doing? (Call on a student. Ideas: *Pulling up his pants; walking behind Mabel.*)

By the time Toby reached the ship, the sun was in the west.

2. If the sun was in the west, what time of day was it? (Call on a student. Ideas: *Late afternoon; sunset; evening.*)

Toby hoped the sailors would let him out of the cage now. He said, "Oh, large and terrible bad," as he bounced along.

2. Everybody, was he happy? (Signal.) *No.*

"Be quiet," Mabel yelled. The sailors carried Toby up the ramp and across the deck of the ship.

2. Everybody, look at the picture. First they took Toby up the ramp. Touch the ramp. ✓
2. Then where did they go? (Call on a student. Idea: *Across the deck of the ship.*)

The sailors put Toby's cage in front of a doorway that led down to the hold of the ship. Mabel yelled, "Put that kangaroo into the hold."

"Yeah," the captain said. "Into the hold."

The two sailors opened the door to the hold and tossed Toby down the stairs. It was so dark inside the hold that Toby couldn't see a thing at first. He looked to the left and looked to the right. He could smell other animals, but he couldn't see a thing.

2. Why couldn't Toby see the other animals? (Call on a student. Idea: *Because it was dark.*)
2. How did he know that other animals were there? (Call on a student. Idea: *He could smell them.*)

Then, after a few minutes, his eyes got used to the dark and he could see the other animals.

1. When you're in the dark for a while, your eyes get used to the dark. That means that you can see things that you could not see at first.

He could see three kangaroos and he could see something else. It was beautiful. Even in the dim light, its feathers shined like a rainbow. It was the biggest, most beautiful peacock you have ever seen.

The peacock puffed itself up. "Aren't I beautiful?" the peacock said. "Even in this terrible place, I am lovely, aren't I?"

2. That peacock is a real show-off, isn't it?

"Oh, bad," Toby said to himself. The peacock kept talking. "I'll bet that you felt bad when they threw you in here, but I know that you're happy now that you can see me. I was worth waiting for, wasn't I?"

"Oh, double bad," Toby said.

2. Everybody, is that peacock proud of himself? (Signal.) *Yes.*
2. Does Toby like to hear the way the peacock keeps talking? (Signal.) *No.*

"Don't you just <u>love</u> my colors?" the peacock continued. "Of course, everybody knows that my tail feathers are the most beautiful things in the world, but look at some of my other feathers."

The peacock strutted out into the middle of the hold, where there was some sunlight that came through a crack. "If you want to see beauty, just take a look at these." The peacock turned around three times.

"Oh, triple bad," Toby said.

2. Everybody, do you think the peacock looked beautiful? (Signal.) *Yes.*
2. Why wasn't Toby happy with the peacock? (Call on a student. Ideas: *The peacock is so vain; it talks about itself all the time; Toby is worried.*)

"Don't listen to that turkey," one of the other kangaroos said.

2. Everybody, who is the kangaroo calling a turkey? (Signal.) *The peacock.*

The kangaroo continued, "That peacock will drive you nuts."

The peacock said, "I am <u>not</u> a turkey. I am the bird of India, the most beautiful thing in the world. I am not plain looking, like you animals from Australia."

2. Everybody, was the peacock from Australia? (Signal.) *No.*
2. Where did he say he was from? (Signal.) *India.*

Toby didn't want to talk about beautiful birds. He said, "When do we eat around here?"

The peacock said, "We get fed once a day. That won't happen until the sun goes all the way down, so you can still look at my feathers for a little while. That's better than eating anyhow."

"Oh, double bad," Toby said to himself. Then he turned to the other kangaroos and said, "Does anybody know where this ship is taking us?"

The peacock said, "I know and I'll tell you as soon as I show you something that you will remember forever." The bird puffed up and turned around very fast in the sunlight. Then he said, "Wasn't that something?"

1. Go back to the beginning of the story. Follow along while I read.
2. Read the rest of the story to yourself. Find out where the ship is going. And find out the fact that Toby didn't know. Raise your hand when you're finished.

Toby still didn't want to talk about beautiful birds. He said, "Where are we going?"

"I'll give you a clue," the peacock said. "The country we're going to is just north of the United States."

Toby said, "I don't know the name of that country."

The peacock said, "My, you animals from Australia don't know much. The country that is just north of the United States is Canada."

MORE NEXT TIME

2. (After all the students have raised their hand:) Where was the ship going? (Call on a student. Ideas: *Across the Pacific Ocean; to Canada.*)
2. What fact didn't Toby know? (Call on a student. Idea: *That Canada is the country that is north of the United States.*)
2. Everybody, was the author's purpose in this story to inform, entertain, or persuade? (Signal) *Entertain.*

EXERCISE 5

PAIRED PRACTICE

You're going to read aloud to your partner. Today the **B** members will read first. Then the **A** members will read from the star to the end of the story.

(Observe students and give feedback.)

End-of-Lesson Activities

INDEPENDENT WORK

Now finish your independent work for lesson 116. Raise your hand when you're finished. (Observe students and give feedback.)

WORKCHECK

a. (Direct students to take out their marking pencils.)
  • We're going to check your independent work. Remember, if you got an item wrong, make an **X** next to the item.
b. (For each item: Read the item. Call on a student to answer it. If the answer is wrong, say the correct answer. Refer to the Answer Key for the correct answers.)
c. Now use your marking pencil to fix up any items you got wrong. Remember, all mistakes must be fixed up before you hand in your work.

WRITING-SPELLING

(Present Writing-Spelling lesson 116 after completing Reading lesson 116. See Writing-Spelling Guide.)

ACTIVITY

(Present Activity 33 after completing Reading lesson 116. See Activities Across the Curriculum.)

LANGUAGE ARTS GUIDE

(Present Language Arts lesson 116 after completing Reading lesson 116. See Language Arts Guide.)

EXERCISE 1

VOCABULARY REVIEW

a. You learned a sentence that tells what surprised the neighbors.
- Everybody, say that sentence. Get ready. (Signal.) *Their amazing effort surprised the neighbors.*
- (Repeat until firm.)

b. You learned a sentence that tells what the police officers checked.
- Say that sentence. Get ready. (Signal.) *The police officers checked the ship's cargo.*
- (Repeat until firm.)

c. Here's the last sentence you learned: The champions performed perfectly.
- Everybody, say that sentence. Get ready. (Signal.) *The champions performed perfectly.*
- (Repeat until firm.)

d. What word means **put on a show?** (Signal.) *Performed.*
- What word means they won the championship? (Signal.) *Champions.*
- What word means **without any mistakes?** (Signal.) *Perfectly.*
- (Repeat step d until firm.)

e. Once more. Say the sentence that tells what the champions did. Get ready. (Signal.) *The champions performed perfectly.*

EXERCISE 2

READING WORDS

Column 1

a. **Find lesson 117 in your textbook.** ✓
- Touch column 1. ✓
- (Teacher reference:)

1. **certain**	3. **imagine**
2. **surprise**	4. **recognize**

b. Word 1 is **certain.** What word? (Signal.) *Certain.*
- Spell **certain.** Get ready. (Tap for each letter.) *C-E-R-T-A-I-N.*

- **Certain** is another word for **sure.** If you are sure about something, you are certain about it. Everybody, what's another word for **sure?** (Signal.) *Certain.*

c. Word 2. What word? (Signal.) *Surprise.*
- Spell **surprise.** Get ready. (Tap for each letter.) *S-U-R-P-R-I-S-E.*

d. Word 3. What word? (Signal.) *Imagine.*
- Spell **imagine.** Get ready. (Tap for each letter.) *I-M-A-G-I-N-E.*

e. Word 4. What word? (Signal.) *Recognize.*

f. Let's read those words again, the fast way.
- Word 1. What word? (Signal.) *Certain.*
- (Repeat for words 2–4.)

g. (Repeat step f until firm.)

Column 2

h. Find column 2. ✓
- (Teacher reference:)

1. **camera**	4. **interesting**
2. **footsteps**	5. **preserve**
3. **blankets**	

- All these words have more than one syllable. The first part of each word is underlined.

i. Word 1. What's the underlined part? (Signal.) *cam.*
- What's the whole word? (Signal.) *Camera.*

j. Word 2. What's the underlined part? (Signal.) *foot.*
- What's the whole word? (Signal.) *Footsteps.*

k. Word 3. What's the underlined part? (Signal.) *blank.*
- What's the whole word? (Signal.) *Blankets.*

l. Word 4. What's the underlined part? (Signal.) *inter.*
- What's the whole word? (Signal.) *Interesting.*

m. Word 5. What's the underlined part? (Signal.) *pre.*
- What's the whole word? (Signal.) *Preserve.*

n. Let's read those words again, the fast way.
- Word 1. What word? (Signal.) *Camera.*
- (Repeat for: **2. footsteps, 3. blankets, 4. interesting, 5. preserve.**)

o. (Repeat step n until firm.)

Column 3

p. Find column 3. ✓
- (Teacher reference:)

1. **breaking**	4. **heading**
2. **liars**	5. **wiggling**
3. **crossed**	

- All these words have endings.

q. Word 1. What word? (Signal.) *Breaking.*
- (Repeat for words 2–5.)

r. (Repeat step q until firm.)

Column 4

s. Find column 4. ✓
- (Teacher reference:)

1. **field**	3. **untied**
2. **law**	4. **entertain**

t. Word 1. What word? (Signal.) *Field.*
- (Repeat for words 2–4.)

u. (Repeat step t until firm.)

Individual Turns

(For columns 1–4: Call on individual students, each to read one to three words per turn.)

EXERCISE 3

STORY READING

a. Find part B in your textbook. ✓
- The error limit for group reading is 11. Read carefully.

b. Everybody, touch the title. ✓
- (Call on a student to read the title.) *[The End of the Trip.]*
- Everybody, what's the title? (Signal.) *The End of the Trip.*
- Everybody, where was the ship when Toby got on the ship? (Signal.) *Australia.*
- Before the ship went to Australia, it stopped in the country where the peacock lived. What's the name of that country? (Signal.) *India.*
- What country was the ship going to after it left Australia? (Signal.) *Canada.*

c. (Call on individual students to read the story, each student reading two or three sentences at a time. Ask questions marked **1.**)

- (Correct errors: Tell the word. Direct the student to reread the sentence.)
- (If the group makes more than 11 errors, direct the students to reread the story.)

d. (After the group has read the selection making no more than 11 errors, read the story to the students and ask questions marked **2.**)

The End of the Trip

The ship was on its way to Canada. The peacock told the others that the trip would take ten days. "But don't worry," the peacock added, "I'll entertain you for the trip. You'll have a lovely time."

2. Everybody, how long would the trip take? (Signal.) *Ten days.*
2. What did the peacock say that he would do during that trip? (Call on a student. Idea: *Entertain the other animals.*)
2. How do you think he would entertain the other animals? (Call on a student. Idea: *By showing off his feathers.*)

"Big and double big bad," Toby said to himself.
But before the trip was over, Toby had become friends with the peacock. The peacock's name was Pip. And Toby learned a lot from Pip. Pip knew the name of the ocean that the ship crossed.

1. Everybody, what ocean did it cross to go from Australia to Canada? (Signal.) *The Pacific Ocean.*

Toby had never heard of the Pacific Ocean before. Pip also knew a lot about the captain and Mabel.
On the day before the ship reached Canada, Pip told Toby, "Mabel and the captain are crooks. When you were in Australia, you lived on a game preserve. It's against the law to hunt on a game preserve."

2. Everybody, what did Toby live on? (Signal.) *A game preserve.*
2. Should people hunt on a game preserve? (Signal.) *No.*
2. Did Mabel and the captain hunt animals on the game preserve? (Signal.) *Yes.*
2. So they were breaking the law. They are crooks. What are crooks? (Call on a student. Idea: *People who break the law.*)

"Oh, that's double bad," Toby said.
Pip said, "Mabel and the captain are also liars. They pretended that they were going to take my picture with a camera. Mabel told me to stand in the middle of a field so that I would be in the bright sun."

1. Everybody, do you think that Pip would like to stand in the bright sun? (Signal.) *Yes.*
1. Why? (Call on a student. Idea: *Because it would show off his feathers.*)

Pip continued, "Then Mabel told me that the captain should stand behind me. That seemed like a good idea. The captain is so ugly that I would look twice as beautiful with him behind me. How did I know that he would drop a net over me?"
Toby mumbled to himself, "Not bad."

2. Everybody, did Toby like what happened to Pip? (Signal.) *Yes.*
2. What did the captain do when he was standing behind Pip? (Call on a student. Idea: *Dropped a net over Pip.*)
2. Why did Pip think it was a good idea for the captain to stand behind him in the picture? (Call on a student. Idea: *Because the captain was so ugly that Pip thought he would look twice as beautiful with the captain behind him.*)

The ship was supposed to dock in Canada the next day. There was a little hole in the side of the hold. The animals took turns looking out of this hole, trying to see the shore. Pip was looking through the hole just after noon. "My, my," he said suddenly. "I don't see the shore, but I do see something that is very interesting."

"What's that?" the other animals asked.
"I'll give you a clue. This thing goes through the water. It carries police officers. And it's probably looking for ships that are breaking the law."

1. Everybody, when the animals ask Pip questions, does he say the answer? (Signal.) *No.*
1. See if you can figure out what Pip was looking at. It goes through water. It carries police officers, and it is looking for ships that are breaking the law. What is it? (Call on a student. Ideas: *A police boat; a patrol boat.*)

Toby pushed the peacock out of the way and looked through the hole. He saw a police boat. And the boat was heading right toward their ship.
"We're saved," Toby shouted. "The police have caught Mabel and the captain."
"Not quite," the peacock said. "You'll discover that Mabel is very smart, even if she is a <u>crook</u>."

2. Everybody, does the peacock think that the police will catch Mabel and the captain? (Signal.) *No.*
2. Why not? (Call on a student. Idea: *Because she is very smart.*)

Two sailors ran into the hold. The sailors slapped tape over the mouth of each animal. Then they quickly tied up the animals and covered them with large blankets. Then they dumped a pile of sacks on top of the animals.

2. Why are they doing all that? (Call on a student. Idea: *To hide the animals.*)
2. Why would they want to hide the animals? (Call on a student. Ideas: *Because they aren't supposed to be carrying animals; so the police wouldn't see them.*)

Toby said to himself, "Very, very bad."
Toby could hear people talking near the doorway to the hold.

> "What do you want, Officer?"
> Mabel said in a sweet voice.
> "We're supposed to look at your
> cargo," the officer said.
> "As you can see," Mabel said,
> "we're just carrying sacks of grain."
> "Yeah," the captain said. "Sacks
> of grain."
> Footsteps moved into the hold.
> Toby tried to make some sound by
> wiggling around.
> The officer said, "Sounds as if
> you have rats in here. Better be
> careful or they'll get into your grain."

2. What did Mabel say the cargo was? (Call on a student. Idea: *Sacks of grain.*)
2. Everybody, what was the real cargo? (Signal.) *Animals.*
2. Did the officer know what the real cargo was? (Signal.) *No.*
2. What did he think was making the noise in the hold? (Signal.) *Rats.*

> "Thank you, Officer," Mabel said.
> "We'll take care of the rats."
> "Yeah," another voice said. "We'll
> take care of the rats."

1. Go back to the beginning of the story. Follow along while I read.
2. Everybody, who said that? (Signal.) *The captain.*
2. Read the rest of the story to yourself. Find out if the police leave the ship. Raise your hand when you're finished.

> Then the footsteps moved up the
> stairs. There was the sound of a
> door closing. A minute or two later,
> there was the sound of a motor that
> moved farther and farther from the
> ship Toby was on.
> When one of the sailors untied the
> animals, Pip said, "What did I tell
> you? Mabel may be a crook, but she
> is very smart."
> Things looked bad for Toby.
> MORE NEXT TIME

2. (After all the students raise their hand:) Did the police leave the ship? (Signal.) *Yes.*

2. What did Mabel do that was so smart? (Call on a student. Ideas: *She tricked the officer; she hid the animals.*)

EXERCISE 4

PAIRED PRACTICE

You're going to read aloud to your partner. Today the **A** members will read first. Then the **B** members will read.
(Observe students and give feedback.)

EXERCISE 5

SEQUENCING

a. **Find lesson 117 in your worksheet.** ✓
 • Touch part A. ✓
b. I'll read the items. You follow along. Item 1: Write the letter of the event that happened near the beginning of the story. Item 2: Write the letter of the event that happened in the middle of the story.
 Item 3: Write the letter of the event that happened near the end of the story.
c. Here's event A: The police boat left and one of the sailors untied the animals. Get ready to tell me if that event is from the **beginning** of the story, the **middle,** or the **end.** Everybody, which part of the story? (Signal.) *End.*
d. Here's event B: Pip told the other animals that the trip to Canada would take 10 days. Get ready to tell me if that event is from the **beginning** of the story, the **middle,** or the **end.** Everybody, which part of the story? (Signal.) *Beginning.*
e. Here's event C: The sailors tied up the animals and covered them with blankets. Get ready to tell me if that event is from the **beginning** of the story, the **middle,** or the **end.** Everybody, which part of the story? (Signal.) *Middle.*

End-of-Lesson Activities

INDEPENDENT WORK

Now finish your independent work for lesson 117. Raise your hand when you're finished.
(Observe students and give feedback.)

WORKCHECK

a. (Direct students to take out their marking pencils.)

- We're going to check your independent work. Remember, if you got an item wrong, make an **X** next to the item.

b. (For each item: Read the item. Call on a student to answer it. If the answer is wrong, say the correct answer. Refer to the Answer Key for the correct answers.)

c. Now use your marking pencil to fix up any items you got wrong. Remember, all mistakes must be fixed up before you hand in your work.

WRITING-SPELLING

(Present Writing-Spelling lesson 117 after completing Reading lesson 117. See Writing–Spelling Guide.)

ACTIVITY

(Present Activity 34 after completing Reading lesson 117. See Activities Across the Curriculum.)

LANGUAGE ARTS GUIDE

(Present Language Arts lesson 117 after completing Reading lesson 117. See Language Arts Guide.)

Lesson 118

EXERCISE 1

VOCABULARY

a. **Find page 342 in your textbook.** ✓
- Touch sentence 29.
- This is a new vocabulary sentence. It says: She paid the correct amount. Everybody, read that sentence. Get ready. (Signal.) *She paid the correct amount.*
- Close your eyes and say the sentence. Get ready. (Signal.) *She paid the correct amount.*
- (Repeat until firm.)

b. The sentence refers to the correct amount. **Correct** is another word for **right.** What's another way of saying **the right address?** (Signal.) *The correct address.*
- What's another way of saying **the right answer?** (Signal.) *The correct answer.*

c. The **amount** of something tells **how much** there is. A large amount of money is a lot of money. A small amount of money is not very much money. What word tells how much there is? (Signal.) *Amount.*

d. Listen to the sentence again: She paid the correct amount. Everybody, say the sentence. Get ready. (Signal.) *She paid the correct amount.*

e. What word means **right?** (Signal.) *Correct.*
- What word tells how much there is? (Signal.) *Amount.*

EXERCISE 2

READING WORDS

Column 1

a. Find lesson 118 in your textbook. ✓
- Touch column 1. ✓
- (Teacher reference:)

1. amount	3. thumping
2. correct	4. recognize

b. Word 1 is **amount.** What word? (Signal.) *Amount.*
- Spell **amount.** Get ready. (Tap for each letter.) *A-M-O-U-N-T.*

c. Word 2 is **correct.** What word? (Signal.) *Correct.*
- Spell **correct.** Get ready. (Tap for each letter.) *C-O-R-R-E-C-T.*

d. Word 3. What word? (Signal.) *Thumping.*
- Spell **thumping.** Get ready. (Tap for each letter.) *T-H-U-M-P-I-N-G.*

e. Word 4. What word? (Signal.) *Recognize.*
- Spell **recognize.** Get ready. (Tap for each letter.) *R-E-C-O-G-N-I-Z-E.*

f. Let's read those words again, the fast way.
- Word 1. What word? (Signal.) *Amount.*
- (Repeat for words 2–4.)

g. (Repeat step f until firm.)

Column 2

h. Find column 2. ✓
- (Teacher reference:)

1. **illegal**	3. **awake**
2. **scolding**	4. **cannon**

- All these words have more than one syllable. The first syllable of each word is underlined.

i. Word 1. What's the first syllable? (Signal.) *ill.*
- What's the whole word? (Signal.) *Illegal.*
- Things that are illegal are not legal. They are against the law. What's another way of saying **It is not legal to ride a bike on the freeway?** (Signal.) *It is illegal to ride a bike on the freeway.*

j. Word 2. What's the first syllable? (Signal.) *scold.*
- What's the whole word? (Signal.) *Scolding.*
- When your mother scolds you, she lets you know what you did wrong. She chews you out. Everybody, what word means **chewing out?** (Signal.) *Scolding.*

k. Word 3. What's the first syllable? (Signal.) *a.*
- What's the whole word? (Signal.) *Awake.*

l. Word 4. What's the first syllable? (Signal.) *can.*
- What's the whole word? (Signal.) *Cannon.*

m. Let's read those words again, the fast way.
- Word 1. What word? (Signal.) *Illegal.*
- (Repeat for: **2. scolding, 3. awake, 4. cannon.**)
n. (Repeat step m until firm.)

Column 3

o. Find column 3. ✓
- (Teacher reference:)

1. <u>road</u>side	3. <u>foot</u>steps
2. <u>worth</u>less	4. <u>gentle</u>man

- All these words are compound words. The first part of each word is underlined.
p. Word 1. What's the underlined part? (Signal.) *road.*
- What's the whole word? (Signal.) *Roadside.*
- A roadside business is a business that is alongside the road.
q. Word 2. What's the underlined part? (Signal.) *worth.*
- What's the whole word? (Signal.) *Worthless.*
- Something that is worthless is not worth anything. A promise that is not worth anything is a worthless promise. Everybody, what do we call a coin that is not worth anything? (Signal.) *A worthless coin.*
r. Word 3. What's the underlined part? (Signal.) *foot.*
- What's the whole word? (Signal.) *Footsteps.*
s. Word 4. What's the underlined part? (Signal.) *gentle.*
- What's the whole word? (Signal.) *Gentleman.*
t. Let's read those words again, the fast way.
- Word 1. What word? (Signal.) *Roadside.*
- (Repeat for words 2–4.)
u. (Repeat step t until firm.)

Column 4

v. Find column 4. ✓
- (Teacher reference:)

1. graph	3. pleasant
2. sped	4. arrives

w. Word 1. What word? (Signal.) *Graph.*

- A graph is a kind of a picture that has lines or parts that show different amounts. Everybody, what do we call a picture that has lines or parts that show different amounts? (Signal.) *Graph.*
x. Word 2. What word? (Signal.) *Sped.*
- When something goes fast, it speeds. When something **went** fast, it sped.
- Everybody, what's another way of saying **The car went fast down the road?** (Signal.) *The car sped down the road.*
- What's another way of saying **The bike went fast down the hill?** (Signal.) *The bike sped down the hill.*
y. Word 3. What word? (Signal.) *Pleasant.*
- (Repeat for word 4.)
z. Let's read those words again.
- Word 1. What word? (Signal.) *Graph.*
- (Repeat for words 2–4.)
a. (Repeat step z until firm.)

Individual Turns

(For columns 1–4: Call on individual students, each to read one to three words per turn.)

EXERCISE 3

VOCABULARY REVIEW

a. Here's the new vocabulary sentence: She paid the correct amount.
- Everybody, say that sentence. Get ready. (Signal.) *She paid the correct amount.*
- (Repeat until firm.)
b. What word tells how much there is? (Signal.) *Amount.*
- What word means **right?** (Signal.) *Correct.*

EXERCISE 4

COMPREHENSION PASSAGE

a. Find part B in your textbook. ✓
- You're going to read the next story about Toby. First you'll read the information passage. It gives some facts about Canada.
b. Everybody, touch the title. ✓
- (Call on a student to read the title.) *[More Facts About Canada.]*
- Everybody, what's the title? (Signal.) *More Facts About Canada.*
c. (Call on individual students to read the passage, each student reading two or three sentences at a time.)

More Facts About Canada

In the story you'll read today, Toby arrives in Canada. You've learned facts about Canada. Which is larger, the United States or Canada?

- Everybody, what's the answer? (Signal.) *Canada.*

Is Canada <u>north</u> of the United States or <u>south</u> of the United States?

- Everybody, what's the answer? (Signal.) *North of the United States.*

Here are two new facts about Canada.
Canada is colder than the United States.

- Everybody, say that fact. Get ready. (Signal.) *Canada is colder than the United States.*
- (Repeat until firm.)
- Canada is colder because Canada is farther north. The farther north you go, the colder the weather gets.

Far more people live in the United States than live in Canada.

- Everybody, where do more people live, in the United States, or in Canada? (Signal.) *In the United States.*
- Remember, Canada is larger than the United States, but Canada has fewer people. Even though Canada is larger, more people live in the United States.

The graph compares the number of people who live in the United States and Canada. This bar shows how many people live in Canada. ■

- Everybody, touch the bar for Canada. ✓

This bar shows how many people live in the United States.

- Everybody, touch the bar for the United States. ✓

- That bar is much longer than the top bar. The longer bar is for the country with more people. Which country has the longer bar? (Signal.) *The United States.*
- So which country has more people? (Signal.) *The United States.*
- Listen: The bottom bar is ten times longer than the top bar. How many times longer is the bottom bar? (Signal.) *Ten.*
- So ten times more people live in the United States than in Canada. The United States has how many times more people than Canada has? (Signal.) *Ten.*

STORY READING

a. Find part C in your textbook. ✓
- The error limit for group reading is 10. Read carefully.
b. Everybody, touch the title. ✓
- (Call on a student to read the title.) [*The Ship Arrives in Canada.*]
- Everybody, what's the title? (Signal.) *The Ship Arrives in Canada.*
c. (Call on individual students to read the story, each student reading two or three sentences at a time. Ask questions marked **1**.)

> - (Correct errors: Tell the word. Direct the student to reread the sentence.)
> - (If the group makes more than 10 errors, direct the students to reread the story.)

d. (After the group has read the selection making no more than 10 errors, read the story to the students and ask questions marked **2**.)

The Ship Arrives in Canada

When the ship docked in Canada, it was night.

2. What time of day was it when the ship docked in Canada? (Call on a student. Idea: *Nighttime.*)

Toby had been sleeping. He heard the sound of footsteps coming down the stairs to the hold.

1. If he heard footsteps coming down the stairs, what was happening? (Call on a student. Idea: *Somebody was coming into the hold.*)

As Toby rubbed his eyes and tried to wake up, he realized that Pip was talking. Pip said, "I'll bet that they're going to try to sneak us into trucks and get us out of here before the police find out that there is illegal cargo on this ship."

2. What did Pip think Mabel and the others were going to do with the animals? (Call on a student. Idea: *Sneak the animals into trucks.*)

2. Why were they in a hurry to get the animals away from the ship? (Call on a student. Ideas: *Because the animals were illegal cargo; because the police might come.*)

Before Toby was completely awake, the three sailors had moved all the other animals from the hold. Toby was the last to go. He could hear Pip on the top deck, scolding the sailors. "Be careful with my feathers. Don't you recognize beauty when you see it?"

2. Everybody, who was the last animal to be removed from the hold? (Signal.) *Toby.*

2. Who was scolding the sailors? (Signal.) *Pip.*

2. Why was Pip complaining? (Call on a student. Idea: *Because the sailors were messing up Pip's feathers.*)

Three sailors started down the stairs for Toby. One of them tripped and fell into the other two. All three sailors fell into the hold. They began yelling at each other.
While the sailors yelled, Toby started to sneak up the stairs.

2. Why didn't the sailors stop him? (Call on a student. Ideas: *Because they had fallen into the hold; they were yelling at each other.*)

Just then, a loud voice from the top of the stairs said, "Throw a net over that kangaroo, you fools."

1. Everybody, who said that? (Signal.) *Mabel.*

A moment later, a net fell over Toby. He tried to free himself, but he couldn't. The sailors hauled him up the stairs and dumped him onto a cart. "Take that kangaroo down the ramp," a voice yelled.
"Yeah, down the ramp," another voice said.

1. Who did those voices belong to? (Call on a student.) *[Mabel and the captain.]*

A sailor started to push the cart down the ramp. Part of the net got caught under the sailor's foot. The sailor tripped and fell forward. When he fell forward, he let go of the cart. The cart sped down the ramp. The cart continued to speed across the dock. It sped past a truck with the other animals in it. As Toby went by the truck, he could hear Pip saying, "Have a pleasant trip."

2. The sailors on this ship seem to be falling all over the place. Listen to that part again and get a picture of what's happening.
   A sailor started to push the cart down the ramp. Part of the net got caught under the sailor's foot. The sailor tripped and fell forward. When he fell forward, he let go of the cart. The cart sped down the ramp. The cart continued to speed across the dock. It sped past a truck with the other animals in it. As Toby went by the truck, he could hear Pip saying, "Have a pleasant trip."

2. Everybody, touch Toby in the picture. ✓
2. Touch the cart. ✓
2. Touch Pip. ✓
2. Touch the sailor who tripped and fell. ✓
2. Everybody, who is that running after the cart? (Signal.) *Mabel.*

Toby's trip was not very pleasant. The cart came to the end of the dock, where there was a large post. The cart hit the post and sent Toby flying through the air. Toby flew right over the post. But the net caught on the top of the post and left Toby hanging above the water.

2. Everybody, touch the post in the picture. ✓
2. What did the net catch on? (Call on a student. Idea: *The top of the post.*)
2. Everybody, who was in the net? (Signal.) *Toby.*
2. Did Toby end up in the water? (Signal.) *No.*
2. Where did he end up? (Call on a student. Idea: *Hanging above the water in the net.*)

"Get that kangaroo," a voice hollered, and Toby could hear footsteps thumping down the dock. Then Toby felt the net being pulled up onto the dock. The sailors carried him to the truck with the other animals. Pip was saying, "Now be careful about my feathers. Don't push against me."

"Oh, triple bad," Toby said.

While it was still dark outside, the truck went to a circus.

1. What do you think Mabel was going to do at a circus? (Call on a student. Idea: *Sell the animals to the circus.*)

"This is where you get off," Mabel said to Toby. "You are going to be one of the stars of this tiny circus. You'll entertain people by being shot from a great cannon."

2. What is Toby going to do at this circus? (Call on a student. Ideas: *Entertain people; get shot from a cannon.*)

"Oh, <u>many</u> kinds of bad," Toby said.

The circus owner put a chain around Toby's neck and led him to a cage. Toby waved goodbye to Pip and the other animals. The circus owner told Toby, "Tomorrow, you will be a star. You will do tricks for people."

1. Go back to the beginning of the story. Follow along while I read.
2. Read the rest of the story to yourself. Find out what things Toby missed. Raise your hand when you're finished.

Toby didn't want to do tricks. He did not want to live in a cage and work for a circus. He wanted to be back home in Australia. As he sat there in that dark cage, he thought about the dust. The dust didn't seem very bad to him now. He missed the thumping sound of the mob. He missed the leader. Toby missed his mother and the other kangaroos. He missed the smell of grass and the sound of the wind.

As he sat there in his cage, he felt a large tear run down the side of his nose and fall off. "Oh, very bad," he said to himself and tried to go to sleep. Poor Toby even missed Pip.

MORE NEXT TIME

2. (After all students have raised their hand:) What are some of the things Toby missed? (Call on different students. Ideas: *Australia; dust; the mob; the leader; his mother; other kangaroos; the smell of the grass; sound of the wind; even Pip.*)
2. Get a picture of Toby in that dark cage, thinking about his home in Australia and try to feel the things that he felt. Listen:

Toby didn't want to do tricks. He did not want to live in a cage and work for a circus. He wanted to be back home in Australia. As he sat there in that dark cage, he thought about the dust. The dust didn't seem very bad to him now. He missed the thumping sound of the mob. He missed the leader. Toby missed his mother and the other kangaroos. He missed the smell of grass and the sound of the wind.

As he sat there in his cage, he felt a large tear run down the side of his nose and fall off. "Oh, very bad," he said to himself and tried to go to sleep. Poor Toby even missed Pip.

2. Where was Toby sitting while he was thinking? (Call on a student. Idea: *In a cage.*)
2. What place was he thinking about? (Call on a student. Ideas: *Australia, home.*)

EXERCISE 6

PAIRED PRACTICE

You're going to read aloud to your partner. Today the **B** members will read first. Then the **A** members will read from the star to the end of the story.
(Observe students and give feedback.)

EXERCISE 7

SEQUENCING

a. **Find lesson 118 on your worksheet.** ✓
• Touch part A. ✓
b. I'll read the items. You follow along.
• Item 1: Write the letter of the event that happened near the beginning of the story. Item 2: Write the letter of the event that happened in the middle of the story.
Item 3: Write the letter of the event that happened near the end of the story.
c. Here's event A: The sailors put Toby on a cart. Get ready to tell me if that event is from the **beginning** of the story, the **middle,** or the **end.** Everybody, which part of the story? (Signal.) *Middle.*
d. Here's event B: The ship docked in Canada. Get ready to tell me if that event is from the **beginning** of the story, the **middle,** or the **end.** Everybody, which part of the story? (Signal.) *Beginning.*
e. Here's event C: Mabel took Toby to a circus. Get ready to tell me if that event is from the **beginning** of the story, the **middle,** or the **end.** Everybody, which part of the story? (Signal.) *End.*

End-of-Lesson Activities

INDEPENDENT WORK

Now finish your independent work for lesson 118. Raise your hand when you're finished.
(Observe students and give feedback.)

WORKCHECK

a. (Direct students to take out their marking pencils.)
• We're going to check your independent work. Remember, if you got an item wrong, make an **X** next to the item.
b. (For each item: Read the item. Call on a student to answer it. If the answer is wrong, say the correct answer. Refer to the Answer Key for the correct answers.)
c. Now use your marking pencil to fix up any items you got wrong. Remember, all mistakes must be fixed up before you hand in your work.

WRITING-SPELLING

(Present Writing-Spelling lesson 118 after completing Reading lesson 118. See Writing-Spelling Guide.)

ACTIVITY

(Present Activity 35 after completing Reading lesson 118. See Activities Across the Curriculum.)

LANGUAGE ARTS GUIDE

(Present Language Arts lesson 118 after completing Reading lesson 118. See Language Arts Guide.)

Lesson 119

VOCABULARY REVIEW

a. Here's the new vocabulary sentence: She paid the correct amount.
- Everybody, say that sentence. Get ready. (Signal.) *She paid the correct amount.*
- (Repeat until firm.)

b. What word means **right?** (Signal.) *Correct.*
- What word tells how much there is? (Signal.) *Amount.*

READING WORDS

Column 1

a. **Find lesson 119 in your textbook.** ✓
- Touch column 1. ✓
- (Teacher reference:)

1. **perform**	4. **umbrella**
2. **presents**	5. **shabby**
3. **rather**	

- All these words have more than one syllable. The first syllable of each word is underlined.

b. Word 1. What's the first syllable? (Signal.) *per.*
- What's the whole word? (Signal.) *Perform.*

c. Word 2. What's the first syllable? (Signal.) *pre.*
- What's the whole word? (Signal.) *Presents.*

d. Word 3. What's the first syllable? (Signal.) *rath.*
- What's the whole word? (Signal.) *Rather.*

e. Word 4. What's the first syllable? (Signal.) *um.*
- What's the whole word? (Signal.) *Umbrella.*

f. Word 5. What's the first syllable? (Signal.) *shabb.*
- What's the whole word? (Signal.) *Shabby.*

- Something that is shabby is not neat and clean. An old run-down house is shabby.

g. Let's read those words again, the fast way.
- Word 1. What word? (Signal.) *Perform.*
- (Repeat for words 2–5.)

h. (Repeat step g until firm.)

Column 2

i. Find column 2. ✓
- (Teacher reference:)

1. **correct**	4. **worse**
2. **rip-off**	5. **amount**
3. **complaining**	

j. Word 1. What word? (Signal.) *Correct.*

k. Word 2. What word? (Signal.) *Rip-off.*
- A rip-off is a bad deal. You don't get what you think you're getting.

l. Word 3. What word? (Signal.) *Complaining.*
- (Repeat for words 4 and 5.)

m. Let's read those words again.
- Word 1. What word? (Signal.) *Correct.*
- (Repeat for words 2–5.)

n. (Repeat step m until firm.)

Individual Turns

(For columns 1 and 2: Call on individual students, each to read one to three words per turn.)

COMPREHENSION PASSAGE

a. Find part B in your textbook. ✓
- You're going to read the next story about Toby. First you'll read the information passage. It gives some facts about circuses.

b. Everybody, touch the title. ✓
- (Call on a student to read the title.) *[Facts About a Circus.]*
- Everybody, what's the title? (Signal.) *Facts About a Circus.*

c. (Call on individual students to read the passage, each student reading two or three sentences at a time.)

Facts About a Circus

In today's lesson, you're going to read about a circus that is not very good. People enjoy a good circus.

Here are some facts about a good circus:

The circus is sometimes held in a large tent.

- Everybody, where is the circus sometimes held? (Signal.) *In a large tent.*
- Where else is a circus sometimes held? (Call on a student. Ideas: *In a building, outside.*)

The picture shows a huge circus tent.

- Everybody, touch the tent in the picture. ✓
- That tent can hold hundreds and hundreds of people.

Two or three acts go on at the same time in a large circus. Some of the acts are on the ground. Other acts take place high in the air.

- Everybody, touch the picture that shows the circus acts. ✓

- Two acts are going on in the rings. What act is going on in ring A? (Call on a student. Idea: *Clowns.*)
- What act is going on in ring B? (Call on a student. Idea: *Elephants doing tricks.*)
- What act is going on above the two rings? (Call on a student. Idea: *A person is riding a bicycle on a tightrope.*)

The favorite acts on the ground are trained animals and clowns. People like to see lions, tigers, and elephants do tricks.

The favorite acts in the air are people diving from one swing to another swing or people walking on wires.

- What is your favorite circus act? (Call on individual students. Student preference.)

EXERCISE 4

STORY READING

a. Find part C in your textbook. ✓
- The error limit for group reading is 10. Read carefully.
b. Everybody, touch the title. ✓
- (Call on a student to read the title.) *[Toby's New Job.]*
- Everybody, what's the title? (Signal.) *Toby's New Job.*
- Where did we leave Toby? (Call on a student. Idea: *In his cage at the circus.*)
- What time of day was it? (Call on a student. Idea: *Nighttime.*)
- How did Toby feel? (Call on a student. Ideas: *Sad; homesick.*)
c. (Call on individual students to read the story, each student reading two or three sentences at a time. Ask questions marked **1.**)

- (Correct errors: Tell the word. Direct the student to reread the sentence.)
- (If the group makes more than 10 errors, direct the students to reread the story.)

d. (After the group has read the selection making no more than 10 errors, read the story to the students and ask questions marked **2.**)

Toby's New Job

The next morning, the circus owner came and took Toby from his cage. The owner said, "You are going to do tricks for the people who have come to see our circus. If you want to eat, you will do tricks.
If you do <u>not</u> do tricks, you will become a <u>very</u> hungry animal."
Toby said, "Oh, bad and super bad."

1. Why would Toby become a very hungry animal if he does not do tricks? (Call on a student. Idea: *Because the circus owner wouldn't feed him.*)
1. Do you think he'll do tricks for the circus owner? (Call on individual students. Student preference.)

The owner took Toby into a tent. In the middle of the tent was a ring.
"What a shabby circus," Toby said to himself.

1. If it's a shabby circus, does it have a lot of good acts? (Signal.) *No.*

This circus did not have many animals and people doing super things. Toby was the only animal in the tent. The owner was dressed up in a black suit with a rip in the back of the coat.
There was no huge crowd of people watching the act. There were about twenty people sitting in the stands. Three of them were sleeping. Two of them were little kids who were crying. The rest of them were complaining.

2. The picture on the next page shows the shabby circus.
2. Touch the circus owner. ✓
2. Look at the rip in the back of his suit.

2. Everybody, about how many people are in the stands? (Signal.) *20.*
2. Touch somebody who is sleeping. ✓

One girl said, "We want to see lions and tigers."
"Yeah," somebody else said. "We don't want to see a dumb kangaroo."
The owner held up his hands. "This kangaroo can do tricks that will surprise you. This kangaroo is the smartest kangaroo in the world. People usually pay as much as a hundred dollars to see this kangaroo perform."

2. Everybody, is the circus owner telling the truth? (Signal.) *No.*

"Boo," the people yelled. "We want lions."
Then a girl yelled, "Make that kangaroo ride a bicycle."
"Make him ride it backward," a boy yelled.
The other people began to clap. "Yes, let's see him ride a bicycle backward."
"Wouldn't you rather see him being shot from a cannon?" the owner asked.
"No," the people agreed. "We want to see that kangaroo ride a bicycle backward."
The owner tried to argue with the crowd, but when people started to throw things at him, he said, "All right, he will ride a bicycle backward."

2. At first the circus owner argued with the crowd. What did he want to do to Toby? (Call on a student. Idea: *Shoot him from a cannon.*)
2. Everybody, did the crowd agree with the circus owner? (Signal.) *No.*
2. So did the circus owner finally agree to have Toby ride a bicycle backward? (Signal.) *Yes.*

The owner got a dusty bicycle. He held up one hand and said to the crowd, "Ladies and gentlemen. Today the Kankan Circus presents Toby, the wonder kangaroo. Toby will amaze you by riding a bicycle backward. And he will do this amazing trick on a high wire ten meters above the floor."

2. Where is Toby supposed to ride the bicycle? (Call on a student. Idea: *On a high wire 10 meters above the floor.*)

Toby looked up at the wire ten meters above the floor. You know what Toby said.

1. Say what he probably said. (Call on a student. Idea: *Oh, double bad.*)

The owner handed Toby the bicycle and said, "Take this bicycle up the ladder. Then ride it backward on the high wire."
Toby shook his head, no.
The owner said, "<u>Do</u> it, you bad kangaroo. Get up there and ride that bicycle."
Toby shook his head, no.
The owner turned to the crowd. "Before Toby, the wonder kangaroo, rides the bicycle on the high wire, he will ride it backward on the floor."

2. The circus owner changed the announcement because Toby wouldn't do it on the high wire.

The owner turned to Toby. "Ride that bicycle on the floor."
Toby shook his head, no.
People were beginning to throw things at Toby and the owner. "This is a rip-off," they were hollering. "That kangaroo can't do anything."
The owner said, "One moment, ladies and gentlemen. Before Toby rides the bicycle backward on the floor, Toby will ride it forward on the floor."
The owner looked at Toby and said, "Do it." Toby shook his head, no.

People were now yelling, "I want my money back," and "Let's call a cop."

1. Go back to the beginning of the story. Follow along while I read.
2. What was the last thing the owner wanted Toby to do? (Signal.) *Ride the bicycle forward on the floor.*
2. Is it easier to ride **forward** or **backward?** (Signal.) *Forward.*
2. Read the rest of the story to yourself. Find out two things. First find out what Toby was supposed to do before he rode the bicycle forward on the floor. Then find out what two boys in the crowd did. Raise your hand when you're done.

The owner held up his hands and said, "Before Toby rides the bicycle forward on the floor, Toby will walk with the bicycle on the floor."
Toby looked at the owner and shook his head no again.
"This is the worst show in the world," people were yelling. A woman was shaking her umbrella at the owner. Two boys were throwing papers at Toby. Toby was saying, "Oh, worse than bad."
MORE NEXT TIME

2. (After all students have raised their hand:) What was Toby supposed to do before he rode the bicycle forward on the floor? (Call on a student. Idea: *Walk with the bicycle on the floor.*)
2. Everybody, is he going to do that? (Signal.) *No.*
2. What were two boys in the crowd doing? (Call on a student. Idea: *Throwing papers at Toby.*)
2. Raise your hand if you remember what Toby said as the boys threw papers at him. (Call on a student.) *[Oh, worse than bad.]*
2. That must be the worst circus in the world.

<hr>

EXERCISE 5

PAIRED PRACTICE

You're going to read aloud to your partner. Today the **B** members will read first. Then the **A** members will read.
(Observe students and give feedback.)

End-of-Lesson Activities

Now finish your independent work for lesson 119. Raise your hand when you're finished. (Observe students and give feedback.)

WORKCHECK

a. (Direct students to take out their marking pencils.)
 • We're going to check your independent work. Remember, if you got an item wrong, make an **X** next to the item.
b. (For each item: Read the item. Call on a student to answer it. If the answer is wrong, say the correct answer. Refer to the Answer Key for the correct answers.)
c. Now use your marking pencil to fix up any items you got wrong. Remember, all mistakes must be fixed up before you hand in your work.

> **Note:** Before presenting lesson 120, you will need to:
> • Reproduce blackline masters for the Fact Game;
> • Preview Literature lesson 12, secure materials and reproduce blackline masters. (See the Literature Guide.)

WRITING-SPELLING

(Present Writing-Spelling lesson 119 after completing Reading lesson 119. See Writing–Spelling Guide.)

ACTIVITY

(Present Activity 36 after completing Reading lesson 119. See Activities Across the Curriculum.)

LANGUAGE ARTS GUIDE

(Present Language Arts lesson 119 after completing Reading lesson 119. See Language Arts Guide.)

Test 12

EXERCISE 1

Materials for Lesson 120

Fact Game

For each team (4 or 5 students):
- pair of number cubes (or dice)
- copy of Fact Game 120

For each student:
- their copy of the scorecard sheet

For each monitor:
- a pencil
- Fact Game 120 answer key (at end of textbook C)

Reading Checkout

Each student needs their thermometer chart.

Literature Lesson 12

See Literature Guide for the materials you will need.

FACT GAME

a. (Divide students into groups of four or five. Assign monitors.)

b. You'll play the fact game for 10 minutes.

- (Circulate as students play the game. Comment on groups that are playing well.)

c. (At the end of 10 minutes, have all students who earned more than 10 points stand up.)

- (Tell the monitor of each game that ran smoothly:) Your group did a good job.

EXERCISE 2

READING CHECKOUTS

a. Today is a test day and a reading-checkout day. While you're writing answers, I'm going to call on you one at a time to read part of the story we read in lesson 119. When I call you to come and do your checkout, bring your thermometer chart.

- Remember, you pass the checkout by reading the passage in less than a minute without making more than 2 mistakes. And when you pass the

checkout, you color the space for lesson 120 on your thermometer chart.

b. (Call on individual students to read the portion of story 119 marked with ❀.)

- (Time the student. Note words that are missed and number of words read.)

- (Teacher reference:)

> ❀**The owner tried to argue with the crowd, but when people started to throw things at him, he said, "All right, he will ride a bicycle backward."**
>
> **The owner got a dusty bicycle. He held up one hand and said to the crowd, "Ladies and gentlemen. Today the Kankan Circus [50] presents Toby, the wonder kangaroo. Toby will amaze you by riding a bicycle backward. And he will do this amazing trick on a high wire [75] ten meters above the floor."**
>
> **Toby looked up at the wire ten meters above the floor. You know what Toby said.**
>
> **The owner handed Toby ❀ [100] the bicycle . . .**

- (If the student reads the passage in one minute or less and makes no more than 2 errors, direct the student to color in the space for lesson 120 on the thermometer chart.)

- (If the student makes any mistakes, point to each word that was misread and identify it.)

- (If the student does not meet the rate-error criterion for the passage, direct the student to practice reading the story with the assigned partner.)

EXERCISE 3

TEST

a. **Find page 141 in your textbook.** ✓

- This is a test. You'll work items you've done before.

b. Work carefully. Raise your hand when you've completed all the items.
(Observe students but do not give feedback on errors.)

EXERCISE 4

MARKING THE TEST

a. (Check students' work before beginning lesson 121. Refer to the Answer Key for the correct answers.)
b. (Record all test 12 results on the Test Summary Sheet and the Group Summary Sheet. Reproducible Summary Sheets are at the back of the Teacher's Guide.)

EXERCISE 5

TEST REMEDIES

• (Provide any necessary remedies for test 12 before presenting lesson 121. Test remedies are discussed in the Teacher's Guide.)

Test 12 Firming Table

Test Item	Introduced in lesson	Test Item	Introduced in lesson	Test Item	Introduced in lesson
1	118	12	114	23	117
2	118	13	114	24	113
3	118	14	114	25	115
4	118	15	114	26	111
5	111	16	114	27	111
6	113	17	115	28	115
7	113	18	115	29	115
8	113	19	113	30	117
9	113	20	113	31	117
10	113	21	117	32	117
11	117	22	117		

LITERATURE

(Present Literature lesson 12 after completing Reading lesson 120. See Literature Guide.)

LANGUAGE ARTS GUIDE

(Present Language Arts lesson 120 after completing Reading lesson 120. See Language Arts Guide.)

Lessons 121–125 • Planning Page

	Lesson 121	Lesson 122	Lesson 123	Lesson 124	Lesson 125
Lesson Events	Vocabulary Review Reading Words Comprehension Passage Story Reading Paired Practice Independent Work Workcheck Writing-Spelling	**Vocabulary Sentence** Reading Words Vocabulary Review Story Reading Paired Practice Independent Work Workcheck Writing-Spelling	Vocabulary Review Reading Words Comprehension Passage Story Reading Paired Practice Independent Work Workcheck Optional Activity Writing-Spelling	Vocabulary Review Reading Words Comprehension Passage Story Reading Paired Practice Independent Work Workcheck Writing-Spelling	Vocabulary Review Reading Words Comprehension Passage Story Reading Reading Checkouts Independent Work Workcheck Writing-Spelling
Vocabulary Sentence	sentence #27 sentence #28 sentence #29	#30: <u>Perhaps</u> they will <u>reply</u> in a few days.	#30: <u>Perhaps</u> they will <u>reply</u> in a few days.	sentence #28 sentence #29 sentence #30	#25: She <u>commented</u> about the <u>still</u> water.
Reading Words: Word Types	modeled words multi-syllable words 2-syllable words mixed words	modeled words words with endings multi-syllable words mixed words	modeled words mixed words multi-syllable words	modeled words mixed words	modeled words mixed words
New Vocabulary	encyclopedia hallelujah refunded	attack behave scar jewels poster project	constantly involved battered	calm describe earplugs	claim
Comprehension Passages	*Facts About Boxing*		*Homonyms*	*Henry Ouch Takes a Vacation*	*A Pilot's Trip*
Story	*Toby Leaves the Circus*	*The Big Fight*	*The Scarred Words in the Word Bank*	*The Number with the Most Scars*	*Some Words Stop Fighting*
Skill Items	Sequencing Vocabulary Sentence	Sequencing Vocabulary Sentences	Alphabetical Order	Vocabulary Sentence Guide Words	Vocabulary Sentences Compare
Special Materials		*Materials for project			Thermometer charts
Special Projects/ Activities		Project after lesson 122	Activity after lesson 123		

* Reference materials (Australia books, animal books, encyclopedias, CD-ROMs); poster-making supplies (butcher paper or poster board, markers, crayons, paints, scissors, paste, magazines for pictures).

Lesson 121

EXERCISE 1

VOCABULARY REVIEW

a. You learned a sentence that tells what the police officers checked.
  - Everybody, say that sentence. Get ready. (Signal.) *Police officers checked the ship's cargo.*
  - (Repeat until firm.)

b. You learned a sentence that tells what she paid.
  - Everybody, say that sentence. Get ready. (Signal.) *She paid the correct amount.*
  - (Repeat until firm.)

c. Here's the last sentence you learned: The champions performed perfectly.
  - Everybody, say that sentence. Get ready. (Signal.) *The champions performed perfectly.*
  - (Repeat until firm.)

d. What word means **put on a show?** (Signal.) *Performed.*
  - What word means they won the championship? (Signal.) *Champions.*
  - What word means **without any mistakes?** (Signal.) *Perfectly.*
  - (Repeat step d until firm.)

e. Once more. Say the sentence that tells what the champions did. Get ready. (Signal.) *The champions performed perfectly.*

EXERCISE 2

READING WORDS

Column 1

a. **Find lesson 121 in your textbook.** ✓
  - Touch column 1. ✓
  - (Teacher reference:)

> 1. encyclopedia 3. truth
> 2. hallelujah 4. homonym

b. Word 1 is **encyclopedia.** What word? (Signal.) *Encyclopedia.*
  - An encyclopedia is a large set of books that gives information about anything you can name. You can find out about anything from aardvarks to Zulus in an encyclopedia.

c. Word 2 is **hallelujah.** What word? (Signal.) *Hallelujah.*
  - People who say "Hallelujah" are feeling great joy. Everybody, what word do people sometimes say when they're feeling great joy? (Signal.) *Hallelujah.*

d. Word 3 is **truth.** What word? (Signal.) *Truth.*

e. Word 4 is **homonym.** What word? (Signal.) *Homonym.*
  - You'll read about what homonyms are.

f. Let's read those words again.
  - Word 1. What word? (Signal.) *Encyclopedia.*
  - (Repeat for words 2–4.)

g. (Repeat step f until firm.)

Column 2

h. Find column 2. ✓
  - (Teacher reference:)

> 1. **re**funded   4. **loud**ly
> 2. **work**er   5. **re**ply
> 3. **per**haps

  - All these words have more than one syllable. The first syllable of each word is underlined.

i. Word 1. What's the first syllable? (Signal.) *re.*
  - What's the whole word? (Signal.) *Refunded.*
  - When money is refunded, it is returned. Here's another way of saying **He returned their money: He refunded their money.** Everybody, what is somebody doing when the person returns money? (Signal.) *Refunding money.*

j. Word 2. What's the first syllable? (Signal.) *work.*
  - What's the whole word? (Signal.) *Worker.*

k. Word 3. What's the first syllable? (Signal.) *per.*
  - What's the whole word? (Signal.) *Perhaps.*

l. Word 4. What's the first syllable? (Signal.) *loud.*
  - What's the whole word? (Signal.) *Loudly.*

m. Word 5. What's the first syllable? (Signal) *re.*
- What's the whole word? (Signal.) *Reply.*

n. Let's read those words again, the fast way.
- Word 1. What word? (Signal.) *Refunded.*
- (Repeat for: **2. worker, 3. perhaps, 4. loudly, 5. reply.**)

o. (Repeat step n until firm.)

Column 3

p. Find column 3. ✓
- (Teacher reference:)

1. **certain**	4. **boxer**
2. **roadside**	5. **amount**
3. **stupid**	

q. Word 1. What word? (Signal.) *Certain.*
- (Repeat for words 2–5.)

r. (Repeat step q until firm.)

Column 4

s. Find column 4. ✓
- (Teacher reference:)

1. **worthless**	3. **mountains**
2. **gloves**	4. **wear**

t. Word 1. What word? (Signal.) *Worthless.*
- Spell **worthless.** Get ready. (Tap for each letter.) *W-O-R-T-H-L-E-S-S.*

u. Word 2. What word? (Signal.) *Gloves.*
- Spell **gloves.** Get ready. (Tap for each letter.) *G-L-O-V-E-S.*

v. Word 3. What word? (Signal.) *Mountains.*
- Spell **mountains.** Get ready. (Tap for each letter.) *M-O-U-N-T-A-I-N-S.*

w. Word 4. What word? (Signal.) *Wear.*
- Spell **wear.** Get ready. (Tap for each letter.) *W-E-A-R.*
- Did you wear a coat today?

x. Let's read those words again, the fast way.
- Word 1. What word? (Signal.) *Worthless.*
- (Repeat for words 2–4.)

y. (Repeat step x until firm.)

Individual Turns

(For columns 1–4: Call on individual students, each to read one to three words per turn.)

COMPREHENSION PASSAGE

a. Find part B in your textbook. ✓
- You're going to read the next story about Toby. First you'll read the information passage. It gives some facts about boxing.

b. Everybody, touch the title. ✓
- (Call on a student to read the title.) *[Facts About Boxing.]*
- Everybody, what's the title? (Signal.) *Facts About Boxing.*

c. (Call on individual students to read the passage, each student reading two or three sentences at a time.)

Facts About Boxing

The story in the next lesson will tell about kangaroos boxing. Here are facts about boxing:
    Two people box.

- Everybody, say that fact. Get ready. (Signal.) *Two people box.*
- (Repeat until firm.)

The boxers wear large mittens called boxing gloves.

- Everybody, what are the large mittens called? (Signal.) *Boxing gloves.*
- Everybody, touch the boxers in the picture. ✓
- Touch their boxing gloves. ✓

The boxers box inside a place that is roped off. Although this place is not round, it is called a ring.

- Everybody, what is the place they box in called? (Signal.) *A ring.*
- Is it round? (Signal.) *No.*
- Touch the ropes in the picture. ✓
- Those ropes mark the outside of the ring. The boxers box inside the ropes.

The boxers hit each other with the gloves.

The fight ends if one boxer knocks out the other boxer.

• How can you tell if a boxer is knocked out? (Call on a student. Idea: *The boxer falls down and doesn't get up.*)

If one of the boxers does not knock out the other, the fight goes on for a certain amount of time.

• Sometimes boxers will box for three minutes and then rest for one minute. They may do that ten times. Then the fight is over.

EXERCISE 4

STORY READING

a. Find part C in your textbook. ✓
• The error limit for group reading is 11. Read carefully.
b. Everybody, touch the title. ✓
• (Call on a student to read the title.) *[Toby Leaves the Circus.]*
• What's going to happen in this story? (Call on a student. Idea: *Toby will leave the circus.*)
c. (Call on individual students to read the story, each student reading two or three sentences at a time. Ask questions marked **1.**)

• (Correct errors: Tell the word. Direct the student to reread the sentence.)
• (If the group makes more than 11 errors, direct the students to reread the story.)

d. (After the group has read the selection making no more than 11 errors, read the story to the students and ask questions marked **2.**)

Toby Leaves the Circus

The circus owner refunded all the money the people had paid to see Toby.

2. What does it mean, he refunded the money? (Call on a student. Idea: *He gave back the money.*)

2. Why did he have to do that? (Call on a student. Ideas: *Because the people were mad; because Toby wouldn't do any tricks.*)

Then the owner led Toby back to his cage. The owner said, "You know how much you're going to eat, don't you?"

Toby knew how much he was going to eat.

1. How much? (Call on a student. Idea: *Nothing.*)
1. How do you know that Toby won't get anything to eat? (Call on a student. Idea: *Because he didn't do any tricks.*)

Toby sat there in his dark little cage, feeling very sad. He could hear the owner on the phone in the other room.

1. The story will just tell what the circus owner says. You have to figure out who he is talking to and what that person is saying.

The owner was saying, "You told me that the kangaroo could do all sorts of tricks. That stupid animal can't do anything. He has almost ruined my circus."

1. Everybody, who is the owner talking to? (Signal.) *Mabel.*
1. What did Mabel tell the owner that the kangaroo could do? (Call on a student. Idea: *All sorts of tricks.*)

The owner stopped talking for a while.

1. Why do you think he stopped talking for a while? (Call on a student. Idea: *Because he was listening to Mabel.*)

Then the owner said, "But I paid you a lot of money for that kangaroo. I want my thousand dollars back."

2. How much did he pay for Toby? (Signal.) *A thousand dollars.*
2. Why does the owner think he should get his money back? (Call on a student. Idea: *Because Toby couldn't do the tricks Mabel said he could do.*)

Again the owner stopped talking. Then the owner said, "All right. It's a deal. But you and the captain are crooks."

2. When the owner said, "It's a deal," what did he mean? (Call on a student. Idea: *That he and Mabel had agreed on something.*)

Later that day, a truck came by. The owner led Toby into the truck. The captain and Mabel got out of the truck, and they talked to the owner for a few minutes. The owner looked very unhappy. Then the captain and Mabel got in the back of the truck with Toby. They were laughing. Mabel said, "We really tricked that circus owner."
The captain said, "Yeah, really tricked him."

1. They tricked the circus owner. I wonder what they did.

Mabel said, "Imagine. We sold him that worthless kangaroo for one thousand dollars. Then we bought him back for one hundred dollars. Not bad."
"Yeah," the captain said. "Not bad."

2. Everybody, how much did Mabel and the captain sell Toby for? (Signal.) *A thousand dollars.*
2. How much did they buy him back for? (Signal.) *One hundred dollars.*
2. So they made 900 dollars on that deal. No wonder they were happy.

Mabel said, "Now we'll sell that kangaroo to the Roadside Zoo for one thousand dollars and we'll make more money."
"Yeah," the captain said. "More money."

2. What are they going to do with Toby? (Call on a student. Idea: *Sell him to the Roadside Zoo.*)

The truck left the city and drove for hours into the mountains. Then it stopped. Toby saw a sign, "Roadside Zoo."

2. Everybody, what did the sign say? (Signal.) *Roadside Zoo.*

Toby saw other signs: "Amazing Animals," "Killer Snakes," "Apes," and "The Beautiful Bird of India." A worker was putting up a new sign. It said, "Boxing Kangaroos."

1. Name some of the animals they have in the Roadside Zoo. (Call on individual students. Ideas: *Snakes; apes; the bird of India; kangaroo.*)
1. Everybody, what is the bird of India? (Signal.) *A peacock.*
1. Do you think it's a peacock we know? (Call on a student. Student preference.)

2. Everybody, what did the new sign say? (Signal.) *Boxing kangaroos.*
2. So what do you think Toby's new job will be? (Call on a student. Idea: *A boxer.*)
2. Everybody, look at the picture. Does that look like a very fancy zoo? (Signal.) *No.*
2. Touch the newest sign. ✓

One of the sailors led Toby into this zoo. The zoo smelled very bad. It wasn't the kind of zoo that has many animals. There were about ten animals. Each was in a small cage. One of them was talking very loudly. "How in the world can I entertain people if I don't even have enough room to spread out my lovely feathers?"

1. Everybody, who talks like that? (Signal.) *Pip.*

"Pip," Toby hollered.

But Toby didn't have a chance to talk with Pip. The sailor led Toby to the end cage, far from Pip. There was already another animal in this cage. It was a kangaroo—a big one. The sailor shoved Toby into the cage.

In the distance, Mabel was saying, "And now you have two boxing kangaroos."

1. Everybody, was Toby alone in his cage? (Signal.) *No.*
1. Who else was in that cage? (Call on a student. Idea: *A big kangaroo.*)

It was very crowded in that small cage. There were legs and tails all over the place. Toby could see two tails. One of them was very big. Along the top of that tail were three white spots. Toby looked at the tail and counted the spots. Then he looked at the kangaroo. There was only one kangaroo in the whole world that had a tail like that. "Daddy," Toby said. "Daddy."

For a moment, the large kangaroo stared at Toby. Then he said, "Are you my little Toby?"

"Yes, Daddy," Toby said. "It's me. They caught me and brought me here."

"Oh, son," Toby's father said, with a tear running down the side of his nose. "I am so glad to see you."

1. Go back to the beginning of the story. Follow along while I read.
2. Read the rest of the story to yourself. Find out two things. Find out the name of the place they talked about. Find out what Toby's father wanted to do. Raise your hand when you're done.

The two kangaroos hugged each other with their short little front legs. Then they talked. They talked about dust and blue skies and the mob and Australia. They talked about Toby's mother and the leader and the other kangaroos from the mob. Then Toby's father said, "Son, we've got to get out of this terrible place and go home."

Toby said, "Double good."
MORE NEXT TIME

2. (After all students have raised their hand:) Everybody, what country did they talk about? (Signal.) *Australia.*
2. Name some things they missed about Australia. (Call on different students. Ideas: *The mob; Toby's mother; other kangaroos.*)
2. What did Toby's father want to do? (Call on a student. Idea: *Go home.*)
2. Raise your hand if you remember what Toby said when his father said that they should get out of the zoo and go home. (Call on a student.) *[Double good.]*

EXERCISE 5

PAIRED PRACTICE

You're going to read aloud to your partner. First the **B** members will read from the moon to the star. Then the **A** members will read from the start to the end of the story. (Observe students and give feedback.)

End-of-Lesson Activities

INDEPENDENT WORK

Now finish your independent work for lesson 121. Raise your hand when you're finished. (Observe students and give feedback.)

WORKCHECK

a. (Direct students to take out their marking pencils.)

• We're going to check your independent work. Remember, if you got an item wrong, make an **X** next to the item.

b. (For each item: Read the item. Call on a student to answer it. If the answer is wrong, say the correct answer. Refer to the Answer Key for the correct answers.)

c. Now use your marking pencil to fix up any items you got wrong. Remember, all mistakes must be fixed up before you hand in your work.

Note: A special project occurs after lesson 122. See page 117 for the materials you'll need.

WRITING-SPELLING

(Present Writing-Spelling lesson 121 after completing Reading lesson 121. See Writing-Spelling Guide.)

LANGUAGE ARTS GUIDE

(Present Language Arts lesson 121 after completing Reading lesson 121. See Language Arts Guide.)

Lesson 122

EXERCISE 1

VOCABULARY

a. **Find page 342 at the back of your textbook.** ✓
- Touch sentence 30. ✓
- This is a new vocabulary sentence. It says: Perhaps they will reply in a few days. Everybody, read that sentence. Get ready. (Signal.) *Perhaps they will reply in a few days.*
- Close your eyes and say the sentence. Get ready. (Signal.) *Perhaps they will reply in a few days.*
- (Repeat until firm.)

b. **Perhaps** is another word for **maybe.** Here's another way of saying **Maybe it will rain: Perhaps it will rain.**
- Everybody, what's another way of saying **Maybe it will be cold tomorrow?** (Signal.) *Perhaps it will be cold tomorrow.*
- What's another way of saying **Maybe the birds were frightened?** (Signal.) *Perhaps the birds were frightened.*

c. **Reply** is another word for **answer.**
- What's another way of saying **They will answer soon?** (Signal.) *They will reply soon.*
- What's another way of saying **Their answer was very rude?** (Signal.) *Their reply was very rude.*

d. Listen to the sentence again: Perhaps they will reply in a few days. Everybody, say the sentence. Get ready. (Signal.) *Perhaps they will reply in a few days.*

e. What word means **maybe?** (Signal.) *Perhaps.*
- What word means **answer?** (Signal.) *Reply.*
- (Repeat step e until firm.)

EXERCISE 2

READING WORDS

Column 1

a. Find lesson 122 in your textbook. ✓
- Touch column 1. ✓
- (Teacher reference:)

1. terrible	4. scar
2. attack	5. scarred
3. behave	6. perhaps

b. Word 1 is **terrible.** What word? (Signal.) *Terrible.*
- Spell **terrible.** Get ready. (Tap for each letter.) *T-E-R-R-I-B-L-E.*

c. Word 2 is **attack.** What word? (Signal.) *Attack.*
- Spell **attack.** Get ready. (Tap for each letter.) *A-T-T-A-C-K.*
- When you attack somebody, you start a fight. Here's another way of saying **The short man started a fight with the tall man: The short man attacked the tall man.**

d. Your turn. What's another way of saying **The short man started a fight with the tall man?** (Signal.) *The short man attacked the tall man.*
- (Repeat step d until firm.)

e. What's another way of saying **The cat started a fight with the dog?** (Signal.) *The cat attacked the dog.*

f. Word 3 is **behave.** What word? (Signal.) *Behave.*
- Spell **behave.** Get ready. (Tap for each letter.) *B-E-H-A-V-E.*
- The way you act is the way you behave. Here's another way of saying **She acted strangely: She behaved strangely.**

g. Your turn. What's another way of saying **She acted strangely?** (Signal.) *She behaved strangely.*
- (Repeat step g until firm.)

h. What's another way of saying **I don't like the way he acts?** (Signal.) *I don't like the way he behaves.*

i. Word 4. What word? (Signal.) *Scar.*
- Spell **scar.** Get ready. (Tap for each letter.) *S-C-A-R.*
- A mark left from a bad cut or burn is called a **scar.**
- Everybody, what do you call a mark left from a bad cut? (Signal.) *A scar.*

j. Word 5. What word? (Signal.) *Scarred.*

k. Word 6. What word? (Signal.) *Perhaps.*

l. Let's read those words again, the fast way.
- Word 1. What word? (Signal.) *Terrible.*
- (Repeat for: **2. attack, 3. behave, 4. scar, 5. scarred, 6. perhaps.**)

m. (Repeat step l until firm.)

Column 2

n. Find column 2. ✓
- (Teacher reference:)

1. **jewels**	4. **prettier**
2. **earned**	5. **returned**
3. **handful**	

- All these words have endings.
o. Word 1. What word? (Signal.) *Jewels.*
- Jewels are valuable stones. Diamonds, emeralds, and rubies are jewels.
p. Word 2. What word? (Signal.) *Earned.*
- (Repeat for words 3–5.)
q. Let's read those words again.
- Word 1. What word? (Signal.) *Jewels.*
- (Repeat for words 2–5.)
r. (Repeat step q until firm.)

Column 3

s. Find column 3. ✓
- (Teacher reference:)

1. <u>post</u>er	4. <u>corr</u>ect
2. <u>hal</u>lelujah	5. <u>plen</u>ty
3. <u>power</u>ful	6. <u>gentle</u>men

- All these words have more than one syllable. The first part of each word is underlined.
t. Word 1. What's the underlined part? (Signal.) *post.*
- What's the whole word? (Signal.) *Poster.*
- A poster is a large picture that tells about something. Some posters tell about movies. Some posters tell about preventing forest fires.
u. Word 2. What's the underlined part? (Signal.) *hal.*
- What's the whole word? (Signal.) *Hallelujah.*
v. Word 3. What's the underlined part? (Signal.) *power.*
- What's the whole word? (Signal.) *Powerful.*
w. Word 4. What's the underlined part? (Signal.) *corr.*

- What's the whole word? (Signal.) *Correct.*
x. Word 5. What's the underlined part? (Signal.) *plen.*
- What's the whole word? (Signal.) *Plenty.*
y. Word 6. What's the underlined part? (Signal.) *gentle.*
- What's the whole word? (Signal.) *Gentlemen.*
z. Let's read those words again, the fast way.
- Word 1. What word? (Signal.) *Poster.*
- (Repeat for words 2–6.)
a. (Repeat step z until firm.)

Column 4

b. Find column 4. ✓
- (Teacher reference:)

1. **project**	4. **truth**
2. **bought**	5. **single**
3. **reply**	6. **homonym**

c. Word 1. What word? (Signal.) *Project.*
- A **project** is a **large job.** For some projects, different people have to work together. Everybody, what's another word for a **large job?** (Signal.) *Project.*
d. Word 2. What word? (Signal.) *Bought.*
- (Repeat for words 3–6.)
e. Let's read those words again.
- Word 1. What word? (Signal.) *Project.*
- (Repeat for words 2–6.)
f. (Repeat step e until firm.)

Individual Turns

(For columns 1–4: Call on individual students, each to read one to three words per turn.)

EXERCISE 3

VOCABULARY REVIEW

a. Here's the new vocabulary sentence: Perhaps they will reply in a few days.
- Everybody, say the sentence. Get ready. (Signal.) *Perhaps they will reply in a few days.*
- (Repeat until firm.)
b. Everybody, what word means **answer?** (Signal.) *Reply.*
- What word means **maybe?** (Signal.) *Perhaps.*

STORY READING

a. Find part B in your textbook. ✓
- The error limit for group reading is 12. Read carefully.

b. Everybody, touch the title. ✓
- (Call on a student to read the title.) [The Big Fight.]
- Everybody, what's the title? (Signal.) *The Big Fight.*
- Who do you think is going to be in that big fight? (Call on a student. Idea: *Toby and his father.*)

c. (Call on individual students to read the story, each student reading two or three sentences at a time. Ask questions marked **1.**)

- (Correct errors: Tell the word. Direct the student to reread the sentence.)
- (If the group makes more than 12 errors, direct the students to reread the story.)

d. (After the group has read the selection making no more than 12 errors, read the story to the students and ask questions marked **2.**)

The Big Fight

It was noon when three workers led Toby and his father from the cage to a small tent. There were about twenty people inside the tent waiting for the boxing kangaroos to put on their show.

1. Who were those boxing kangaroos? (Call on a student. Idea: *Toby and his father.*)

One of the workers put boxing gloves on both kangaroos. Then the owner of the zoo stood between the two kangaroos and said, "Ladies and gentlemen—boxing kangaroos. You will see them box like champions. You will see them fight until one of them knocks the other out. They will use their gloves, but these powerful animals will also use their tails."

The owner of the zoo was right about some of the things he said but not all of them. The crowd did see the kangaroos use their gloves. The crowd also saw them use their tails.

But the two kangaroos did not hit each other. They had a plan. Toby's father winked at Toby. That was the signal for the two kangaroos to swing their little front legs as hard as they could. They both hit the owner of the zoo.

2. Everybody, who gave the signal? (Signal.) *Toby's father.*
2. How did he signal? (Call on a student. Idea: *He winked.*)
2. Everybody, show me a wink. ✓
2. What did the kangaroos do when Toby's father winked? (Call on a student. Idea: *Hit the owner of the zoo.*)

Then the kangaroos swung their tails as hard as they could. Both tails hit the owner at the same time, and he went flying through the air.

2. Everybody, look at the picture. Touch the owner. ✓
2. What's he doing in that picture? (Call on a student. Idea: *Flying through the air.*)
2. How do you think he feels? (Call on a student. Ideas: *Surprised, in pain.*)
2. Everybody, touch Toby. ✓
2. How do you know that the other kangaroo is Toby's father? (Call on a student. Idea: *Because he has spots on his tail.*)

Quickly Toby ran over to the people in the crowd. "Please, listen to me," he said, but they were not listening. They were clapping and cheering.

One person said, "This is the best act we ever saw. What boxing kangaroos."

1. What do you think Toby was trying to tell the people? (Call on a student. Ideas: *Help us; this is a terrible place.*)

1. Why didn't the people listen to Toby? (Call on a student. Ideas: *Because they were making too much noise to hear him; they were watching the act.*)

> "Please listen," Toby said. "We were taken from Australia by crooks . . . ."
>
> The people were still laughing and clapping. "What an act," they were shouting.
>
> Suddenly, there was a terrible screech. The crowd became quiet. Then a very loud voice said, "The kangaroo is telling you the truth."

1. Everybody, who made the terrible screech? (Signal.) *Pip.*

> Toby said, "Good for Pip."
>
> Pip was in his cage, but he had such a loud voice that the people could easily hear what he was saying. "I was taken from my home in India. For me, this was terrible. For you, of course, it is very nice because you get to look at me. But the people who brought us here are crooks. Somebody should call the police."

1. Do you think the people will do it? (Call on individual students. Student preference.)

> Somebody did call the police. By the time the police came to the zoo, four people were sitting on the owner so that he did not escape. The people had let out all the animals. One platypus kept shouting, "Hallelujah!" A small bear was eating a handful of peanuts. Toby and his father were standing next to Pip. And Pip was entertaining the people.
>
> "Here's one that will amaze you," Pip said and turned around with his tail feathers shining. "Notice how the sunlight catches the feathers and makes them shine like jewels."
>
> When the police started to take the owner away, the owner said, "You can't blame me for this. I bought these animals from Mabel."

> "That's correct," Pip said. "Mabel is a crook."
>
> The owner said, "I'll tell you where you can find Mabel and the captain." And he did.

1. Why did the owner tell on Mabel and the captain? (Call on a student. Idea: *Because Mabel and the captain sold him stolen animals.*)
1. There are dots in the story. What does that mean? (Call on a student. Idea: *Part of the story is missing.*)

> • • •
> Mabel is in jail. So are the captain and the three sailors.

1. This part tells what's going on now. Everybody, where is Mabel now? (Signal.) *In jail.*
1. Where is the captain? (Signal.) *In jail.*
1. What part of the story is missing? (Call on a student. Idea: *The part that tells how Mabel and the captain got to jail.*)

> Pip is still in Canada. When he thought about going back to India, he realized that there were many peacocks there, and some of them were even prettier than he was. So he decided that he would continue to entertain the people of Canada. He has a nice place in a real zoo. He has plenty of room to turn around and to show off.

1. How happy do you think he is if he can entertain people all the time? (Call on a student. Idea: *Very happy.*)

> The platypus went back to Australia. All the way back he kept saying, "Hallelujah!" The police took the bears, the snakes, and the apes to their homes.

1. Go back to the beginning of the story. Follow along while I read.
2. Read the rest of the story to yourself. Find out two things. Find out where Toby and his father went and what happened to them. Raise your hand when you're done.

That took care of just about everybody except Toby and his father. They went back to Australia too, where they found their mob.

When the other kangaroos saw Toby and his father, they cheered. "Toby saved us from hunters," they shouted. "Hooray for Toby!"

The leader said, "We are glad that two very important kangaroos have returned to our mob. Both these kangaroos have earned our thanks."

Now, when the mob moves from place to place, the leader hops first. Right behind him is a kangaroo with a very long tail that has three white spots on it. And right next to that kangaroo is a kangaroo that used to be called a joey. And right next to that kangaroo is Toby's mother.

And when the mob moves along, you may be able to hear one of the kangaroos saying, "Oh, good, good, good."

THE END

2. (After all students have raised their hand:) Everybody, what country did Toby and his father go to? *Australia.*
2. Everybody, did the mob treat Toby like a joey? (Signal.) *No.*
2. How had Toby saved the other kangaroos? (Call on a student. Idea: *By warning the mob about the hunters.*)
2. Where are Toby and his mother and father in the mob? (Call on a student. Idea: *Right behind the leader.*)
2. Which kangaroo says "Oh, good, good, good"? (Signal.) *Toby.*
2. Touch Toby's father in the picture on the next page. ✓
2. Touch Toby. ✓
2. Touch his mother. ✓
2. How do you think they feel? (Call on a student. Idea: *Happy.*)

2. Did you like these stories about Toby? (Call on individual students. Student preference.)
2. What part did you like the best? (Call on individual students. Student preference.)

EXERCISE 5

PAIRED PRACTICE

You're going to read aloud to your partner. Today the **A** members will read first. Then the **B** members will read from the star to the end of the story.
(Observe students and give feedback.)

End-of-Lesson Activities

INDEPENDENT WORK

Now finish your independent work for lesson 122. Raise your hand when you're finished.
(Observe students and give feedback.)

WORKCHECK

a. (Direct students to take out their marking pencils.)
• We're going to check your independent work. Remember, if you got an item wrong, make an **X** next to the item.
b. (For each item: Read the item. Call on a student to answer it. If the answer is wrong, say the correct answer. Refer to the Answer Key for the correct answers.)
c. Now use your marking pencil to fix up any items you got wrong. Remember, all mistakes must be fixed up before you hand in your work.

WRITING-SPELLING

(Present Writing-Spelling lesson 122 after completing Reading lesson 122. See Writing-Spelling Guide.)

LANGUAGE ARTS GUIDE

(Present Language Arts lesson 122 after completing Reading lesson 122. See Language Arts Guide.)

Special Project

Note: After completing lesson 122, do this special project with the students. You may do this project during another part of the school day.

Materials: Reference materials (Australia books, animal books, encyclopedias, CD-ROMs) and poster-making supplies (butcher paper or poster board, markers, crayons, paints, scissors, paste, magazines for pictures)

a. Everybody, find page 159 in your textbook. ✔
- (Call on individual students to read two or three sentences.)
- (Teacher reference:)

Special Project

Make a large poster that shows some of the animals that live in Australia. You may find pictures of animals of Australia in an encyclopedia or in other books. Your teacher will help you find some good pictures.

Make copies of the pictures you find. Put the pictures on a large poster. At the top of the poster write the title of the poster. Write the name of each animal near the picture of that animal. Below each animal write some facts about that animal.

- ✦ Tell what it eats.
- ✦ Tell what color it is.
- ✦ Tell how big it is.

---

b. (Divide the group into subgroups, each of which is responsible for finding pictures and information for one or two animals. Use encyclopedias [such as *World Book*] or CD-ROMs and magazines [such as *National Geographic*] for pictures and information.)
c. (Help each group find the information and pictures needed for the poster. Then ask the students for ideas about how to display the information and pictures.)

Lesson 123

EXERCISE 1

VOCABULARY REVIEW

a. Here's the new vocabulary sentence: Perhaps they will reply in a few days.
- Everybody, say the sentence. Get ready. (Signal.) *Perhaps they will reply in a few days.*
- (Repeat until firm.)

b. Everybody, what word means **maybe?** (Signal.) *Perhaps.*
- What word means **answer?** (Signal.) *Reply.*

EXERCISE 2

READING WORDS

Column 1

a. **Find lesson 123 in your textbook.** ✓
- Touch column 1. ✓
- (Teacher reference:)

1. involve	3. among
2. perhaps	4. constantly

b. Word 1 is **involve.** What word? (Signal.) *Involve.*
- Spell **involve.** Get ready. (Tap for each letter.) *I-N-V-O-L-V-E.*

c. Word 2 is **perhaps.** What word? (Signal.) *Perhaps.*
- Spell **perhaps.** Get ready. (Tap for each letter.) *P-E-R-H-A-P-S.*

d. Word 3 is **among.** What word? (Signal.) *Among.*
- Spell **among.** Get ready. (Tap for each letter.) *A-M-O-N-G.*

e. Word 4 is **constantly.** What word? (Signal.) *Constantly.*
- Things that go on constantly go on **all the time.** Here's another way of saying **He talked all the time: He talked constantly.**

f. Your turn. What's another way of saying **He talked all the time?** (Signal.) *He talked constantly.*
- (Repeat step f until firm.)

g. What's another way of saying **She eats all the time?** (Signal.) *She eats constantly.*

h. Let's read those words again, the fast way.
- Word 1. What word? (Signal.) *Involve.*
- (Repeat for words 2–4.)
i. (Repeat step h until firm.)

Column 2

j. Find column 2. ✓
- (Teacher reference:)

1. involved	4. scarred
2. scar	5. terrible
3. single	

k. Word 1. What word? (Signal.) *Involved.*
- People who **take part** in a game are **involved** in the game. Here's another way of saying **They are taking part in a meeting: They are involved in a meeting.**

l. Your turn. What's another way of saying **They are taking part in a meeting?** (Signal.) *They are involved in a meeting.*
- (Repeat step l until firm.)

m. What's another way of saying **Two boys took part in an argument?** (Signal.) *Two boys were involved in an argument.*

n. Word 2. What word? (Signal.) *Scar.*
- (Repeat for words 3–5.)

o. Let's read those words again.
- Word 1. What word? (Signal.) *Involved.*
- (Repeat for words 2–5.)
p. (Repeat step o until firm.)

Column 3

q. Find column 3. ✓
- (Teacher reference:)

1. batter	4. behave
2. homonym	5. attack
3. battered	6. reply

r. Word 1. What word? (Signal.) *Batter.*
- Word 2. What word? (Signal.) *Homonym.*

s. Word 3. What word? (Signal.) *Battered.*
- When something is battered, it is beat up.
- What's another way of saying a beat-up car? (Signal.) *A battered car.*

t. Word 4. What word? (Signal.) *Behave.*
  • (Repeat for: **5, attack, 6. reply.**)
u. Let's read those words again.
  • Word 1. What word? (Signal.) *Batter.*
  • (Repeat for: **2. homonym, 3. battered, 4. behave, 5. attack, 6. reply.**)
v. (Repeat step u until firm.)

Individual Turns

(For columns 1–3: Call on individual students, each to read one to three words.)

EXERCISE 3

COMPREHENSION PASSAGE

a. Find part B in your textbook. ✓
  • You're going to read another story about Hohoboho. First you'll read the information passage. It gives information about words that sound the same as other words.
b. Everybody, touch the title. ✓
  • (Call on a student to read the title.) *[Homonyms.]*
  • Everybody, what's the title? (Signal.) *Homonyms.*
c. (Call on individual students to read the passage, each student reading two or three sentences at a time.)

> **Homonyms**
>
> You're going to read a story about words that sometimes confuse people. These words are called <u>homonyms</u>.

  • Everybody, what are they called? (Signal.) *Homonyms.*

> A homonym sounds the same as some other word. But a homonym is spelled differently. Remember, two homonyms sound the same, but their spelling is different.

  • In what way are two homonyms the same? (Call on a student. Idea: *They sound the same.*)
  • In what way are two homonyms different? (Call on a student. Idea: *How they're spelled.*)

> Here are two homonyms: <u>four</u> and <u>for</u>.

  • Everybody, say the first homonym. Get ready. (Signal.) *Four.*

  • Say the second homonym. Get ready. (Signal.) *For.*
  • Do they sound **the same** or sound **different?** (Signal.) *The same.*
  • Spell the first homonym. Get ready. (Tap for each letter.) *F-O-U-R.*
  • Spell the second homonym. Get ready. (Tap for each letter.) *F-O-R.*
  • Do they have the **same spelling** or **different spelling?** (Signal.) *Different spelling.*

> Here are two other homonyms: <u>new</u> and <u>knew</u>.

  • Everybody, are the words **new** and **knew** spelled the same way? (Signal.) *No.*

> The word <u>eight</u> has a homonym.

  • Everybody, spell the word **eight** that is in that sentence. Get ready. (Signal.) *E-I-G-H-T.*
  • Everybody, say the homonym. Get ready. (Signal.) *Ate.*
  • Is that homonym spelled E-I-G-H-T? (Signal.) *No.*

> Other numbers have homonyms.
> The sentence below has four words that are homonyms: <u>She rode for one hour.</u>
> The first homonym is the word <u>rode.</u>
> What's the next homonym?

  • Everybody, what's the answer? (Signal.) *For.*

> What's the next homonym?

  • Everybody, what's the answer? (Signal.) *One.*

> What's the last homonym?

  • Everybody, what's the answer? (Signal.) *Hour.*

> You'll read more about those homonyms.
> Remember the name we use for words that sound the same as other words.

  • Everybody, what do we call those words? (Signal.) *Homonyms.*

STORY READING

a. Find part C in your textbook. ✓
• The error limit for this story is 7. Read carefully.
b. Everybody, touch the title. ✓
• (Call on a student to read the title.) *[The Scarred Words in the Word Bank.]*
• What's this story going to tell about? (Call on a student. Idea: *The scarred words in the word bank.*)
• What would words look like if they were scarred? (Call on a student. Idea: *They would have marks from scratches and cuts on them.*)
c. (Call on individual students to read the story, each student reading two or three sentences at a time. Ask questions marked **1**.)

> • (Correct errors: Tell the word. Direct the student to reread the sentence.)
> • (If the group makes more than 7 errors, direct the students to reread the story.)

d. (After the group has read the selection making no more than 7 errors, read the story to the students and ask questions marked **2**.)

The Scarred Words in the Word Bank

If you look at the words in the word bank, you'll notice that some of them have scars. These scars came from great fights that used to take place right in the word bank. The words no longer fight, but thousands of years ago when Hohoboho was a very young country, there were hundreds of terrible fights.

2. When did these fights take place? (Call on a student. Idea: *Thousands of years ago.*)
2. Everybody, do they still go on? (Signal.) *No.*

Words would leap out of their seats and attack other words. They would hit and fight and scratch and yell and throw things and behave like a bunch of animals. From these fights some words got their scars.

Not all the words have scars. The word <u>wash</u> does not have one single scar. Neither does the word <u>only</u> or the word <u>run.</u> But the word <u>red</u> has scars. The word <u>their</u> is covered with scars. So is the word <u>two.</u>

Here's the story about why some words are scarred: When the word bank opened for the first time, the words were given their seats. The people in Hohoboho would talk, and every time one of the words was said, that word would get one point. But there was a very bad problem. Some words sounded just like other words. When somebody in Hohoboho said, "It is over <u>there,</u>" the word <u>there</u> would say, "That's me. I get that point." The word <u>their</u> would say, "No, that's me. The person said <u>their.</u>"

By now both words would be standing up and hollering at each other.

2. Everybody, name the two words that were fighting. Get ready. (Signal.) *Their and there.*
2. Why were they fighting? (Call on a student. Idea: *Because they both wanted the point.*)
2. How are **there** and **their** different from each other? (Call on a student. Ideas: *They're spelled differently; they have different meanings.*)

And then the words would start swinging and scratching and throwing things.

2. What does that mean, they started swinging? (Call on a student. Idea: *They started to fight.*)

The fight would continue until the words were tired out.

2. Everybody, when would they stop fighting? (Signal.) *When they were tired out.*

By then somebody in Hohoboho would say something like, "Do they have a radio in <u>their</u> car?"

The word <u>their</u> would jump up, "That's me."

2. Everybody, spell the word that said that. Get ready. (Tap for each letter.) *T-H-E-I-R.*

2. Spell the word that's going to fight with **T-H-E-I-R.** Get ready. (Tap for each letter.) *T-H-E-R-E.*

> **"No way," the word <u>there</u> would reply. "Somebody said <u>there</u> and that's me."**
> **Soon, the two words would be fighting again.**
> **As <u>their</u> and <u>there</u> fought, somebody in Hohoboho would say, "Speak louder. I can't <u>hear</u> you."**

2. Everybody, how is that **hear** spelled? (Tap for each letter.) *H-E-A-R.*

> **The word <u>hear</u> would jump up and say, "That's me." The word <u>here</u> would jump up and say, "That's me." Then <u>here</u> and <u>hear</u> would get into a terrible fight.**

2. What would the word **H-E-R-E** say to start the fight? (Call on a student.) *[That's me.]*

> **In other parts of the word bank, other words would be shouting and fighting.**
> **MORE NEXT TIME**

1. Go back to the beginning of the story. Follow along while I read.
2. Can you think of any other two words that would be fighting because they sound the same? (Call on individual students. Ideas: *To and too; one and won;* etc.)

EXERCISE 5

PAIRED PRACTICE

You're going to read aloud to your partner. Today the **B** members will read first. Then the **A** members will read from the star to the end of the story.
(Observe students and give feedback.)

End-of-Lesson Activities

INDEPENDENT WORK

Now finish your independent work for lesson 123. Raise your hand when you're finished.
(Observe students and give feedback.)

WORKCHECK

a. (Direct students to take out their marking pencils.)
• We're going to check your independent work. Remember, if you got an item wrong, make an **X** next to the item. Don't change any answers.
b. (For each item: Read the item. Call on a student to answer it. If the answer is wrong, say the correct answer. Refer to the Answer Key for the correct answers.)
c. Now use your marking pencil to fix up any items you got wrong. Remember, all mistakes must be fixed up before you hand in your independent work.

OPTIONAL ACTIVITY

MORE HOMONYMS

a. You're going to learn more homonyms.
b. Listen: We drove **by** the school. The word **by** means **near.** Who can think of another word **by** that does not mean **near?** When you think of a word, tell me how you use it in a sentence. (Prompt if necessary: Tell me about the kind of **buy** you might do in a store.)
• Who can spell the word **buy** that you would do in a store? (Call on a student.) *[B-U-Y.]*
c. (Repeat step b for:) I **know** a lot of things. That **know** tells about things that I understand. Tell me about the **no** that does not mean **understand.**
d. (Repeat step b for:) The **dew** was on the lawn. That **dew** tells about drops of water. Tell me about the **do** that does not refer to drops of water.
e. (Repeat step b for:) She was trying to lose **weight.** That **weight** tells about pounds. Tell me about the **wait** that does not tell about pounds.

WRITING-SPELLING

(Present Writing-Spelling lesson 123 after completing Reading lesson 123. See Writing-Spelling Guide.)

ACTIVITY

(Present Activity 37 after completing Reading lesson 123. See Activities Across the Curriculum.)

LANGUAGE ARTS GUIDE

(Present Language Arts lesson 123 after completing Reading lesson 123. See Language Arts Guide.)

VOCABULARY REVIEW

a. You learned a sentence that tells what the champions did.

- Everybody, say that sentence. Get ready. (Signal.) *The champions performed perfectly.*
- (Repeat until firm.)

b. You learned a sentence that tells how much she paid.

- Say that sentence. Get ready. (Signal.) *She paid the correct amount.*
- (Repeat until firm.)

c. Here's the last sentence you learned: Perhaps they will reply in a few days.

- Everybody, say that sentence. Get ready. (Signal.) *Perhaps they will reply in a few days.*
- (Repeat until firm.)

d. Everybody, what word means **answer?** (Signal.) *Reply.*

- What word means **maybe?** (Signal.) *Perhaps.*

e. Once more. Say the sentence that tells when they might reply. Get ready. (Signal.) *Perhaps they will reply in a few days.*

READING WORDS

Column 1

a. **Find lesson 124 in your textbook.** ✓

- Touch column 1. ✓
- (Teacher reference:)

1. calm	3. among
2. describe	4. eight

b. Word 1 is **calm.** What word? (Signal.) *Calm.*

- Spell **calm.** Get ready. (Tap for each letter.) *C-A-L-M.*
- When things are **calm,** they are **very quiet and peaceful.** Here's another way of saying **The water was peaceful: The water was calm.**

c. Your turn. What's another way of saying **The water was peaceful?** (Signal.) *The water was calm.*

- (Repeat step c until firm.)

d. What's another way of saying **The children were quiet and peaceful?** (Signal.) *The children were calm.*

e. Word 2. What word? (Signal.) *Describe.*

- Spell **describe.** Get ready. (Tap for each letter.) *D-E-S-C-R-I-B-E.*
- When you **describe** something, you tell **how it looks** or **how it works.** Here's another way of saying **She told how her car looks: She described her car.**

f. Your turn. What's another way of saying **She told how her car looks?** (Signal.) *She described her car.*

- (Repeat step f until firm.)

g. What's another way of saying **She told how her plan works?** (Signal.) *She described her plan.*

h. Word 3. What word? (Signal.) *Among.*

- Spell **among.** Get ready. (Tap for each letter.) *A-M-O-N-G.*

i. Word 4. What word? (Signal.) *Eight.*

- Spell **eight.** Get ready. (Tap for each letter.) *E-I-G-H-T.*

j. Let's read those words again, the fast way.

- Word 1. What word? (Signal.) *Calm.*
- (Repeat for words 2–4.)

k. (Repeat step j until firm.)

Column 2

l. Find column 2. ✓

- (Teacher reference:)

1. plugs	4. constantly
2. earplugs	5. battered
3. involved	

m. Word 1. What word? (Signal.) *Plugs.*

n. Word 2. What word? (Signal.) *Earplugs.*

- **Earplugs** are rubber things that you stick in your ears. It's hard to hear things when you're wearing earplugs.

o. Word 3. What word? (Signal.) *Involved.*

- (Repeat for words 4 and 5.)

p. Let's read those words again.
- Word 1. What word? (Signal.) *Plugs.*
- (Repeat for: **2. earplugs, 3. involved, 4. constantly, 5 battered.**)

q. (Repeat step p until firm.)

Individual Turns

(For columns 1 and 2: Call on individual students, each to read one to three words per turn.)

EXERCISE 3

COMPREHENSION PASSAGE

a. Find part B in your textbook. ✓
- You're going to read the next story about Hohoboho. First you'll read the information passage. It reviews some facts you have learned.

b. Everybody, touch the title. ✓
- (Call on a student to read the title.) *[Henry Ouch Takes a Vacation.]*
- Everybody, what's the title? (Signal.) *Henry Ouch Takes a Vacation.*

c. (Call on individual students to read the passage, each student reading two or three sentences at a time.)

Henry Ouch Takes a Vacation

Henry Ouch went for a vacation.

- Everybody, what kind of animal is Henry Ouch? (Signal.) *A flea.*

He left San Francisco on a large ship. That ship went to Japan. You know which direction it went.

- Everybody, if it went from San Francisco to Japan, in which direction did it go? (Signal.) *West.*

How far was that trip?

- Everybody, how far is it from San Francisco to Japan? (Signal.) *5 thousand miles.*

What ocean did Henry cross?

- Everybody, what's the answer? (Signal.) *Pacific Ocean.*

The ship passed some islands. How did Henry know they were islands?

- What's the answer? (Call on a student. Idea: *They were surrounded by water.*)

Henry could see palm trees on some islands. He knew the name for branches of a palm tree.

- Everybody, what are those branches called? (Signal.) *Fronds.*

He also knew the name of the large hard things that grow on some palm trees.

- Everybody, what are those large hard things called? (Signal.) *Coconuts.*

When Henry got thirsty, he drank little drops of water that formed on the deck early in the morning. What are those drops called?

- Everybody, what's the answer? (Signal.) *Dew.*

Henry did not drink water from the ocean. Why not?

- What's the answer? (Call on a student. Idea: *It would make him thirstier.*)

Henry did not like it when the temperature dropped down because Henry's body worked like the bodies of other insects. Henry was ▮▮▮-blooded.

- Everybody, what kind of blood? (Signal.) *Cold.*
- What does that mean? (Call on a student. Idea: *The temperature inside his body changes when the outside temperature changes.*)

Sometimes the temperature inside his body was higher than your normal temperature.

- Everybody, what's your normal body temperature? (Signal.) *98 degrees.*

Sometimes the temperature inside his body was lower than your normal temperature.

- When would the temperature inside his body get lower? (Call on a student. Idea: *When it gets colder outside.*)

STORY READING

a. Find part C in your textbook. ✓
- The error limit for this story is 9. Read carefully.

b. Everybody, touch the title. ✓
- (Call on a student to read the title.) *[The Number with the Most Scars.]*
- What's this story going to tell about? (Call on a student. Idea: *The number with the most scars.*)
- What number do you think that is? (Call on individual students. Ideas: *One, two, four, or eight.*)

c. (Call on individual students to read the story, each student reading two or three sentences at a time. Ask questions marked **1**.)

- (Correct errors: Tell the word. Direct the student to reread the sentence.)
- (If the group makes more than 9 errors, direct the students to reread the story.)

d. (After the group has read the selection making no more than 9 errors, read the story to the students and ask questions marked **2**.)

The Number with the Most Scars

The words in the word bank had a problem because they listened to the words that were said by the people in Hohoboho.

2. What kind of words had a problem? (Call on a student. Ideas: *Words that sounded the same; homonyms.*)

Some words sound the same. When the people in Hohoboho said these words, the words that sounded the same would fight over who got the point. The words **their** and **there** were always fighting. But they were not the only ones.

2. Tell me another pair of homonyms. (Call on individual students. Ideas: *Won and one; there and their; eight and ate; read and red; etc.*)

The words for numbers were involved in some of the worst fights you could imagine.

1. Name a number that might get in a fight because it sounds like another word. (Call on individual students. Ideas: *One, two, four, eight.*)

The word **three** never fought.

2. Why not? (Call on a student. Idea: *Because it doesn't sound the same as another word.*)

Nor did the words **five**, **six**, or **seven**. But **one**, **two**, **four**, and **eight** went from one fight to another.
The word **one** fought with the word **won**.

2. Why? (Call on a student. Idea: *Because they sounded the same.*)

Every time somebody in Hohoboho said, "I **won**," a fight would take place. Every time somebody in Hohoboho said, "You have **one** more turn," another fight would take place.

2. Spell the words that would be in that fight. (Call on a student.) *[O-N-E and W-O-N.]*

The word **four** was always fighting with **for**. If somebody in Hohoboho said, "I will do something **for** you," the words **for** and **four** would fight. They also fought when somebody said, "I have **four** spoons."
The word **eight** was always fighting with the word **ate**. If somebody said, "A man **ate** an egg," there would be a fight. The word **eight** would say, "Somebody said **eight**. That's me." The word **ate** would say, "You're crazy. Somebody said **ate**." And the fight would start.
Eight, **four**, and **one** had terrible fights and lots of them, but their fights could not compare to the fights that the word **two** used to have.

1. What does that mean, their fights could not compare to the fights that **two** had? (Call on a student. Idea: *It means that the fights **two** had were much worse than the fights the others had.*)

1. Everybody, which word had the worst fights? (Signal.) *Two.*

> **If you look at <u>two</u> now, you can get some idea of how bad those fights were. <u>Two</u> has scars and scars and scars. The reason is that two used to fight constantly.**

1. Can you spell any words that **two** fought with? (Call on a student.)
[T-O and T-O-O.]
2. How often did **two** fight? (Call on a student. Idea: *Constantly.*)

> **<u>Two</u> used to fight with the word <u>to</u>. Every time somebody would say, "Go <u>to</u> the store," <u>two</u> would say, "That's me. She said <u>two</u>." Soon, <u>two</u> and <u>to</u> would be fighting.**
>   **But <u>two</u> also had fights with <u>too</u>. If somebody said, "I'll go, <u>too</u>," <u>two</u> would say, "Another point for me. She said <u>two</u>."**
>   **"No," <u>too</u> would say. "She said <u>too</u>."**
>   **By now the word <u>to</u> would say, "You're both crazy," and a *big* fight would start.**

2. Everybody, who was the word spelled T-O talking to when it said, "You're both crazy"? (Call on a student. Ideas: *Two and too; T-W-O and T-O-O.*)
2. Spell those 3 words that fought. (Call on a student.) [T-O, T-O-O, T-W-O.]

> **By the end of the day, when the people in Hohoboho stopped talking and went to bed, some of the words in the word bank were pretty battered up.**

2. Why? (Call on a student. Idea: *Because they'd been fighting a lot.*)

> **The word <u>two</u> was always among the words that were the most battered. <u>Two</u> was usually glad when the day was over. <u>Two</u> needed the rest before starting another day of battles with <u>too</u> and <u>to</u>.**
>   **MORE NEXT TIME**

1. Go back to the beginning of the story. Follow along while I read.

PAIRED PRACTICE

You're going to read aloud to your partner. Today the **A** members will read first. Then the **B** members will read from the star to the end of the story.
(Observe students and give feedback.)

End-of-Lesson Activities

INDEPENDENT WORK

Now finish your independent work for lesson 124. Raise your hand when you're finished. (Observe students and give feedback.)

WORKCHECK

a. (Direct students to take out their marking pencils.)
 • We're going to check your independent work. Remember, if you got an item wrong, make an **X** next to the item. Don't change any answers.
b. (For each item: Read the item. Call on a student to answer it. If the answer is wrong, say the correct answer. Refer to the Answer Key for the correct answers.)
c. Now use your marking pencil to fix up any items you got wrong. Remember, all mistakes must be fixed up before you hand in your independent work.

WRITING-SPELLING

(Present Writing-Spelling lesson 124 after completing Reading lesson 124. See Writing-Spelling Guide.)

LANGUAGE ARTS GUIDE

(Present Language Arts lesson 124 after completing Reading lesson 124. See Language Arts Guide.)

Materials: Each student will need their thermometer chart for exercise 5.

EXERCISE 1

VOCABULARY REVIEW

a. You learned a sentence that tells what she commented about.
  • Everybody, say that sentence. Get ready. (Signal.) *She commented about the still water.*
  • (Repeat until firm.)

b. I'll say part of the sentence. When I stop, you say the next word. Listen: She . . . Everybody, what's the next word? (Signal.) *Commented.*

c. Listen: She commented about the . . . Everybody, what's the next word? (Signal.) *Still.*
  • Say the whole sentence. Get ready. (Signal.) *She commented about the still water.*

EXERCISE 2

READING WORDS

Column 1

a. **Find lesson 125 in your textbook.** ✓
  • Touch column 1. ✓
  • (Teacher reference:)

1. **guard**	4. **calm**
2. **language**	5. **earplugs**
3. **describe**	

b. Word 1 is **guard.** What word? (Signal.) *Guard.*
  • Spell **guard.** Get ready. (Tap for each letter.) *G-U-A-R-D.*

c. Word 2 is **language.** What word? (Signal.) *Language.*
  • Spell **language.** Get ready. (Tap for each letter.) *L-A-N-G-U-A-G-E.*

d. Word 3. What word? (Signal.) *Describe.*
  • Spell **describe.** Get ready. (Tap for each letter.) *D-E-S-C-R-I-B-E.*

e. Word 4. What word? (Signal.) *Calm.*
  • Spell **calm.** Get ready. (Tap for each letter.) *C-A-L-M.*

f. Word 5. What word? (Signal.) *Earplugs.*

g. Let's read those words again, the fast way.
  • Word 1. What word? (Signal.) *Guard.*
  • (Repeat for words 2–5.)

h. (Repeat step g until firm.)

Column 2

i. Find column 2. ✓
  • (Teacher reference:)

1. **claim**	4. **spelling**
2. **difference**	5. **noisy**
3. **screen**	6. **rhyme**

j. Word 1. What word? (Signal.) *Claim.*
  • When you **claim** something, you say it's yours. Here's another way of saying **She said the coat was hers: She claimed the coat.**

k. Your turn. What's another way of saying **She said the coat was hers?** (Signal.) *She claimed the coat.*
  • (Repeat step k until firm.)

l. What's another way of saying **He said the point was his?** (Signal.) *He claimed the point.*

m. Word 2. What word? (Signal.) *Difference.*
  • (Repeat for words 3–6.)

n. Let's read those words again.
  • Word 1. What word? (Signal.) *Claim.*
  • (Repeat for words 2–6.)

o. (Repeat step n until firm.)

Individual Turns

(For columns 1 and 2: Call on individual students, each to read one to three words per turn.)

COMPREHENSION PASSAGE

a. Find part B in your textbook. ✓
 • You're going to read the next story about Hohoboho. First you'll read the information passage. It reviews some facts you have learned.
b. Everybody, touch the title. ✓
 • (Call on a student to read the title.) *[A Pilot's Trip.]*
 • Everybody, what's the title? (Signal.) *A Pilot's Trip.*
c. (Call on individual students to read the passage, each student reading two or three sentences at a time.)

A Pilot's Trip

A jet pilot went around the world. She went from the country of Japan. She flew over China and Turkey and she landed in Italy. In what direction was she going?

 • Everybody, what's the answer? (Signal.) *West.*

Then she continued in the same direction until she came to a country that is much larger than Japan or Italy.

 • Everybody, which direction was she going? (Signal.) *West.*
 • What's the name of that large country? (Call on a student. Ideas: *Canada; the United States.*)

She landed her jet plane in a city on the east coast of the country.

 • Name the city on the east coast of the United States. (Call on a student. Ideas: *New York City or another east coast city.*)

The pilot was not feeling well. She thought she had a slight fever.

 • What would her temperature be if she had a slight fever? (Call on a student. Idea: *A little over 98 degrees.*)

So she went to a doctor. The doctor told her that her temperature was normal.

 • Everybody, so what was her temperature? (Signal.) *98 degrees.*

The doctor said, "You need more exercise. You should walk more than 5 thousand feet every day." The pilot knew the name of a unit that is a little more than 5 thousand feet.

 • Everybody, what name? (Signal.) *Mile.*

The pilot took off and flew to a country where kangaroos live.

 • Everybody, what's the name of that country? (Signal.) *Australia.*
 • Is that country on the **east side** of the Pacific Ocean or the **west side** of the Pacific Ocean? (Signal.) *West side.*

There she saw a large group of kangaroos.

 • Everybody, what is a large group of kangaroos called? (Signal.) *Mob.*
 • What other kinds of animals could she see in Australia? (Call on a student. Ideas: *Koalas, platypus.*)

She had a nice vacation.

STORY READING

a. Find part C in your textbook. ✓
 • The error limit for this story is 10. Read carefully.
b. Everybody, touch the title. ✓
 • (Call on a student to read the title.) *[Some Words Stop Fighting.]*
 • What's going to happen in this story? (Call on a student. Idea: *Some words will stop fighting.*)
c. (Call on individual students to read the story, each student reading two or three sentences at a time. Ask questions marked **1.**)

 • (Correct errors: Tell the word. Direct the student to reread the sentence.)
 • (If the group makes more than 10 errors, direct the students to reread the story.)

d. (After the group has read the selection making no more than 10 errors, read the story to the students and ask questions marked **2.**)

Some Words Stop Fighting

The word bank was a mess. That's the best way to describe it.

1. Why was it a mess? (Call on a student. Idea: *Because some words fought and threw things.*)

Early in the morning, before the people in Hohoboho started to talk, things in the word bank would be calm.

1. What does that mean? (Call on a student. Idea: *It was quiet, and no words were fighting.*)

But before long a fight would start. Somebody in Hohoboho would say, "I have <u>new</u> shoes," and the fight would start between <u>new</u> and <u>knew</u>.

2. What would the word spelled **N-E-W** say? (Call on a student. Idea: *"That's me."*)
2. Then what would happen? (Call on a student. Idea: *Then **knew** would say, "No, that's me," and they would fight.*)

Then the people in Hohoboho would start talking more and more and more. And fights would start all over the word bank. It would become so noisy that some of the words wore earplugs.

1. Why would they do that? (Call on a student. Idea: *So they couldn't hear all the noise.*)

When a word wore earplugs it could not hear if it was said, but the words in the back of the bank didn't care.

2. Why didn't those words care? (Call on a student. Idea: *Because they weren't said very often.*)

The word <u>billows</u> almost always wore earplugs. The word <u>usually</u> sat near <u>billows</u>. Once <u>usually</u> pulled an earplug from <u>billows'</u> ear and asked, "Why do you wear earplugs? Don't you want to hear your name said?"

"Sure," <u>billows</u> replied. "But I'm not going to be said more than once or twice a day, and I'd rather have it quiet than listen to all this fighting and shouting."

2. Everybody, who is talking in the picture? (Signal.) *Usually.*
2. Who is **usually** talking to? (Signal.) *Billows.*
2. Are they sitting in the front part of the word bank? (Signal.) *No.*
2. Why aren't they sitting in the front part? (Call on a student. Idea: *Because they aren't said very often.*)
2. What is **moment** doing? (Call on a student. Idea: *Looking at his watch.*)
2. Why is **moment** doing that? (Call on a student. Ideas: *He's bored; to find out the time.*)

After a while, things got so bad in the word bank that a change was made.

1. What does that mean, a change was made? (Call on a student. Idea: *Something happened so things would be better.*)

If that change hadn't been made, some of the words might have been battered to pieces in the terrible fights they had. But one morning there was an announcement. A voice came over the loudspeaker and said, "From now on, the words will appear on the screen when the people of Hohoboho say them. You will not hear what the people say. But you will see how the words are spelled. If you are spelled the same way as a word on the screen, you get a point."

1. Everybody, would this solve the problem of the words that sound the same? (Signal.) *Yes.*

2. Everybody, will the words in the word bank hear the words that are said by the people in Hohoboho? (Signal.) *No.*
2. How will a word know if it gets a point? (Call on a student. Idea: *By looking at the spelling of the word on the screen.*)

> **The words looked at each other. The word <u>their</u> looked at <u>there</u>. The word <u>their</u> said, "I think that will work. My spelling is different from your spelling. If they write the words, we will be able to tell if the word is <u>their</u> or <u>there</u>."**
>
> **And that's just what happened. When the words were said by the people in Hohoboho, the words would appear on a large screen. And that was the very last fight that <u>two</u> had or that <u>there</u> had or that <u>eight</u> had. The word <u>one</u> shook hands with the word <u>won</u>. "This is great," the word <u>one</u> said. The word <u>hear</u> and the word <u>here</u> also shook hands.**

2. What did it mean when they shook hands? (Call on a student. Idea: *It meant they were friends.*)

> **There wasn't any word happier about this change than the word <u>two</u>.**

1. Why? (Call on a student. Idea: *Because <u>two</u> had the worst fights.*)

> **For the first time since the word bank opened, the word <u>two</u> could jump up and say, "That's me. They said <u>two</u>," without getting into a fight with <u>to</u> and <u>too</u>.**
>
> **The change in the word bank stopped the fights among words that sound the same. But there was a new problem. As soon as the words appeared on the screen, fights started among words that had never fought before. Can you think of why these fights would take place?**
> **MORE NEXT TIME**

1. Go back to the beginning of the story. Follow along while I read.
2. Everybody, did fights still go on between words like **T-W-O** and **T-O**? (Signal.) *No.*

2. New fights took place. Do you have any idea why? (Call on a student. Accept reasonable responses.)

READING CHECKOUTS

> **Note:** There is a reading checkout in this lesson; therefore, there is no paired practice.

a. Today is a reading-checkout day. While you're doing your independent work, I'm going to call on you one at a time to read part of the story from lesson 124. When I call on you to come and do your checkout, bring your thermometer chart.
• Remember, you pass the checkout by reading the passage in less than a minute without making more than 2 mistakes. And when you pass the checkout, you'll color the space for lesson 125 on your thermometer chart.
b. (Call on individual students to read the portion of story 124 marked with ❀.)
• (Time the student. Note words that are missed and total number of words read.)
• (Teacher reference:)

> ❀ **The words in the word bank had a problem because they listened to the words that were said by the people in Hohoboho. Some words sound the same. When the people in Hohoboho said these words, the words that sounded the same would fight over who got the point. The [50] words <u>their</u> and <u>there</u> were always fighting. But they were not the only ones. The words for numbers were involved in some of the worst [75] fights you could imagine. The word <u>three</u> never fought. Nor did the words <u>five</u>, <u>six</u>, or <u>seven</u>. But <u>one</u>, <u>two</u>, <u>four</u>, and <u>eight</u> went from ❀ [100] one fight to another.**

• (If the student reads the passage in one minute or less and makes no more than 2 errors, direct the student to color in the space for lesson 125 on the thermometer chart.)

- (If the student makes any mistakes, point to each word that was misread and identify it.)

- (If the student does not meet the time-error criterion for the passage, direct the student to practice reading the story with the assigned partner.)

End-of-Lesson Activities

INDEPENDENT WORK

Now finish your independent work for lesson 125. Raise your hand when you're finished. (Observe students and give feedback.)

WORKCHECK

a. (Direct students to take out their marking pencils.)
- We're going to check your independent work. Remember, if you got an item wrong, make an **X** next to the item. Don't change any answers.

b. (For each item: Read the item. Call on a student to answer it. If the answer is wrong, say the correct answer. Refer to the Answer Key for the correct answers.)

c. Now use your marking pencil to fix up any items you got wrong. Remember, all mistakes must be fixed up before you hand in your independent work.

WRITING-SPELLING

(Present Writing-Spelling lesson 125 after completing Reading lesson 125. See Writing-Spelling Guide.)

LANGUAGE ARTS GUIDE

(Present Language Arts lesson 125 after completing Reading lesson 125. See Language Arts Guide.)

	Lesson 126	Lesson 127	Lesson 128	Lesson 129	Lesson 130
Lesson Events	Vocabulary Review Reading Words Story Reading Paired Practice Independent Work Workcheck Writing-Spelling	**Vocabulary Sentence** Reading Words Vocabulary Review Comprehension Passage Story Reading Paired Practice Independent Work Workcheck Writing-Spelling	Vocabulary Review Reading Words Comprehension Passages Paired Practice Independent Work Workcheck Writing-Spelling	Vocabulary Review Reading Words Story Reading Paired Practice Independent Work Workcheck Writing-Spelling	Fact Game Reading Checkouts Test Marking the Test Test Remedies Literature Lesson
Vocabulary Sentence	#26: Their <u>amazing effort</u> surprised the <u>neighbors</u>.	#31: The <u>palace guards</u> spoke different <u>languages.</u>	#31: The <u>palace guards</u> spoke different <u>languages</u>.	sentence #29 sentence #30 sentence #31	
Reading Words: Word Types	modeled words mixed words	modeled words mixed words 2-part words	modeled words **e-a** words multi-syllable words	modeled words mixed words	
New Vocabulary		smooth and quiet			
Comprehension Passages		*Contractions*	1) *Wooden Buildings* 2) *Time Machines* 3) *More About a Time Line*		
Story	*Another Change is Made*	*The Last Problem in the Word Bank is Solved*		*Eric and Tom Find a Time Machine*	
Skill Items	Vocabulary	Deductions	Vocabulary	Sequencing Vocabulary Sentence	Test: Vocabulary sentences #29, 30
Special Materials		3 copies of page 143; blank cards; writing materials for Activity			Thermometer charts, dice, Fact Game 130, Fact Game Answer Key, scorecard sheets, *materials for literature project.
Special Projects/ Activities		Project and activity after lesson 127			

* Literature anthology; blackline master 13A; modeling clay; sources for researching Southwest Native Americans; materials for making displays (poster board, markers, scissors, glue, etc.); copy of *Not Just Any Ring*.

VOCABULARY REVIEW

a. You learned a sentence that tells what surprised the neighbors.
  • Everybody, say that sentence. Get ready. (Signal.) *Their amazing effort surprised the neighbors.*
  • (Repeat until firm.)

b. I'll say part of the sentence. When I stop, you say the next word. Listen: Their amazing . . . Everybody, what's the next word? (Signal.) *Effort.*

c. Listen: Their amazing effort surprised the . . . Everybody, what's the next word? (Signal.) *Neighbors.*
  • Say the whole sentence. Get ready. (Signal.) *Their amazing effort surprised the neighbors.*

d. Listen: Their . . . Everybody, what's the next word? (Signal.) *Amazing.*

READING WORDS

Column 1

a. **Find lesson 126 in your textbook.** ✓
  • Touch column 1. ✓
  • (Teacher reference:)

1. contraction	3. guard
2. palace	4. language

b. Word 1 is **contraction.** What word? (Signal.) *Contraction.*
  • Spell **contraction.** Get ready. (Tap for each letter.) *C-O-N-T-R-A-C-T-I-O-N.*

c. Word 2 is **palace.** What word? (Signal.) *Palace.*
  • Spell **palace.** Get ready. (Tap for each letter.) *P-A-L-A-C-E.*

d. Word 3. What word? (Signal.) *Guard.*
  • Spell **guard.** Get ready. (Tap for each letter.) *G-U-A-R-D.*

e. Word 4. What word? (Signal.) *Language.*
  • Spell **language.** Get ready. (Tap for each letter.) *L-A-N-G-U-A-G-E.*

f. Let's read those words again, the fast way.
  • Word 1. What word? (Signal.) *Contraction.*
  • (Repeat for words 2–4.)
g. (Repeat step f until firm.)

Column 2

h. Find column 2. ✓
  • (Teacher reference:)

1. difference	3. rhyme
2. finger	4. smoothly

i. Word 1. What word? (Signal.) *Difference.*
  • (Repeat for words 2–4.)
j. (Repeat step i until firm.)

Column 3

k. Find column 3. ✓
  • (Teacher reference:)

1. whisper	4. whispered
2. aren't	5. claim
3. she'd	

l. Word 1. What word? (Signal.) *Whisper.*
  • Show me how to whisper. ✓
m. Word 2. What word? (Signal.) *Aren't.*
  • (Repeat for words 3–5.)
n. Let's read those words again.
  • Word 1. What word? (Signal.) *Whisper.*
  • (Repeat for words 2–5.)
o. (Repeat step n until firm.)

Individual Turns

(For columns 1–3: Call on individual students, each to read one to three words per turn.)

STORY READING

a. Find part B in your textbook. ✓
  • The error limit for this story is 13. Read carefully.
b. Everybody, touch the title. ✓
  • (Call on a student to read the title.) *[Another Change is Made.]*

- What's going to happen in this story? (Call on a student. Idea: *Another change will be made.*)
- Why would the word bank need another change? (Call on a student. Idea: *Because there were new fights in the word bank.*)

c. (Call on individual students to read the story, each student reading two or three sentences at a time. Ask questions marked **1**.)

- (Correct errors: Tell the word. Direct the student to reread the sentence.)
- (If the group makes more than 13 errors, direct the students to reread the story.)

d. (After the group has read the selection making no more than 13 errors, read the story to the students and ask questions marked **2**.)

Another Change Is Made

New fights started in the word bank as soon as the words were written on the screen. To understand the problem that took place in the word bank, you have to understand that some words are spelled the same way but are not said the same way. They sound different.

1. What's the same about the words that started to fight? (Call on a student. Idea: *The way they're spelled.*)
1. What's different about those words? (Call on a student. Idea: *The way they sound.*)
1. Everybody, the next sentence shows a word that you must spell, not read. I'll read that sentence:

> Two words are spelled with the letters r-o-w.

1. Now you read that sentence. (Call on a student.)

Two words are spelled with the letters <u>r-o-w</u>. One of those words rhymes with <u>now</u>. Say that word.

1. Everybody, say the word that is spelled **R-O-W** and rhymes with **now**. Get ready. (Signal.) *Rŏw.*
1. A row is a fight.

The other word that is spelled <u>r-o-w</u> rhymes with <u>go</u>. Say that word.

1. Everybody, say the word that is spelled **R-O-W** and rhymes with **go**. Get ready. (Signal.) *Rōw.*

The two words that are spelled <u>r-o-w</u> never fought until the words were written on the screen. But as soon as the words appeared on the screen, these words fought.

When somebody in Hohoboho would say, "Let's plant these seeds in a <u>row</u>," the two words spelled <u>r-o-w</u> would jump up. "That's me," they would start yelling. Soon they would be fighting.

2. Everybody, did these words fight **before** the words were written on the screen? (Signal.) *No.*
2. Why not? (Call on a student. Idea: *Because they could hear how they were said.*)
2. Why do they fight now? (Call on a student. Idea: *Because they can't hear how they're said.*)

Two other words that are spelled the same are spelled <u>w-i-n-d</u>. One of those words rhymes with <u>find</u>.

1. Everybody, say the word that is spelled **W-I-N-D** and rhymes with **find**. Get ready. (Signal.) *Wīnd.*

The other word rhymes with <u>pinned</u>.

1. Everybody, say the word that is spelled **W-I-N-D** and rhymes with **pinned**. Get ready. (Signal.) *Wĭnd.*

But every time the word spelled <u>w-i-n-d</u> appeared on the screen, these two words started to fight over who got the point.

2. Say the two words that fought. (Call on a student.) *[Wĭnd and Wīnd.]*
2. How are those words the same? (Call on a student. Idea: *They're spelled the same.*)
2. How are they different? (Call on a student. Idea: *They sound different.*)

Some terrible fights took place over the word spelled <u>r-e-a-d</u>.

2. Say the two words that are spelled **R-E-A-D.** (Call on a student.) *[Rēad and rĕad.]*

Somebody in Hohoboho would say, "Did you <u>read</u> that?" The other person would answer, "Yes, I <u>read</u> that." Both words spelled <u>r-e-a-d</u> would get into a terrible row.

1. Yes, a terrible **rŏw** is a terrible fight.

Another pair of words that had some bad fights are spelled <u>t-e-a-r</u>.

2. Say those words. (Call on a student.) *[Tēar and tĕar.]*

Somebody in Hohoboho would say, "I think you're crying. Is that a <u>tear</u> in your eye?" And both words would try to claim the point.

1. What would these words say when trying to claim the point? (Call on a student. Idea: *That's me.*)

"That's me," they would shout. The same words would fight when somebody said, "Take that paper and <u>tear</u> it up."
   If you looked at the words that were involved in these fights, you'd see that they have some small scars, but not many scars and not very bad ones.

2. So what does that tell you about how hard they fought and how long they fought? (Call on a student. Idea: *They didn't fight very hard or very long.*)

Compared to the word <u>two</u>, the words spelled <u>t-e-a-r</u> would look as if they had never been in a fight.

2. What does that mean, compared to **two** they looked as if they had never been in a fight? (Call on a student. Ideas: *Two had been in much harder and longer fights; **two** had lots of scars.*)

Here's the reason that the words with the same spelling are not very scarred: A few days after the fights started another announcement was made. The voice said, "From now on, the words will go on the screen. Then a voice will read the words.

2. What two things will happen to the words that are spoken in Hohoboho? (Call on a student. Idea: *They will go on a screen and a voice will read them.*)

Here's how a word in the word bank gets a point. That word must be spelled the same as the word on the screen. The word must also sound the same as the word the voice reads."

2. What two things must happen before the word gets a point? (Call on a student. Idea: *It must be spelled the same as the word on the screen, and it must also sound the same.*)

The word <u>slow</u> said, "I don't understand that rule."
   The word <u>smart</u> said, "It's easy. If you're spelled like the word on the screen and if you sound like that word, you get a point."
   The word <u>confusion</u> said, "It sounds too hard."
   The word <u>clear</u> said, "Look at it this way. If you get mixed up, I'll tell you if you get the point."
   <u>Lazy</u> said, "That sounds good to me."
   Then the words with problems began to talk.

2. Which words are these? (Call on a student. Idea: *The words that are spelled the same.*)

One of the words spelled <u>t-e-a-r</u> said, "That makes sense. If somebody says my name, we will hear it. We don't have to fight."

2. How do you say the two words that are spelled **T-E-A-R?** (Call on a student.) *[Tēar and tĕar.]*

2. Everybody, which one refers to drops that come out of your eyes? (Signal.) *Tēar.*

The words spelled r-e-a-d agreed.

2. Say those two words. (Call on a student.) *[Rēad and rĕad.]*

"You can hear the difference when somebody says, 'I will read a book' or says 'Yesterday, I read a book.'"
So there was a big change in the word bank. The words that sound the same didn't fight because they could look at the screen to see how the word was spelled. The word two didn't fight with the words that sounded the same.

2. Spell those words. (Call on a student.) *[T-O and T-O-O.]*

And the words that are spelled the same never had a problem because they listened to the voice. If the voice said, "That is a live fish," the sound of the word would tell who got the point.

2. Everybody, what word would fight with līve if there was no voice? (Signal.) *Lĭve.*

Most of the problems in the word bank were solved.
MORE NEXT TIME

1. Go back to the beginning of the story. Follow along while I read.

EXERCISE 4
PAIRED PRACTICE

You're going to read aloud to your partner. Today the **B** members will read first. Then the **A** members will read from the star to the end of the story.
(Observe students and give feedback.)

End-of-Lesson Activities

INDEPENDENT WORK

Now finish your independent work for lesson 126. Raise your hand when you're finished. (Observe students and give feedback.)

WORKCHECK

a. (Direct students to take out their marking pencils.)
 • We're going to check your independent work. Remember, if you got an item wrong, make an **X** next to the item. Don't change any answers.
b. (For each item: Read the item. Call on a student to answer it. If the answer is wrong, say the correct answer. Refer to the Answer Key for the correct answers.)
c. Now use your marking pencil to fix up any items you got wrong. Remember, all mistakes must be fixed up before you hand in your independent work.

Note: A special project occurs after lesson 127. See page 142 for the materials you'll need.

WRITING-SPELLING

(Present Writing-Spelling lesson 126 after completing Reading lesson 126. See Writing-Spelling Guide.)

LANGUAGE ARTS GUIDE

(Present Language Arts lesson 126 after completing Reading lesson 126. See Language Arts Guide.)

EXERCISE 1

VOCABULARY

a. **Find page 342 at the back of your textbook.** ✓
- Touch sentence 31. ✓
- This is a new vocabulary sentence. It says: The palace guards spoke different languages. Everybody, read that sentence. Get ready. (Signal.) *The palace guards spoke different languages.*
- Close your eyes and say the sentence. Get ready. (Signal.) *The palace guards spoke different languages.*
- (Repeat until firm.)

b. A king and queen live in a **palace.** A palace is a very large and fancy place. The palace **guards** are the **soldiers** who guard the palace.

c. The sentence says: The palace guards spoke different **languages.** The language is the words that people in a country use to say things. We speak English in the United States. If English is the only language you know, you can't understand other languages like Chinese, Spanish or German.
- Everybody, what do we call the words that people in a country use to say things? (Signal.) *Language.*
- If the guards spoke different languages, they could not understand each other. One guard spoke one language; another guard spoke a different language.

d. Listen to the sentence again: The palace guards spoke different languages. Everybody, say the sentence. Get ready. (Signal.) *The palace guards spoke different languages.*

e. What's the name of the place where a king and a queen live? (Signal.) *Palace.*
- What word names the people who protect the palace? (Signal.) *Guards.*
- What word refers to the words that people in a country use to say things? (Signal.) *Language.*
- (Repeat step e until firm.)

EXERCISE 2

READING WORDS

Column 1

a. Find lesson 127 in your textbook. ✓
- Touch column 1. ✓
- (Teacher reference:)

1. future	4. travel
2. possible	5. traveler
3. guards	6. brick

b. Word 1 is **future.** What word? (Signal.) *Future.*
- Spell **future.** Get ready. (Tap for each letter.) *F-U-T-U-R-E.*
c. Word 2 is **possible.** What word? (Signal.) *Possible.*
- Spell **possible.** Get ready. (Tap for each letter.) *P-O-S-S-I-B-L-E.*
d. Word 3. What word? (Signal.) *Guards.*
- Spell **guards.** Get ready. (Tap for each letter.) *G-U-A-R-D-S.*
e. Word 4. What word? (Signal.) *Travel.*
- Spell **travel.** Get ready. (Tap for each letter.) *T-R-A-V-E-L.*
f. Word 5. What word? (Signal.) *Traveler.*
g. Word 6. What word? (Signal.) *Brick.*
h. Let's read those words again, the fast way.
- Word 1. What word? (Signal.) *Future.*
- (Repeat for words 2–6.)
i. (Repeat step h until firm.)

Column 2

j. Find column 2. ✓
- (Teacher reference:)

1. <u>pal</u>ace	4. <u>aren</u>'t
2. <u>near</u>by	5. <u>whisper</u>
3. <u>she</u>'d	

- First you'll read the underlined part. Then you'll read the whole word.
k. Word 1. What's the underlined part? (Signal.) *pal.*
- What's the whole word? (Signal.) *Palace.*
l. Word 2. What's the underlined part? (Signal.) *near.*

- What's the whole word? (Signal.) *Nearby.*

m. Word 3. What's the underlined part? (Signal.) *she.*
- What's the whole word? (Signal.) *She'd.*

n. Word 4. What's the underlined part? (Signal.) *are.*
- What's the whole word? (Signal.) *Aren't.*

o. Word 5. What's the underlined part? (Signal.) *whis.*
- What's the whole word? (Signal.) *Whisper.*

p. Let's read those words again, the fast way.
- Word 1. What word? (Signal.) *Palace.*
- (Repeat for: **2. nearby, 3. she'd, 4. aren't, 5. whisper.**)

q. (Repeat step p until firm.)

Column 3

r. Find column 3. ✓
- (Teacher reference:)

1. **smooth and quiet**	3. **yesterday**
2. **contractions**	4. **languages**

s. Number 1. What words? (Signal.) *Smooth and quiet.*
- When things are **smooth and quiet**, they are very **calm**.

t. Word 2. What word? (Signal.) *Contractions.*
- (Repeat for words 3 and 4.)

u. Let's read those words again.
- Number 1. What words? (Signal.) *Smooth and quiet.*

v. Word 2. What word? (Signal.) *Contractions.*
- (Repeat for words 3 and 4.)

w. (Repeat steps u and v until firm.)

Individual Turns

(For columns 1–3: Call on individual students, each to read one to three words per turn.)

VOCABULARY REVIEW

a. Here's the new vocabulary sentence: The palace guards spoke different languages.

- Everybody, say the sentence. Get ready. (Signal.) *The palace guards spoke different languages.*
- (Repeat until firm.)

b. What word refers to the words that people in a country use to say things? (Signal.) *Language.*
- What's the name of a place where a king and a queen live? (Signal.) *Palace.*
- What word names the people who protect the palace? (Signal.) *Guards.*

COMPREHENSION PASSAGE

a. Find part B in your textbook. ✓
- You're going to read the next story about Hohoboho. First you'll read the information passage. It gives some facts about contractions.

b. Everybody, touch the title. ✓
- (Call on a student to read the title.) *[Contractions.]*
- Everybody, what's the title? (Signal.) *Contractions.*

c. (Call on individual students to read the passage, each student reading two or three sentences at a time.)

Contractions

Contractions are words made by joining two words together.

- How are contractions made? (Call on a student. Idea: *By joining two words together.*)

Part of one word is missing. This mark ' is called an **apostrophe**. It is used to show where part of the word is missing.

- What does the mark show? (Call on a student. Idea: *Where the part is missing.*)

Here are some contractions and the words that make them up:
- **Couldn't is made up of could and not.**

- Everybody, what words make up **couldn't?** (Signal.) *Could and not.*
- Touch **couldn't.** ✓

- I'll spell **could not.** You figure out the missing part. C-O-U-L-D N-O-T. Everybody, what part is missing? (Signal.) *O.*
- What's in its place? (Signal.) *Apostrophe.*

> • <u>He'll</u> is made up of <u>he</u> and <u>will</u>.

- Everybody, what words make up **he'll?** (Signal.) *He and will.*
- Touch **he'll.** ✓
- I'll spell **he will.** You figure out the missing part. H-E W-I-L-L. Everybody, what part is missing? (Signal.) *W-I.*
- What's in its place? (Signal.) *Apostrophe.*

> • <u>You've</u> is made up of <u>you</u> and <u>have</u>.

- Everybody, what words make up **you've?** (Signal.) *You and have.*
- Touch **you've.** ✓
- I'll spell **you have.** You figure out the missing part. Y-O-U H-A-V-E. Everybody, what part is missing? (Signal.) *H-A.*
- What's in its place? (Signal.) *Apostrophe.*

> **Say the words that make up each contraction below.**

- Say **blank** when you come to a missing word.

> **a.** <u>We've</u> is made up of ▭ and ▭.

- Everybody, what words go in the blanks? (Signal.) *We and have.*

> **b.** <u>You're</u> is made up of ▭ and ▭.

- Everybody, what words go in the blanks? (Signal.) *You and are.*

> **c.** <u>Can't</u> is made up of ▭ and ▭.

- Everybody, what words go in the blanks? (Signal.) *Can and not.*

> **d.** <u>I'll</u> is made up of ▭ and ▭.

- Everybody, what words go in the blanks? (Signal.) *I and will.*

EXERCISE 5

STORY READING

a. Find part C in your textbook. ✓
- The error limit for this story is 10. Read carefully.
b. Everybody, touch the title. ✓
- (Call on a student to read the title.) *[The Last Problem in the Word Bank Is Solved.]*
- What's going to happen in this story? (Call on a student. Idea: *The last problem in the word bank will be solved.*)
c. (Call on individual students to read the story, each student reading two or three sentences at a time. Ask questions marked **1.**)

> - (Correct errors: Tell the word. Direct the student to reread the sentence.)
> - (If the group makes more than 10 errors, direct the students to reread the story.)

d. (After the group has read the selection making no more than 10 errors, read the story to the students and ask questions marked **2.**)

> **The Last Problem in the Word Bank Is Solved**
>
> **Perhaps you think that all the problems in the word bank had been solved. The words that sound the same as other words were no longer fighting.**

2. Here are two words that sound the same: R-O-D-E and R-O-A-D. Why weren't they fighting? (Call on a student. Idea: *Because they could see their names printed on the screen.*)

> **The words that are spelled the same as other words were friends again.**

1. Say a pair of words that are spelled the same. (Call on individual students. Ideas: *Rōw and rŏw; līve and lĭve; etc.*)
1. Why weren't they fighting? (Call on a student. Idea: *Because they could hear their names.*)

Almost everything was going smoothly. There was still one problem, however. Words that are contractions had fights. Here are some contractions: you're, I'll, can't, couldn't, shouldn't, aren't, she'd. Can you name some other contractions?

2. Name some. (Call on individual students. Ideas: *Hasn't, don't, wouldn't,* etc.)

The contractions fought because contractions are made up of two words. The contraction couldn't is made up of the words could and not.

The contraction you're is made up of the words you and are. The contraction I'll is made of two other words.

1. What words? (Call on a student. Idea: *I and will.*)

What words make up the contraction shouldn't?

1. Everybody, what's the answer? (Signal.) *Should and not.*

Here's what used to happen in the word bank. Whenever a contraction was named, the two words that make up the contraction would fight. For example, when the contraction you'll was said, the word you would say, "That's me." The word will would say, "No, that's me." A third word would join the fight. That word was the contraction you'll. So a big row would go on between you'll, you, and will.

Which three words would fight when someone in Hohoboho said, she'll?

2. What's the answer? (Call on a student.) *[She, will, and she'll.]*

Which three words would fight when someone said shouldn't?

2. What's the answer? (Call on a student.) *[Should, not, and shouldn't.]*

By now, the other words in the word bank were tired of seeing words fight. "Come on," the word calm said. "Why don't you figure out some way of solving the problem? Do you have to wait for another announcement?"

"Yeah," the word smart said. "We can work out a plan that will make everybody happy."

The word question asked, "What kind of plan would that be?"

So the word smart thought for a moment and then came up with this plan: every time a contraction is said, three words get points. The contraction that is said gets one point. The word in the contraction that has all its letters gets one point. The word in the contraction that has some letters missing does not get one point. That word gets half a point.

2. Which word gets half a point? (Call on a student. Idea: *The word in the contraction that has a part missing.*)

Smart said, "Remember, the contraction and the full word each get one point."

2. Which two words get one point? (Call on a student. Idea: *The contraction and the word in the contraction that has all of its letters.*)

The contraction shouldn't said, "I think I understand. If somebody says shouldn't, I get one point. And should gets one point because it has all its letters."

The word not said, "And I only get half a point because one of my letters is missing in the word shouldn't."

2. Which words get one point? (Call on a student.) *[Shouldn't and should.]*
2. Everybody, what does the word **not** get? (Signal.) *Half a point.*
2. Why only half a point? (Call on a student. Idea: *Because it has a part missing.*)

> The plan worked, and the fighting finally ended in the word bank. When a word like you'll is said, the contraction you'll gets one point. The word you gets one point because it has no part missing. The word will gets half a point because it has a part missing.

2. Everybody, what part of **will** is missing in **you'll**? (Signal.) *W-I.*

> "Things are very nice in the word bank now," the word calm said when the plan was first used.
> "Yes, things are nice," the word quiet whispered.
> ## THE END

1. Go back to the beginning of the story. Follow along while I read.

EXERCISE 6

PAIRED PRACTICE

You're going to read aloud to your partner. Today the **A** members will read first. Then the **B** members will read from the star to the end of the story.
(Observe students and give feedback.)

End-of-Lesson Activities

INDEPENDENT WORK

Now finish your independent work for lesson 127. Raise your hand when you're finished.
(Observe students and give feedback.)

WORKCHECK

a. (Direct students to take out their marking pencils.)
• We're going to check your independent work. Remember, if you got an item wrong, make an **X** next to the item. Don't change any answers.
b. (For each item: Read the item. Call on a student to answer it. If the answer is wrong, say the correct answer. Refer to the Answer Key for the correct answers.)
c. Now use your marking pencil to fix up any items you got wrong. Remember, all mistakes must be fixed up before you hand in your independent work.

WRITING-SPELLING

(Present Writing-Spelling lesson 127 after completing Reading lesson 127. See Writing-Spelling Guide.)

ACTIVITY

(Present Activity 38 after completing Reading lesson 127. See Activities Across the Curriculum.)

LANGUAGE ARTS GUIDE

(Present Language Arts lesson 127 after completing Reading lesson 127. See Language Arts Guide.)

Special Project

Note: After completing lesson 127, do this special project with the students. You may do the project during another part of the school day.
Purpose: To make up a word game.
Materials: 3 copies of page 143; blank cards.

a. (Tell the students that they are going to make up a game and then play the game. For this game, each student will draw a card on which a pair of words is written. The words are either synonyms, opposites, or homonyms. The student will categorize the words by saying they are synonyms, opposites, or homonyms.)

b. (Divide students into three teams. One team will create pairs of synonyms, one team will create pairs of opposites, and one team will create pairs of homonyms.)

• (Pass out a word list (page 143) to each team and assign a column (synonyms, opposites, or homonyms) to each team.)

• (Tell each team:) After each word in your column, write the (synonym/opposite/ homonym). When you finish all the pairs for your column, make up 4 new pairs.

synonyms	opposites	homonyms
hear	small	hear
happy	fast	their
sad	big	new
big	sad	through
perhaps	new	would
fast	hard	wait
cheap	hot	road
hard	tall	know
small	thin	by
thin	long	cell
start	smooth	one
finish	quiet	ate
reply	dark	two
grown-ups	heavy	four
correct	start	do
often	find	write

• (Each team is to write the missing word for each pair and then write four more pairs.)

c. (After all the teams have twenty pairs, direct students to write each pair on a card. Shuffle the cards and play the game with the group.)

d. (The cards are presented in a stack with the blank side showing. Students take turns drawing a card and then identifying whether the words in the pair are **synonyms, opposites,** or **homonyms.** For each correct response, the team the student is on gets one point. The team with the most points at the end of the game is the winner.)

e. (A variation of the game can be played with homographs. [Don't play this game until the students have played the basic game at least three times.])

• (For the variation, add five cards, each with a pair of homographs [e.g. bōw/bōw; ob'ject/object'; tēar/tĕar; wīnd/wĭnd; rēad/rĕad]. You draw a card for a student's turn and read the pair of words. [For the homograph, you would simply read the same pronunciation twice.] The student identifies the words in each pair as either **synonyms, opposites, homonyms,** or **words that are spelled the same.** Continue with other students, awarding points for correct answers as above.)

synonyms	opposites	homonyms
hear	small	hear
happy	fast	their
sad	big	new
big	sad	through
perhaps	new	would
fast	hard	wait
cheap	hot	road
hard	tall	know
small	thin	by
thin	long	cell
start	smooth	one
finish	quiet	ate
reply	dark	two
grown-ups	heavy	four
correct	start	do
often	find	write

Lesson 128

EXERCISE 1

VOCABULARY REVIEW

a. Here's the new vocabulary sentence:
The palace guards spoke different languages.
- Everybody, say the sentence. Get ready. (Signal.) *The palace guards spoke different languages.*
- (Repeat until firm.)

b. What's the name of a place where a king and a queen live? (Signal.) *Palace.*
- What word names the people who protect the palace? (Signal.) *Guards.*
- What word refers to the words that people in a country use to say things? (Signal.) *Language.*

EXERCISE 2

READING WORDS

Column 1

a. **Find lesson 128 in your textbook.** ✓
- Touch column 1. ✓
- (Teacher reference:)

1. bicycle	3. wooden
2. fruit	4. brick

b. Word 1 is **bicycle.** What word? (Signal.) *Bicycle.*
- Spell **bicycle.** Get ready. (Tap for each letter.) *B-I-C-Y-C-L-E.*
c. Word 2 is **fruit.** What word? (Signal.) *Fruit.*
- Spell **fruit.** Get ready. (Tap for each letter.) *F-R-U-I-T.*
d. Word 3. What word? (Signal.) *Wooden.*
- Spell **wooden.** Get ready. (Tap for each letter.) *W-O-O-D-E-N.*
e. Word 4. What word? (Signal.) *Brick.*
- Spell **brick.** Get ready. (Tap for each letter.) *B-R-I-C-K.*
f. Let's read those words again, the fast way.
- Word 1. What word? (Signal.) *Bicycle.*
- (Repeat for words 2–4.)
g. (Repeat step f until firm.)

Column 2

h. Find column 2. ✓
- (Teacher reference:)

1. heart	4. reasons
2. nearby	5. greater
3. spread	

- All these words have the letters **E-A.** Those letters make different sounds in the words.
i. Word 1. What word? (Signal.) *Heart.*
- (Repeat for words 2–5.)
j. (Repeat step i until firm.)

Column 3

k. Find column 3. ✓
- (Teacher reference:)

1. future	4. travelers
2. Chicago	5. yesterday
3. possible	

l. Word 1. What word? (Signal.) *Future.*
- (Repeat for words 2–5.)
m. (Repeat step l until firm.)

Individual Turns
(For columns 1–3: Call on individual students, each to read one to three words per turn.)

EXERCISE 3

COMPREHENSION PASSAGES

Passage B

a. Find part B in your textbook. ✓
- Today you'll read three information passages.
b. Everybody, touch the title. ✓
- (Call on a student to read the title.) [*Wooden Buildings.*]
- Everybody, what's the title? (Signal.) *Wooden Buildings.*
c. (Call on individual students to read the passage, each student reading two or three sentences at a time.)

Wooden Buildings

In large cities, houses may be made of wood, but most of the other buildings are not made of wood.

- Everybody, what kind of buildings may be made of wood? (Signal.) *Houses.*
- What kind of buildings are not made of wood? (Call on a student. Ideas: *Buildings that are not houses*; *stores*; *office buildings*; *factories*; etc.)
- What are those buildings made of? (Call on a student. Ideas: *Steel, brick.*)

There are a lot of reasons that office buildings and stores are not made of wood. Buildings made of steel, concrete, and brick are stronger than buildings made of wood. Some office buildings are very tall, but it would not be possible to make such tall buildings out of wood.

- Everybody, which makes a stronger building, wood or steel? (Signal.) *Steel.*
- Would it be possible to make a very tall building out of wood? (Signal.) *No.*

Another reason that stores and office buildings are not made of wood is that wooden buildings may burn. The buildings in a city are close together, so when a building catches on fire, the fire may spread to buildings that are nearby. In a city with many wooden buildings, a fire could burn down the whole city.

- Why would the fire be able to spread through wooden buildings in a city? (Call on a student. Idea: *The buildings are close together.*)

That is what happened in Chicago in the year 1871. The buildings were made of wood and a fire spread through the whole city.

- Everybody, in what year was the great fire in Chicago? (Signal.) *1871.*

Chicago is not the only city that had a great fire that spread through wooden buildings. You will soon read about another one of those cities.

Passage C

d. Find part C in your textbook. ✓
- This passage gives some information about time machines.
e. Everybody, touch the title. ✓
- (Call on a student to read the title.) [*Time Machines.*]
- Everybody, what's the title? (Signal.) *Time Machines.*
f. (Call on individual students to read the passage, each student reading two or three sentences at a time.)

Time Machines

In the next lesson, you'll read about a time machine. There are no real time machines, but there are stories about them. In these stories, the time machine takes people into the future or the past. You could go back to the year men first landed on the moon. Or you could go to the year 2050. When time travelers go into the past, they see how things were years ago. When they go into the future, they see how things will be years from now.

- Everybody, are time machines **real** or **make-believe?** (Signal.) *Make-believe.*
- If you went to the year men first landed on the moon, would you go into the **past** or the **future?** (Signal.) *Past.*
- If you went to the year 2050, would you go into the **past** or the **future?** (Signal.) *Future.*

In the story you will read, the people in the time machine feel a great force as they go through time. A force is a push. The greater the force, the harder the push. If you put a book on top of your hand, your hand will feel the force of that book pushing down on your hand. If you pile ten books on your hand, your hand will feel much more force. If you were in the time machine that you will read about, you might feel the force of 500 books pushing against parts of your body.

- Everybody, press against your hand with a small force. ✓
- Press against your hand with a larger force. ✓

- Remember, a force is a push. The greater the force, the harder the push.

Passage D

g. Find part D in your textbook. ✓
- This passage gives some information about time lines.

h. Everybody, touch the title. ✓
- (Call on a student to read the title.) [More About a Time Line.]
- Everybody, what's the title? (Signal.) *More About a Time Line.*

i. (Call on individual students to read the passage, each student reading two or three sentences at a time.)

More About a Time Line

You're going to read about some things that took place a long time ago and other things that will take place in the future.

The future is the time that has not happened yet. Tomorrow is part of the future. Next week is part of the future. Yesterday is not part of the future. It is part of the past.

- Listen: Everybody, is last week part of the **future** or part of the **past**? (Signal.) *Past.*
- Is last year part of the **future** or part of the **past**? (Signal.) *Past.*
- Is tomorrow part of the **future** or part of the **past**? (Signal.) *Future.*

What year is it now?

- Everybody, what's the answer? (Signal.) (Accept appropriate response.)

A year with a larger number is in the future. A year with a smaller number is in the past. The year 2300 is about 300 years in the future. The year 1700 is about 300 years in the past.

- Everybody, listen: What year is it now? (Signal. Accept appropriate response.)
- What year will it be next year? (Signal. Accept appropriate response.)
- What year was it last year? (Signal. Accept appropriate response.)

Let's say a girl was living in the year 1997. For her, the year 1996 would be in the past. For her, the year 1998 would be in the future.

Remember the rule about time: The numbers for the years get smaller as you go back in the past.

Look at time line 1. This is like a time line you have seen. The word now is at the top of this time line.

TIME LINE 1

- Everybody, touch the word **now**. ✓

Touch dot A. That's the year for now. What is it?

- Everybody, what year do we live in now? (Signal. Accept appropriate response.)

Touch dot B.

- Everybody, do it. ✓

That dot shows when you were born. What year goes at dot B?

- (Call on a student.) What year? (Accept appropriate birth year response.)
- Everybody, is that year in the **past** or in the **future**? (Signal.) *Past.*

Touch dot C.

- Everybody, do it. ✓

That dot shows when men landed on the moon. What year was that?

- Everybody, what's the answer? (Signal.) *1969.*
- Did that happen **before** you were born or **after** you were born? (Signal.) *Before.*

Touch dot D.

- Everybody, do it. ✓

That dot shows when the first airplane was made. What year was that?

- Everybody, what's the answer? (Signal.) *1903.*
- 1903. That was about 100 years ago. Everybody, was the first airplane made **before** or **after** men landed on the moon? (Signal.) *Before.*

Touch dot E.

- Everybody, do it. ✓

That dot shows the year the United States became a country. What year was that?

- Everybody, what's the answer? (Signal.) *1776.*

Time line 2 shows the future. The future is the part above <u>now.</u>

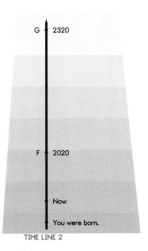

- Everybody, touch the dot for **now** on the time line. ✓

On the time line, dot F is the year 2020.

- Everybody, is that dot in the **past** or the **future?** (Signal.) *Future.*
- You'll be an adult when the year is 2020.

What year is dot G?

- Everybody, what's the answer? (Signal.) *2320.*

Which is farther in the future, the year 2020 or the year 2320?

- Everybody, what's the answer? (Signal.) *2320.*

EXERCISE 4

PAIRED PRACTICE

You're going to read aloud to your partner. Today the **B** members will read first. Then the **A** members will read from the star to the end of the story.
(Observe students and give feedback.)

End-of-Lesson Activities

INDEPENDENT WORK

Now finish your independent work for lesson 128. Raise your hand when you're finished. (Observe students and give feedback.)

WORKCHECK

a. (Direct students to take out their marking pencils.)
- We're going to check your independent work. Remember, if you got an item wrong, make an **X** next to the item.

b. (For each item: Read the item. Call on a student to answer it. If the answer is wrong, say the correct answer. Refer to the Answer Key for the correct answers.)

c. Now use your pencil to fix up any items you got wrong. Remember, all mistakes must be fixed up before you hand in your work.

WRITING-SPELLING

(Present Writing-Spelling lesson 128 after completing Reading lesson 128. See Writing-Spelling Guide.)

LANGUAGE ARTS GUIDE

(Present Language Arts lesson 128 after completing Reading lesson 128. See Language Arts Guide.)

Lesson 129

EXERCISE 1

VOCABULARY REVIEW

a. You learned a sentence that tells when they will reply.

- Everybody, say that sentence. Get ready. (Signal.) *Perhaps they will reply in a few days.*
- (Repeat until firm.)

b. You learned a sentence that tells how much she paid.

- Everybody, say that sentence. Get ready. (Signal.) *She paid the correct amount.*
- (Repeat until firm.)

c. Here's the last sentence you learned: The palace guards spoke different languages.

- Everybody, say that sentence. Get ready. (Signal.) *The palace guards spoke different languages.*
- (Repeat until firm.)

d. What word refers to the words that people in a country use to say things? (Signal.) *Language.*

- What's the name of the place where a king and a queen live? (Signal.) *Palace.*
- What word names the people who protect the palace? (Signal.) *Guards.*
- (Repeat step d until firm.)

e. Once more. Say the sentence that tells about the palace guards. Get ready. (Signal.) *The palace guards spoke different languages.*

EXERCISE 2

READING WORDS

Column 1

a. **Find lesson 129 in your textbook.** ✓

- Touch column 1. ✓
- (Teacher reference:)

1. argument	4. clicked
2. convince	5. dials
3. appliance	6. flashing

b. Word 1 is **argument.** What word? (Signal.) *Argument.*

- Spell argument. Get ready. (Tap for each letter.) *A-R-G-U-M-E-N-T.*

c. Word 2 is **convince.** What word? (Signal.) *Convince.*

- Spell **convince.** Get ready. (Tap for each letter.) *C-O-N-V-I-N-C-E.*

d. Word 3 is **appliance.** What word? (Signal.) *Appliance.*

- Spell **appliance.** Get ready. (Tap for each letter.) *A-P-P-L-I-A-N-C-E.*

e. Word 4. What word? (Signal.) *Clicked.*

- Spell **clicked.** Get ready. (Tap for each letter.) *C-L-I-C-K-E-D.*

f. Word 5. What word? (Signal.) *Dials.*

g. Word 6. What word? (Signal.) *Flashing.*

h. Let's read those words again, the fast way.

- Word 1. What word? (Signal.) *Argument.*
- (Repeat for words 2–6.)

i. (Repeat step h until firm.)

Column 2

j. Find column 2. ✓

- (Teacher reference:)

1. Thrig	4. fruit
2. metal	5. Eric
3. heart	6. bicycles

k. Word 1. What word? (Signal.) *Thrig.*

- That's the name of someone in today's story.
- Word 2. What word? (Signal.) *Metal.*
- (Repeat for words 3–6.)

l. Let's read those words again.

- Word 1. What word? (Signal.) *Thrig.*
- (Repeat for words 2–6.)

m. (Repeat step l until firm.)

Individual Turns

(For columns 1 and 2: Call on individual students, each to read one to three words per turn.)

STORY READING

a. Find part B in your textbook. ✓
- The error limit for group reading is 16. Read carefully.

b. Everybody, touch the title. ✓
- (Call on a student to read the title.) *[Eric and Tom Find a Time Machine.]*
- Everybody, what's the title? (Signal.) *Eric and Tom Find a Time Machine.*

c. (Call on individual students to read the story, each student reading two or three sentences at a time. Ask questions marked **1**.)

- (Correct errors: Tell the word. Direct the student to reread the sentence.)
- If the group makes more than 16 errors, direct the students to reread the story.

d. (After the group has read the selection making no more than 16 errors, read the story to the students and ask questions marked **2**.)

Eric and Tom Find a Time Machine

Eric and Tom were with some other boys and girls. They had been at a picnic that was halfway up the mountain. Now they were walking home with the other boys and girls. As they walked down the mountain, they could see the town off in the distance.

2. Everybody, was the town **close** or **far away**? (Signal.) *Far away.*

Eric was tired. "Tom," he said, "let's rest."

Tom said, "I don't think that's a good idea. It's going to get dark pretty soon, and we might get lost."

1. What time of day was it in this story? (Call on a student. Idea: *Late afternoon, early evening.*)

"That's silly," Eric said. "All we have to do is follow the path. It goes right back to town. Are you scared?"

Tom said, "I'm not scared of anything."

It was very quiet up there on the side of the mountain—very quiet. The lights in the town were coming on. The ther kids were far away by now. A cool breeze was blowing down the side of the mountain.

2. I'll read that part again. Everybody, close your eyes and imagine that you are there. Try to see the town and get a feel of that cool breeze.

It was very quiet up there on the side of the mountain—very quiet. The lights in the town were coming on. The other kids were far away by now. A cool breeze was blowing down the side of the mountain.

Then suddenly there was a loud sound. "Crrrrsssssk."

Tom jumped up. "Wh—what was that?"

Tom saw something flash through the sky.

It landed on the side of the mountain right above them. It looked like a metal pill. And it was as big as some of the trees on the mountain.

1. How big was that thing? (Call on a student. Ideas: *Very big; as big as some trees.*)
1. What did it look like? (Call on a student. Idea: *A big metal pill.*)
1. How do you think Tom and Eric felt? (Call on a student. Ideas: *Afraid, surprised.*)

"Let's get out of here," Tom said. He grabbed Eric's arm, but Eric didn't move. He was standing there with his mouth open, looking at the pill.

1. Why was his mouth open? (Call on a student. Idea: *He was surprised.*)

Just then a door on the side of the thing opened, and an old man stepped out. He waved to Eric and Tom. "Hello," he called.

"Let's get out of here," Tom said again. Tom's heart was beating so hard that his shirt was shaking.

2. Why was his heart beating so hard? (Call on a student. Idea: *He was afraid.*)

Eric waved to the old man. "Hello," Eric called and started running toward the metal pill.

"Come back," Tom called. But Eric ran up to the old man. The old man was sitting on the ground. He did not look well. He was wearing a strange metal coat.

"Who are you?" Eric asked.

The old man said, "My name is Thrig."

1. That seems like a strange name, doesn't it?

Eric said, "Where do you live?"

Thrig said, "I live on Earth. But I live in a different time than you."

1. Everybody, what year is it right now? (Signal. Accept appropriate response.)
1. That's when this story takes place. If Thrig is from a different time, he isn't from this year.

Tom and Eric looked at each other. Tom thought, "How can somebody live in a different time?"

Thrig then told Eric and Tom a very strange story. Thrig told them that he lived in the year 2400.

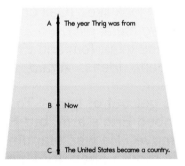

2. Everybody, look at the time line. Touch the year that shows now. ✓
2. What year is it? (Signal. Accept appropriate response.)
2. Touch the year that the United States became a country. ✓
2. That happened many years ago. Everybody, in what year did it happen? (Signal.) *1776.*
2. Now touch the year that Thrig was from. ✓
2. What year is that? (Signal.) *2400.*
2. Thrig didn't live many years **ago.** Thrig hasn't even lived yet. The year 2400 is many years **in the future.**

Tom said, "The year 2400 will not be here for 4 hundred years. That year is 4 hundred years in the future."

2. When is the year 2400? (Call on a student. Idea: *400 years in the future.*)

Thrig nodded. "Yes, I live in the future," he said. He told the boys that he had made a time machine. This machine was the large metal pill. It could take him into the past or into the future. Thrig had just gone back in time 4 hundred years.

1. Now we know what that strange machine is. Everybody, what is it? (Signal.) *A time machine.*
2. Everybody, what year did Thrig start in? (Signal.) *2400.*
2. Then he went back to the year it is now. Everybody, what year is that? (Signal. Accept appropriate response.)

Thrig said, "But now I cannot go back to the year 2400. I am old. And when the machine goes through time, it puts a great force on a person's body. I do not think that I have enough strength to return to 2400."

2. Why didn't he think that he could take the trip to 2400? (Call on a student. Idea: *He wasn't strong enough.*)

Thrig said, "I will spend the rest of my life here. I will never see my friends again."

Thrig looked very sad. "And now I must rest. The trip through time has made me very tired." Thrig closed his eyes.

"He's asleep," Eric said after a moment. Then Eric walked toward the time machine.

1. What do you think Eric wants to do? (Call on a student. Idea: *Look at the time machine.*)

Tom grabbed his arm and said, "Let's get out of here before something happens."

Eric laughed. He said, "That time machine won't bite you." Eric pulled away and started toward the door of the giant machine.

1. What door? (Call on a student. Idea: *The door of the time machine.*)

Tom ran after Eric. He caught up just as Eric was going through the door.

The inside of the time machine was filled with dials and lights. There were red lights and green lights and orange lights. There were big dials and little dials. There were dials that buzzed and dials that clicked.

2. Everybody, touch a dial in the picture. ✓
2. There sure are a lot of dials in that time machine. I'll read that part again. Everybody, close your eyes and imagine what it's like inside that machine.

The inside of the time machine was filled with dials and lights. There were red lights and green lights and orange lights. There were big dials and little dials. There were dials that buzzed and dials that clicked.

"Let's get out of here," Tom said.
Eric walked over to a seat in the middle of the machine. He sat down. As soon as he sat down, the door closed. "Swwwwwshshshsh."

1. What do you think made the door close? (Call on a student. Ideas: *Sitting in the seat; electronic eye.*)

Eric grabbed one of the handles. "I wonder what this handle does."
"Don't touch it," Tom said. "Don't touch it."

1. Go back to the beginning of the story. Follow along while I read.
2. Tom was afraid of what that handle might do. What might happen if Eric moves the handle? (Call on a student. Idea: *The machine might take them somewhere.*)
2. Read the rest of the story to yourself. Find out what happened to the boys. Raise your hand when you're finished.

Eric pulled the handle down a little bit. Suddenly more lights started going on. Dials started moving and clicking and buzzing. And then Tom felt a great force. He could feel it push against his face and his chest.

"We—we're going through time," Tom announced.

He heard Eric's voice. It sounded very far away. "Oh, no," Eric cried.

And then everything was quiet. The dials slowed down. Most of the lights stopped flashing.

Eric stood up and the door opened. The boys looked outside. For a long time they looked. They could not believe what they saw.
MORE NEXT TIME

2. (After all students have raised their hand:) When Eric stood up, something happened. What was that? (Call on a student. Idea: *The door of the time machine opened.*)
2. What were the boys doing at the end of this story? (Call on a student. Idea: *Looking outside.*)
2. I wonder if they traveled through time.

EXERCISE 4

PAIRED PRACTICE

You're going to read aloud to your partner. Today the **A** members will read first. Then the **B** members will read from the star to the end of the story.
(Observe students and give feedback.)

End-of-Lesson Activities

INDEPENDENT WORK

Now finish your independent work for lesson 129. Raise your hand when you're finished. (Observe students and give feedback.)

WORKCHECK

a. (Direct students to take out their marking pencils.)
  • We're going to check your independent work. Remember, if you got an item wrong, make an **X** next to the item.
b. (For each item: Read the item. Call on a student to answer it. If the answer is wrong, say the correct answer. Refer to the Answer Key for the correct answers.)
c. Now use your pencil to fix up any items you got wrong. Remember, all mistakes must be fixed up before you hand in your work.

Note: Before presenting lesson 130, you will need to:
• Reproduce blackline masters for the Fact Game;
• Preview Literature lesson 13, secure materials and reproduce blackline masters. (See the Literature Guide.)

WRITING-SPELLING

(Present Writing-Spelling lesson 129 after completing Reading lesson 129. See Writing-Spelling Guide.)

LANGUAGE ARTS GUIDE

(Present Language Arts lesson 129 after completing Reading lesson 129. See Language Arts Guide.)

Materials: Each student will need their thermometer chart for exercise 2.

EXERCISE 1

Materials for Lesson 130
Fact Game

For each team (4 or 5 students):
- pair of number cubes (or dice)
- copy of Fact Game 130

For each student:
- their copy of the scorecard sheet

For each monitor:
- a pencil
- Fact Game 130 answer key (at end of textbook C)

Reading Checkout

Each student needs their thermometer chart.

Literature Lesson 13

See Literature Guide for the materials you will need.

FACT GAME

a. (Divide students into groups of four or five. Assign monitors. Direct the monitors to write the correct answers for item 9a on their lined paper.)

b. You'll play the game for 10 minutes. (Circulate as students play the game. Comment on groups that are playing well.)

c. (At the end of 10 minutes, have all students who earned more than 10 points stand up.)

- (Tell the monitor of each game that ran smoothly:) Your group did a good job.

EXERCISE 2

READING CHECKOUTS

a. Today is a test day and a reading-checkout day. While you're writing answers, I'm going to call on you one at a time to read part of the story we read in lesson 129. When I call on you to come and do your checkout, bring your thermometer chart.

- Remember, you pass the checkout by reading the passage in less than a minute without making more than 2 mistakes. And when you pass the checkout, you color the space for lesson 130 on your thermometer chart.

b. (Call on individual students to read the portion of story 129 marked with ✿.)

- (Time the student. Note words that are missed and number of words read.)

- (Teacher reference:)

> ✿ Eric grabbed one of the handles. "I wonder what this handle does."
>
> "Don't touch it," Tom said. "Don't touch it."
>
> Eric pulled the handle down a little bit. Suddenly more lights started going on. Dials started moving and clicking and buzzing. And then Tom felt a great force. He could [50] feel it push against his face and his chest.
>
> "We—we're going through time," Tom announced.
>
> He heard Eric's voice. It sounded very far away. [75] "Oh, no," Eric cried.
>
> And then everything was quiet. The dials slowed down. Most of the lights stopped flashing.
>
> Eric stood up and the door ✿ [100] opened.

- (If the student reads the passage in one minute or less and makes no more than 2 errors, direct the student to color in the space for lesson 130 on the thermometer chart.)

- (If the student makes any mistakes, point to each word that was misread and identify it.)

- (If the student does not meet the rate-error criterion for the passage, direct the student to practice reading the story with the assigned partner.)

TEST

a. **Find page 207 in your textbook.** ✓
* This is a test. You'll work items you've done before.
b. Work carefully. Raise your hand when you've completed all the items.
(Observe students but do not give feedback on errors.)

Test 13 Firming Table

Test Item	Introduced in lesson	Test Item	Introduced in lesson	Test Item	Introduced in lesson
1	121	13	127	25	128
2	123	14	127	26	128
3	126	15	127	27	128
4	126	16	128	28	128
5	126	17	128	29	128
6	123	18	128	30	122
7	123	19	129	31	118
8	123	20	129	32	122
9	123	21	129	33	118
10	123	22	129		
11	123	23	129		
12	127	24	128		

MARKING THE TEST

a. (Check students' work before beginning lesson 131. Refer to the Answer Key for the correct answers.)
b. (Record all test 13 results on the Test Summary Sheet and the Group Summary Sheet. Reproducible Summary Sheets are at the back of the Teacher's Guide.)

TEST REMEDIES

* (Provide any necessary remedies for test 13 before presenting lesson 131. Test remedies are discussed in the Teacher's Guide.)

LITERATURE

(Present Literature lesson 13, after completing Reading lesson 130. See Literature Guide.)

LANGUAGE ARTS GUIDE

(Present Language Arts lesson 130, after completing Reading lesson 130. See Language Arts Guide.)

Lessons 131–135 · Planning Page

	Lesson 131	Lesson 132	Lesson 133	Lesson 134	Lesson 135
Lesson Events	**Vocabulary Sentence** Reading Words Vocabulary Review Comprehension Passage Story Reading Paired Practice Independent Work Workcheck Writing-Spelling	Vocabulary Review Reading Words Comprehension Passages Globe Review Story Reading Paired Practice Independent Work Workcheck Writing-Spelling	Vocabulary Review Reading Words Comprehension Passage Story Reading Paired Practice Independent Work Workcheck Writing-Spelling	Vocabulary Review Reading Words Comprehension Passage Story Reading Paired Practice Independent work Workcheck Writing-Spelling	Vocabulary Review Reading Words Globe Story Reading Reading Checkouts Independent Work Workcheck Writing-Spelling
Vocabulary Sentence	#32: His <u>argument</u> <u>convinced</u> them to buy an <u>appliance</u>.	#32: His <u>argument</u> <u>convinced</u> them to buy an <u>appliance</u>.	sentence #30 sentence #31 sentence #32	#27: <u>Police officers</u> checked the ship's <u>cargo</u>.	#28: The <u>champions</u> <u>performed</u> <u>perfectly</u>.
Reading Words: Word Types	modeled words compound words words with endings mixed words	modeled words multi-syllable words words with endings mixed words	modeled words mixed words	modeled words multi-syllable words words with endings –ed words	modeled words mixed words
New Vocabulary	buried pyramid slave earthquake clomping we'd center hay lean Egypt	electric computer forever raft queens blade	ton bowed	ancient	grain
Comprehension Passages	*More About Time*	1) *More About Time* 2) *Facts About Egypt*	*More About Time*	*Inventing*	
Story	*The San Francisco Earthquake*	*Eric and Tom in Egypt*	*Eric and Tom Meet the King of Egypt*	*Eric and Tom Meet the King*	*Eric and Tom Leave Egypt*
Skill Items	Vocabulary Sentences Vocabulary	Alphabetical Order	Sequencing Vocabulary Sentence	Vocabulary Vocabulary sentences	Vocabulary
Special Materials		Globe			Globe, thermometer charts
Special Projects/ Activities	Scavenger hunt				

Lesson 131

VOCABULARY

a. **Find page 342 at the back of your textbook.** ✓
- Touch sentence 32. ✓
- This is a new vocabulary sentence. It says: His argument convinced them to buy an appliance. Everybody, read that sentence. Get ready. (Signal.) *His argument convinced them to buy an appliance.*
- Close your eyes and say the sentence. Get ready. (Signal.) *His argument convinced them to buy an appliance.*
- (Repeat until firm.)

b. When you convince people, you make them believe something.

c. The argument is the things he said to make people believe him.

d. Appliances are machines that are used around the house. Some appliances are toasters, blenders, hair dryers, washers, dryers, refrigerators.
- Everybody, what do we call these things? (Signal.) *Appliances.*

e. Listen to the sentence again: His argument convinced them to buy an appliance. Everybody, say the sentence. Get ready. (Signal.) *His argument convinced them to buy an appliance.*

f. What word means he **made somebody believe something?** (Signal.) *Convinced.*
- What word names a machine that's used around the house? (Signal.) *Appliance.*
- What word refers to what he said to convince people? (Signal.) *Argument.*
- (Repeat step f until firm.)

READING WORDS

Column 1

a. Find lesson 131 in your textbook. ✓
- Touch column 1. ✓
- (Teacher reference:)

1. buried	4. pocket
2. Egypt	5. slave
3. pyramid	6. argument

b. Word 1 is **buried.** What word? (Signal.) *Buried.*
- Spell **buried.** Get ready. (Tap for each letter.) *B-U-R-I-E-D.*
- When something is buried, it has things piled on top of it. If a person is buried in the ground, there is earth on top of the person.

c. Word 2 is **Egypt.** What word? (Signal.) *Egypt.*
- Spell **Egypt.** Get ready. (Tap for each letter.) *E-G-Y-P-T.*
- Egypt is the name of a country.

d. Word 3 is **pyramid.** What word? (Signal.) *Pyramid.*
- A pyramid is a type of building that you'll learn about.
- Spell **pyramid.** Get ready. (Tap for each letter.) *P-Y-R-A-M-I-D.*

e. Word 4 is **pocket.** What word? (Signal.) *Pocket.*
- Spell **pocket.** Get ready. (Tap for each letter.) *P-O-C-K-E-T.*

f. Word 5. What word? (Signal.) *Slave.*
- A slave is a person who has very few rights. People used to own slaves the same way they owned cattle or horses. The slaves had to do everything their owner told them to do.

g. Word 6. What word? (Signal.) *Argument.*

h. Let's read those words again, the fast way.
- Word 1. What word? (Signal.) *Buried.*
- (Repeat for words 2–6.)

i. (Repeat step h until firm.)

Column 2

j. Find column 2. ✓
- (Teacher reference:)

1. **earth**quake	3. **news**paper
2. **street**light	4. **tug**boat

- All these words are compound words. The first part of each word is underlined.

k. Word 1. What's the underlined part? (Signal.) *earth.*
- What's the whole word? (Signal.) *Earthquake.*

- When an earthquake takes place, the ground moves and shakes and splits open. Everybody, what do we call it when the ground moves and shakes and splits open? (Signal.) *Earthquake.*
l. Word 2. What's the underlined part? (Signal.) *street.*
- What's the whole word? (Signal.) *Streetlight.*
m. Word 3. What's the underlined part? (Signal.) *news.*
- What's the whole word? (Signal.) *Newspaper.*
n. Word 4. What's the underlined part? (Signal.) *tug.*
- What's the whole word? (Signal.) *Tugboat.*
o. Let's read those words again.
- Word 1. What word? (Signal.) *Earthquake.*
- (Repeat for: **2. streetlight, 3. newspaper, 4. tugboat.**)
p. (Repeat step o until firm.)

Column 3
q. Find column 3. ✓
- (Teacher reference:)

1. **clomping**	4. **bicycles**
2. **wider**	5. **words**
3. **waking**	6. **convinced**

- All these words have an ending.
r. Word 1. What word? (Signal.) *Clomping.*
- A clomping sound is the sound a horse makes when it walks on a street. Clomp, clomp.
s. Word 2. What word? (Signal.) *Wider.*
- (Repeat for words 3–6.)
t. Let's read those words again.
- Word 1. What word? (Signal.) *Clomping.*
- (Repeat for words 2–6.)
u. (Repeat step t until firm.)

Column 4
v. Find column 4. ✓
- (Teacher reference:)

1. **we'd**	4. **lean**
2. **center**	5. **April**
3. **hay**	6. **fruit**

w. Word 1. What word? (Signal.) *We'd.*
- **We'd** is a contraction for the words **we would.** Everybody, what's another way of saying **We would go there every Saturday?** (Signal.) *We'd go there every Saturday.*
x. Word 2. What word? (Signal.) *Center.*
- The center of something is the middle of the thing. What's another way of saying **They marked the middle of the circle?** (Signal.) *They marked the center of the circle.*
y. Word 3. What word? (Signal.) *Hay.*
- Hay is dried grass that horses and cows eat.
z. Word 4. What word? (Signal.) *Lean.*
- Something that leans does not stand straight up and down. It is tilted to one side. Everybody, what's another way of saying **The building started to tilt?** (Signal.) *The building started to lean.*
a. Word 5. What word? (Signal.) *April.*
b. Word 6. What word? (Signal.) *Fruit.*
c. Let's read those words again.
- Word 1. What word? (Signal.) *We'd.*
- (Repeat for words 2–6.)
d. (Repeat step c until firm.)

Individual Turns
(For columns 1–4: Call on individual students, each to read one to three words per turn.)

EXERCISE 3

VOCABULARY REVIEW

a. Here's the new vocabulary sentence: His argument convinced them to buy an appliance.
- Everybody, say the sentence. Get ready. (Signal.) *His argument convinced them to buy an appliance.*
b. What word refers to what he said to convince people? (Signal.) *Argument.*
- What word names a machine that's used around the house? (Signal.) *Appliance.*
- What word means he **made somebody believe something?** (Signal.) *Convinced.*
- (Repeat step b until firm.)

COMPREHENSION PASSAGE

a. Find part B in your textbook. ✓
 • You're going to read the next story about Eric and Tom. First you'll read the information passage. It gives some more facts about time.
b. Everybody, touch the title. ✓
 • (Call on a student to read the title.) *[More About Time.]*
 • Everybody, what's the title? (Signal.) *More About Time.*
c. (Call on individual students to read the passage, each student reading two or three sentences at a time.)

> ### More About Time
>
> In today's story, you'll find out what year Tom and Eric went to in the time machine.
> That year was in the past, not in the future.

 • What do we know about the year? (Call on a student. Idea: *It was in the past.*)

> So you know that they did not go to some of the years below. Tell which years they did not go to.
>
> a. 2450 b. 1880 c. 1900 d. 2600

 • Everybody, read each year and tell me **future** or **past.** Year A. Read it. (Signal.) *2450.*
 • Is that year in the **future** or the **past?** (Signal.) *Future.*
 • Remember, they went to the **past,** not the future. So could they have gone to that year? (Signal.) *No.*
 • Year B. Read it. (Signal). *1880.*
 • Is that year in the **future** or the **past?** (Signal.) *Past.*
 • Could they have gone to that year? (Signal.) *Yes.*
 • Year C. Read it. (Signal). *1900.*
 • Is that year in the **future** or the **past?** (Signal.) *Past.*
 • Could they have gone to that year? (Signal.) *Yes.*
 • Year D. Read it. (Signal). *2600.*

 • Is that year in the **future** or the **past?** (Signal.) *Future.*
 • Could they have gone to that year? (Signal.) *No.*

> ### Touch dot B on the time line.

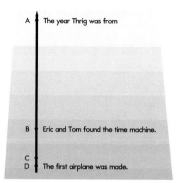

 • Everybody, do it. ✓

> That is the year that Eric and Tom found the time machine. What year is that?

 • Everybody, tell me. (Signal. Accept current year.)

> ### Touch dot A on the time line.

 • Everybody, do it. ✓

> That is the year that Thrig was from. What year is that?

 • Everybody, tell me. (Signal.) *2400.*

> Is that year in the past or in the future?

 • Everybody, tell me. (Signal.) *In the future.*

> About how many years in the future?

 • Everybody, tell me. (Signal.) *Four hundred.*

> ### Touch dot C.

 • Everybody, do it. ✓

That is the year Tom and Eric went to. It is very close to the year the first airplane was made. What year was the first airplane made?

- Everybody, tell me. (Signal.) *1903.*

Did Tom and Eric go to a time that was <u>before</u> or <u>after</u> the first airplane?

- Dot D shows when the first airplane was made. Everybody is dot C **before** or **after** that time? (Signal.) *After.*

EXERCISE 5

STORY READING

a. Find part C in your textbook. ✓
- The error limit for group reading is 12. Read carefully.

b. Everybody, touch the title. ✓
- (Call on a student to read the title.) [*The San Francisco Earthquake.*]
- Everybody, what's the title? (Signal.) *The San Francisco Earthquake.*

c. (Call on individual students to read the story, each student reading two or three sentences at a time. Ask questions marked **1.**)

- (Correct errors: Tell the word. Direct the student to reread the sentence.)
- (If the group makes more than 12 errors, direct the students to reread the story.)

d. (After the group has read the selection making no more than 12 errors, read the story to the students and ask questions marked **2.**)

The San Francisco Earthquake

Tom and Eric looked out of the time machine. They were on the side of a mountain. Tom could see a large city in the distance. Lights were on all over the city, but they did not look very bright.

1. If the lights were not bright, they were not the kind of lights that we have now.
1. If lights were on, what time of day was it? (Call on a student. Ideas: *Nighttime; early morning.*)

"Let's go down there," Eric said.
Tom said, "Remember, we don't know where we are. Let's be careful."
By the time the boys got to the city, the sky was very dark. The city had buildings and streets, but there was something strange about the city.
"I know what's funny," Tom said. "Most of the streets are made of dirt." Tom pointed to the streetlights. "Those are gas streetlights," he said. "Those are the kind of streetlights they had a long time ago."

1. Gas streetlights gave off light by burning gas. We don't use gas streetlights today. We use electric streetlights.

Just then a clomping sound came down the street. The boys hid behind a fence. The sound came from a wagon that was pulled by a horse.

1. What do you think made the clomping sound? (Call on a student. Idea: *A horse.*)
1. The streets are dirt. The streetlights are gas lights. And the people use wagons and horses to get around. These are clues about the time that Tom and Eric are in.

After the wagon went by, Tom said, "We've gone back in time, all right."
Eric said, "Things don't look very different."
Tom said, "You don't see any cars or trucks, do you?"

1. Why do you think they didn't see cars or trucks? (Call on a student. Idea: *Maybe no cars or trucks had been made yet.*)

Then Tom said, "We'd better find a place to sleep."
They found a barn outside the city. They slept in the hay. Tom did not sleep very well. He had bad dreams.

Very early in the morning, the boys started to walk toward the center of the city. On the way they saw a newspaper in the street. They looked at the first page of the newspaper. The words that were at the top of the page said, "San Francisco Times."

1. Everybody, say those words. (Signal.) *San Francisco Times.*
1. So where were they? (Signal.) *San Francisco.*

Eric asked, "What's San Francisco?"
"San Francisco is a city," Tom said. "It is near the Pacific Ocean." Tom looked at the date at the top of the newspaper: April 18, 1906.

1. Everybody, what year was it? (Signal.) *1906.*

Tom felt dizzy. He said, "We've gone back in time about a hundred years." Just then Tom remembered that something happened in San Francisco in 1906, but he couldn't remember what.
Tom looked up. Three boys were standing in the street. They were wearing funny pants that stopped just below their knees. They were laughing at Tom and Eric. The tallest boy said to Tom, "You sure have funny clothes."
Tom looked at the clothes he and Eric were wearing. They didn't look funny to him.

2. Everybody, touch the three boys in the picture who are laughing at Tom and Eric. ✓

2. Tell how their outfits are different from the way boys dress today. (Call on a student. Ideas: *They have short pants, not long; they wear suspenders, not belts; long socks and caps.*)
2. The three boys thought that Tom and Eric were dressed funny. But what do you think Tom and Eric thought about the way the three boys were dressed? (Call on a student. Idea: *The three boys had funny clothes.*)

"Let's get out of here," Eric said. "Let's go downtown."
The boys walked past blocks and blocks of buildings. Some of the buildings were little and some were pretty big. But most of them were made of wood.

1. In cities today, are most of the downtown buildings made of **wood** or of **brick, steel, and concrete?** (Signal.) *Brick, steel, and concrete.*
1. What's the problem with buildings that are made of wood? (Call on a student. Ideas: *They burn easily; they can't be built as tall.*)

Most people were riding horses or they were riding in wagons pulled by horses. Some boys and girls rode bicycles. Tom and Eric saw only one car. It was one of the very first cars ever made. When the car went by, a horse went wild and started to run down the street.

2. Name the vehicles that people used to get from place to place. (Call on a student. Ideas: *Horses, horse-drawn wagons, bicycles, cars.*)

2. The picture shows the car Eric and Tom saw. Everybody, does that car look much like cars you see today? (Signal.) *No.*

2. Do you think those horses had seen a lot of cars before? (Signal.) *No.*

2. Do you think those horses had seen a lot of cars before? (Signal.) *No.*

2. What do you think those horses thought the car was? (Call on a student. Idea: *A monster.*)

The horse was pulling a wagon full of fruit. Fruit spilled all over the street. Tom and Eric picked up some apples.

2. Why do you think they picked up the apples? (Call on a student. Idea: *They were hungry.*)

Just then, the street shook. The ground moved to one side. It moved so fast that Eric fell down. Then the ground moved the other way, and Tom could see a large crack starting to form right in the middle of the street.

1. What do you think is happening? (Call on a student. Idea: *The earthquake is starting.*)

Tom yelled, "I remember what happened in 1906. The earthquake! The San Francisco earthquake!"

2. Everybody, in what year was the San Francisco earthquake? (Signal.) *1906.*

2. And Tom and Eric were there.

Tom could hardly hear his own voice. People were screaming and running from buildings. A building on the corner started to lean and then it fell into the street. The crack in the middle of the street suddenly got wider and longer. The crack ran down the street. A horse and wagon slid and fell into the crack.

1. Go back to the beginning of the story. Follow along while I read.

2. Read the rest of the story to yourself. Find out what happened to Eric. Raise your hand when you're finished.

Suddenly, fires started to break out all along the crack. The crack had broken the gas lines, and now the gas was burning. Buildings were burning. The ground was shaking. People were running and screaming. Buildings were falling. "We've got to get out of here," Tom yelled.

Hundreds of men and women pushed this way and that way. The ground shook again. Another great crack formed in the street. It ran across the street and ran right between Eric and Tom. The crack got wider and wider. And suddenly Eric fell into the crack.
MORE NEXT TIME

2. (After all students have raised their hand:)

2. Let me read the last part to you again. Close your eyes and get a picture of what Tom and Eric must have felt during that earthquake.

Suddenly, fires started to break out all along the crack. The crack had broken the gas lines, and now the gas was burning. Buildings were burning. The ground was shaking. People were running and screaming. Buildings were falling. "We've got to get out of here," Tom yelled.

Hundreds of men and women pushed this way and that way. The ground shook again. Another great crack formed in the street. It ran across the street and ran right between Eric and Tom. The crack got wider and wider. And suddenly Eric fell into the crack.

2. The fires started because of broken gas lines. Gas lines are pipes underground that bring gas to the streetlights and buildings. That gas burns very easily.

2. What happened to Eric? (Call on a student. Idea: *He fell into a crack in the street.*)

2. I'll name some events. You tell me if each event happened in the part you read to yourself. Hundreds of men and women pushed this way and that way. Everybody, did that happen? (Signal.) *Yes.*

2. A train blew up and started the fires. Did that happen? (Signal.) *No.*

2. A second crack formed after the first one formed. Did that happen? (Signal.) *Yes.*

2. A dog fell in the second crack. Did that happen? (Signal.) *No.*

2. Gas lines broke and the fires started. Did that happen? (Signal.) *Yes.*

EXERCISE 6
PAIRED PRACTICE

You're going to read aloud to your partner. Today the **B** members will read first. Then the **A** members will read from the star to the end of the story.
(Observe students and give feedback.)

End-of-Lesson Activities

INDEPENDENT WORK

Now finish your independent work for lesson 131. Start with the worksheet then finish the textbook. Raise your hand when you're finished.
(Observe students and give feedback.)

WORKCHECK

a. (Direct students to take out their marking pencils.)
 • We're going to check your independent work. Remember, if you got an item wrong, make an **X** next to the item.
b. (For each item: Read the item. Call on a student to answer it. If the answer is wrong, say the correct answer. Refer to the Answer Key for the correct answers.)
c. Now use your pencil to fix up any items you got wrong. Remember, all mistakes must be fixed up before you hand in your work.

WRITING-SPELLING

(Present Writing-Spelling lesson 131 after completing Reading lesson 131. See Writing-Spelling Guide.)

LANGUAGE ARTS GUIDE

(Present Language Arts lesson 131 after completing Reading lesson 131. See Language Arts Guide.)

ACTIVITY

SCAVENGER HUNT

a. (Divide the group into teams of three.)
b. (Explain the rules of the hunt: Each team will have the same list of things to find about the San Francisco 1906 earthquake. Some of the things may be found on a computer. You may find some in magazines or newspapers.)
 Things to be found
 A photograph of San Francisco around the time of the 1906 earthquake.
 A map that shows San Francisco around that time and that shows where the earthquake occurred.
 A magazine article that tells something about the earthquake.
 A chart that shows the population of some major U.S. cities around 1900. (Check census records.)
c. (Go over the list of items each team is to find. Answer questions about where or how to locate some information. You may want to alert librarians and/or computer labs to be prepared to assist students. Tell teams that they can ask parents or anyone else for help in finding these items. To receive credit for an item, they must bring it (or a copy) to the classroom.)
 • (Arrange for a librarian or volunteer to show students how to find answers to some of these questions using the internet. Tell teams that if they get stuck they should ask this person to help them.)

Materials: You will need a globe for exercise 4.

EXERCISE 1

VOCABULARY REVIEW

a. Here's the new vocabulary sentence: His argument convinced them to buy an appliance.
 • Everybody, say the sentence. Get ready. (Signal.) *His argument convinced them to buy an appliance.*
b. What word names a machine that's used around the house? (Signal.) *Appliance.*
 • What word refers to what he said to convince people? (Signal.) *Argument.*
 • What word means he **made somebody believe something?** (Signal.) *Convinced.*
 • (Repeat step b until firm.)

EXERCISE 2

READING WORDS

Column 1

a. **Find lesson 132 in your textbook.** ✓
 • Touch column 1. ✓
 • (Teacher reference:)

1. **electric**	3. **appliance**
2. **computer**	4. **pyramid**

b. Word 1 is **electric.** What word? (Signal.) *Electric.*
 • Spell **electric.** Get ready. (Tap for each letter.) *E-L-E-C-T-R-I-C.*
 • Things that are electric run on electricity, not on fuel. You plug some of these things into the wall. An electric toaster runs on electricity. So does a TV set.
c. Word 2 is **computer.** What word? (Signal.) *Computer.*
 • Spell **computer.** Get ready. (Tap for each letter.) *C-O-M-P-U-T-E-R.*
 • Computers are machines that you can use to work problems and play games.
d. Word 3. What word? (Signal.) *Appliance.*

e. Word 4. What word? (Signal.) *Pyramid.*
f. Let's read those words again, the fast way.
 • Word 1. What word? (Signal.) *Electric.*
 • (Repeat for words 2–4.)
g. (Repeat step f until firm.)

Column 2

h. Find column 2. ✓
 • (Teacher reference:)

1. **forever**	4. **soldier**
2. **palace**	5. **flashlight**
3. **pocket**	

 • All these words have more than one syllable. The first part of each word is underlined.
i. Word 1. What's the underlined part? (Signal.) *for.*
 • What's the whole word? (Signal.) *Forever.*
 • If something lasts forever, it never never ends. It just keeps on going. Everybody, what word means that something never ends? (Signal.) *Forever.*
j. Word 2. What's the underlined part? (Signal.) *pal.*
 • What's the whole word? (Signal.) *Palace.*
k. Word 3. What's the underlined part? (Signal.) *pock.*
 • What's the whole word? (Signal.) *Pocket.*
l. Word 4. What's the underlined part? (Signal.) *sold.*
 • What's the whole word? (Signal.) *Soldier.*
m. Word 5. What's the underlined part? (Signal.) *flash.*
 • What's the whole word? (Signal.) *Flashlight.*
n. Let's read those words again, the fast way.
 • Word 1. What word? (Signal.) *Forever.*
 • (Repeat for words 2–5.)
o. (Repeat step n until firm.)

Column 3

p. Find column 3. ✓
- (Teacher reference:)

1. slaves	4. buried
2. rafts	5. recorder
3. queens	

- All these words have endings.
q. Word 1. What word? (Signal.) *Slaves.*
r. Word 2. What word? (Signal.) *Rafts.*
- A raft is a flat boat. A simple raft is just a bunch of logs that are tied together.
s. Word 3. What word? (Signal.) *Queens.*
- Usually, a queen is the wife of a king. Everybody, what's a queen? (Signal.) *The wife of a king.*
t. Word 4. What word? (Signal.) *Buried.*
u. Word 5. What word? (Signal.) *Recorder.*
v. Let's read those words again.
- Word 1. What word? (Signal.) *Slaves.*
- (Repeat for words 2–5.)
w. (Repeat step v until firm.)

Column 4

x. Find column 4. ✓
- (Teacher reference:)

1. blade	3. Egypt
2. Nile	4. sword

y. Word 1. What word? (Signal.) *Blade.*
- The blade is the flat part of a tool that is connected to a handle. The blade of a knife is the part that cuts. The blade of a shovel is the part that digs.
z. Word 2. What word? (Signal.) *Nile.*
- (Repeat for words 3 and 4.)
a. Let's read those words again.
- Word 1. What word? (Signal.) *Blade.*
- (Repeat for words 2–4.)
b. (Repeat step a until firm.)

Individual Turns

(For columns 1–4: Call on individual students, each to read one to three words per turn.)

COMPREHENSION PASSAGES

Passage B

a. Find part B in your textbook. ✓
- You're going to read the next story about Eric and Tom. First you'll read two information passages.
b. Everybody, touch the title. ✓
- (Call on a student to read the title.) [More About Time.]
- Everybody, what's the title? (Signal.) *More About Time.*
c. (Call on individual students to read the passage, each student reading two or three sentences at a time.)

> **More About Time**
>
> In today's story, you'll find out more about the trip that Eric and Tom took through time.
> Touch dot B on the time line.

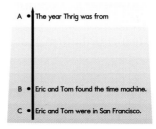

- Everybody, do it. ✓

> **That is the year Eric and Tom found the time machine.**

- Everybody, in what year did they find it? (Signal. Accept current year.)

> **Touch dot A.**

- Everybody, do it. ✓

> **That's the year Thrig was from.**

- Everybody, what year was that? (Signal.) *2400.*

> **Touch dot C.**

- Everybody, do it. ✓

> **That was the year Eric and Tom were in San Francisco.**

- Everybody, what year was that? (Signal.) *1906.*

> **You learned about things that were first made around the year 1900. Name those things.**

- Name something that was first made around the year 1900. (Call on a student. Responses: *Airplane; car.*)

Passage C

d. Find part C in your textbook. ✓
e. Everybody, touch the title. ✓
- (Call on a student to read the title.) *[Facts About Egypt.]*
- Everybody, what's the title? (Signal.) *Facts About Egypt.*
f. (Call on individual students to read the passage, each student reading two or three sentences at a time.)

> **Facts About Egypt**
>
> **The story that you will read today tells about Egypt.**

- Everybody, what does it tell about? (Signal.) *Egypt.*

> **Egypt is a country that is close to Greece and Turkey.**

- Everybody, look at the map. Touch Turkey. ✓
- Now move south until you come to Egypt. ✓

> **Here are facts about Egypt: Egypt has a great river running through it. That river is named the Nile. Touch the Nile River on the map.**

- Everybody, do it. ✓

> **Egypt is famous for its pyramids and palaces.**
>
> **Pyramids are huge stone buildings that are over five thousand years old. The picture shows pyramids.**

- Everybody, what's the name of those buildings that look like pointed piles? (Signal.) *Pyramids.*
- Touch a pyramid. ✓

> **Dead kings and queens of Egypt were made into mummies and buried in pyramids.**

- What were pyramids used for? (Call on a student. Idea: *Burying dead kings and queens of Egypt.*)
- Everybody, what is the name of the great river that runs through Egypt? (Signal.) *Nile River.*
- What is the name of those buildings that look like pointed piles? (Signal.) *Pyramids.*
- If you went from Turkey to Egypt, in which direction would you go? (Call on a student.) *[South.]*

EXERCISE 4

GLOBE REVIEW

a. (Present a globe. Touch New York City.) Everybody, what's this place? (Signal.) *New York City.*
- I'll show you where Egypt is on the globe. (Trace the route from New York City to Egypt.) Here's Egypt. Your turn.
b. (Spin the globe. Call on a student.) Touch New York City. ✓
- Touch Egypt. ✓
- (Repeat step b with other students.)

STORY READING

a. Find part D in your textbook. ✓
- The error limit for group reading is 13. Read carefully.

b. Everybody, touch the title. ✓
- (Call on a student to read the title.) [Eric and Tom in Egypt.]
- Everybody, what's the title? (Signal.) *Eric and Tom in Egypt.*

c. (Call on individual students to read the story, each student reading two or three sentences at a time. Ask questions marked **1**.)

- (Correct errors: Tell the word. Direct the student to reread the sentence.)
- (If the group makes more than 13 errors, direct the students to reread the story.

d. (After the group has read the selection making no more than 13 errors, read the story to the students and ask questions marked **2**.)

Eric and Tom in Egypt

1. Where do you think the time machine will take them this time? (Call on a student.) *Egypt.*

Eric had fallen into the crack in the ground. But Tom held on to Eric's hand. Tom looked down into the crack. It seemed to go down forever.

2. Everybody, could Tom see the bottom of that crack? (Signal.) *No.*

Tom almost slipped. He pulled and pulled, and he finally pulled Eric out of the crack.
Then they ran. They pushed through crowds. From time to time, the earth would shake and knock them down. They ran past houses that were burning. They ran past houses that had fallen over.

2. What started the fire? (Call on a student. Idea: *The gas lines broke.*)

2. What made the houses fall over? (Call on a student. Ideas: *The fire weakened them; the earthquake knocked them down.*)

When the boys got to the mountain outside the city, they looked back as they ran. The whole city was burning. They could hear people screaming in the distance. The boys ran up the side of the mountain to the time machine.
After they caught their breath, Tom said, "Let's figure out a way to get back to the right time."

2. Everybody, what year is the right time? (Signal. Accept current year.)

They went inside the time machine. Dials were clicking and lights were flashing inside the machine. Tom sat down in the seat.

1. What do you think will happen now? (Call on a student. Idea: *The door will shut.*)

The door shut: "Swwwshshsh." Tom pointed to the handle that Eric had pulled. "This makes the time machine work," Tom said.
Eric said, "When I pulled down on it, we went back in time."
Tom said, "I'll bet we will go forward in time if we push the handle up."

1. Raise your hand if you think they'll go forward in time this time.

2. What does Tom think happens if you pull **down** on the handle? (Call on a student. Idea: *The machine goes back in time.*)

2. What does Tom think will happen if you push **up** on the handle? (Call on a student. Idea: *The machine will go forward in time.*)

2. Tom and Eric were in the year 1906. Everybody, did they want to go **back in time** or **forward in time**? (Signal.) *Forward in time.*

2. So which way did they want to move the handle? (Signal.) *Up.*

> "Push it up," Eric said.
> Tom grabbed the handle. It felt very cold. He tried to push it up, but it wouldn't move. "It's stuck," he said. "The handle won't move."
> Eric pushed on the handle, but the outcome was the same.

2. What happened if the outcome was the same? (Call on a student. Ideas: *Nothing happened; the handle didn't move.*)

> "It's got to move," Tom said. He pushed and pulled with all his strength. Suddenly, the handle moved down. A force pushed against him.

1. Raise your hand if you think they'll go forward in time this time.
1. If the handle moved down, what was going to happen? (Call on a student. Idea: *They would go back in time.*)
1. Everybody, is that what the boys wanted? (Signal.) *No.*

> Eric's voice sounded far away as he said, "Oh, no."
> Lights went on and off. Dials clicked and buzzed. Then things began to quiet down.

2. Were they still moving in time when things quieted down? (Call on a student. Idea: *No.*)

> Eric said, "I'm afraid to look outside."
> Tom stood up. The door opened.

2. What made the door open? (Call on a student. Idea: *Tom stood up.*)

> It was very bright outside. At first, Tom couldn't believe what he saw.
> The time machine was on the side of a mountain above a great river. There were many rafts and boats on the river. But they did not look like any rafts or boats that Tom had ever seen before. Next to the river was a city. But it did not look like any city that Tom had ever seen before. All the buildings in the city were white. And next to the city were two great pyramids. One of them was already built and the other one was almost finished. Hundreds of men were dragging great stones toward this pyramid.

1. They saw a great river, a city with white buildings and pyramids. Everybody, in what country were they? (Signal.) *Egypt.*

> "We're in Egypt," Tom said. "We're in Egypt five thousand years ago! Look over there. The men are building a pyramid."

2. Everybody, how long ago were they in Egypt? (Signal.) *5000 years ago.*
2. How did Tom know it was 5000 years ago? (Call on a student. Idea: *He saw men building a pyramid.*)

> "What are pyramids for?" Eric asked.
> Tom said, "When a king dies, they put him in a pyramid along with all of his slaves and his goats and everything else he owned."

2. What did they use pyramids for? (Call on a student. Idea: *To bury kings in.*)
2. What did they put inside pyramids? (Call on a student. Ideas: *Kings, slaves, goats, everything the kings owned.*)

> Eric said, "Let's not leave the time machine now. We could take a nap. When it's dark, we'll go down to the city."

1. Go back to the beginning of the story. Follow along while I read.
2. Why did they want to wait until it was dark? (Call on a student. Idea: *So no one would see them.*)
2. Read the rest of the story to yourself. Find out what objects Tom took from the time machine. Raise your hand when you're finished.

> Tom and Eric slept. They woke up just as the sun was setting. Tom looked inside the time machine for a flashlight. He found one on a shelf. Next to it was a tiny tape recorder. He put the flashlight in one pocket and the tape recorder in the other.
> Then Eric and Tom started down the mountain. They were very hungry. Down, down they went. They found a road at the bottom of the mountain. The road led into the city.
> It was very quiet and very dark in the city. Tom took his flashlight out and was ready to turn it on when something happened.
> ### MORE NEXT TIME

2. (After all students have raised their hand:) What was the sun doing when Tom and Eric woke up? (Call on a student. Idea: *Setting.*)
2. So what time of day was it? (Call on a student. Ideas: *Evening, sunset.*)
2. Everybody, which two objects did Tom take from the time machine? (Signal.) *Flashlight and tape recorder.*
2. Were there any streetlights in the city? (Signal.) *No.*
2. How do you know? (Call on a student. Idea: *Because the city was very dark.*)
2. Everybody, what was Tom getting ready to use at the end of the story? (Signal.) *Flashlight.*

PAIRED PRACTICE

You're going to read aloud to your partner. Today the **A** members will read first. Then the **B** members will read from the star to the end of the story.
(Observe students and give feedback.)

End-of-Lesson Activities

INDEPENDENT WORK

Now finish your independent work for lesson 132. Raise your hand when you're finished. (Observe students and give feedback.)

WORKCHECK

a. (Direct students to take out their marking pencils.)
  • We're going to check your independent work. Remember, if you got an item wrong, make an **X** next to the item.
b. (For each item: Read the item. Call on a student to answer it. If the answer is wrong, say the correct answer. Refer to the Answer Key for the correct answers.)
c. Now use your pencil to fix up any items you got wrong. Remember, all mistakes must be fixed up before you hand in your work.

WRITING-SPELLING

(Present Writing-Spelling lesson 132 after completing Reading lesson 132. See Writing-Spelling Guide.)

LANGUAGE ARTS GUIDE

(Present Language Arts lesson 132 after completing Reading lesson 132. See Language Arts Guide.)

EXERCISE 1

VOCABULARY REVIEW

a. You learned a sentence that tells when they might reply.
- Everybody, say that sentence. Get ready. (Signal.) *Perhaps they will reply in a few days.*
- (Repeat until firm.)

b. You learned a sentence that tells about the palace guards.
- Everybody, say that sentence. Get ready. (Signal.) *The palace guards spoke different languages.*
- (Repeat until firm.)

c. Here's the last sentence you learned: His argument convinced them to buy an appliance.
- Everybody, say that sentence. Get ready. (Signal.) *His argument convinced them to buy an appliance.*
- (Repeat until firm.)

d. What word names a machine that's used around the house? (Signal.) *Appliance.*
- What word means he **made somebody believe something?** (Signal.) *Convinced.*
- What word refers to what he said to convince people? (Signal.) *Argument.*
- (Repeat step d until firm.)

e. Once more. Say the sentence that tells what his argument did. Get ready. (Signal.) *His argument convinced them to buy an appliance.*

EXERCISE 2

READING WORDS

Column 1

a. **Find lesson 133 in your textbook.** ✓
- Touch column 1. ✓
- (Teacher reference:)

1. radio	3. refrigerator
2. telephone	4. snapped

b. Word 1 is **radio.** What word? (Signal.) *Radio.*
- Spell **radio.** Get ready. (Tap for each letter.) *R-A-D-I-O.*

c. Word 2 is **telephone.** What word? (Signal.) *Telephone.*

d. Word 3 is **refrigerator.** What word? (Signal.) *Refrigerator.*

e. Word 4. What word? (Signal.) *Snapped.*

f. Let's read those words again, the fast way.
- Word 1. What word? (Signal.) *Radio.*
- (Repeat for words 2–4.)

g. (Repeat step f until firm.)

Column 2

h. Find column 2. ✓
- (Teacher reference:)

1. ton	4. guard
2. bowed	5. pretend
3. lead	

i. Word 1. What word? (Signal.) *Ton.*
- Spell **ton.** Get ready. (Tap for each letter.) *T-O-N.*
- A ton is two thousand pounds. It would take about forty children to weigh one ton. Everybody, what unit of weight is two thousand pounds? (Signal.) *Ton.*

j. Word 2 rhymes with **loud.** What word? (Signal.) *Bowed.*
- Spell **bowed.** Get ready. (Tap for each letter.) *B-O-W-E-D.*
- Here is how you bow. (Demonstrate a bow.) When you bow, you bend forward. People bow when they approach a king or queen.

k. Word 3 rhymes with **bead.** What word? (Signal.) *Lead.*
- Spell **lead.** Get ready. (Tap for each letter.) *L-E-A-D.*

l. Word 4. What word? (Signal.) *Guard.*
- Word 5. What word? (Signal.) *Pretend.*

m. Let's read those words again, the fast way.
- Word 1. What word? (Signal.) *Ton.*
- (Repeat for words 2–5.)

n. (Repeat step m until firm.)

Column 3

o. Find column 3. ✓
- (Teacher reference:)

1. wonderful	4. computer
2. appliance	5. toast
3. electric	6. toaster

p. Word 1. What word? (Signal.)
Wonderful.
- (Repeat for words 2–6.)
q. Let's read those words again.
- Word 1. What word? (Signal.)
Wonderful.
- (Repeat for words 2–6.)
r. (Repeat step q until firm.)

Individual Turns

(For columns 1–3: Call on individual students, each to read one to three words per turn.)

EXERCISE 3

COMPREHENSION PASSAGE

a. Find part B in your textbook. ✓
- You're going to read the next story about Eric and Tom. First you'll read the information passage.
b. Everybody, touch the title. ✓
- (Call on a student to read the title.)
[More About Time.]
- Everybody, what's the title? (Signal.)
More About Time.
c. (Call on individual students to read the passage, each student reading two or three sentences at a time.)

More About Time

- (Teacher reference:)

A The year Thrig was from

B Eric and Tom found the time machine.
C Eric and Tom were in San Francisco.
D The United States became a country.
E Eric and Tom were in Egypt.

**Look at the time line.
Touch dot B.**

- Everybody, do it. ✓

Dot B shows the year that Eric and Tom found the time machine. What year was that?

- Everybody, what's the answer? (Signal. Accept current year.)

Touch dot A.

- Everybody, do it. ✓

Dot A shows the year that Thrig was from. What year was that?

- Everybody, what's the answer? (Signal.)
2400.

Touch dot C.

- Everybody, do it. ✓

Dot C shows the year that Eric and Tom were in San Francisco. When was that?

- Everybody, what's the answer? (Signal.)
1906.

Touch dot D.

- Everybody, do it. ✓

Dot D shows the year that the United States became a country. What year was that?

- Everybody, what's the answer? (Signal.)
1776.

Touch dot E.

- Everybody, do it. ✓

Dot E shows when Eric and Tom were in Egypt. How long ago was that?

- Everybody, what's the answer? (Signal.)
5,000 years ago.

STORY READING

a. Find part C in your textbook. ✓
  • The error limit for group reading is 8. Read carefully.

b. Everybody, touch the title. ✓
  • (Call on a student to read the title.) *[Eric and Tom Meet the King of Egypt.]*
  • Everybody, what's the title? (Signal.) *Eric and Tom Meet the King of Egypt.*
  • Where did we leave Tom and Eric? (Call on a student. Idea: *In Egypt.*)

c. (Call on individual students to read the story, each student reading two or three sentences at a time. Ask questions marked **1.**)

  • (Correct errors: Tell the word. Direct the student to reread the sentence.)
  • (If the group makes more than 8 errors, direct the students to reread the story.)

d. (After the group has read the selection making no more than 8 errors, read the story to the students and ask questions marked **2.**)

> **Eric and Tom Go to a Palace**
> Tom was ready to turn his flashlight on. Suddenly, a soldier was standing in front of him. The soldier had metal bands on his arms, and he held a large sword. He pointed the sword at Tom. "Ha hu ru," he said.

1. Everybody, did the soldier say things that Tom and Eric understood? (Signal.) *No.*
1. The soldier speaks a different language. What do you think he was trying to tell Tom when he said, "Ha hu ru?" (Call on a student. Ideas: *Stop; where do you think you're going?*)

> Tom looked at the soldier and said, "I don't know what you said."
> The soldier moved the sword closer to Tom. Tom could see little marks on the blade. He could see a big scar on the soldier's hand. "Ha hu ru," the soldier said again.

> Eric said, "He looks mad. We'd better do something."
> The soldier yelled, "Ha hu ru," and shook his sword. But Tom still couldn't understand him.
> The blade of the sword was only inches from Tom's face.

1. What did the soldier do? (Call on a student. Ideas: *Moved the sword closer to Tom; yelled; shook the sword.*)
1. What did Tom try to explain to the soldier? (Call on a student. Idea: *That he couldn't understand what the soldier was saying.*)
1. Everybody, did the soldier understand what Tom said? (Signal.) *No.*
1. How did Tom feel? (Call on a student. Idea: *Frightened.*)
1. The story has given some clues about how Tom might get out of trouble. Do you have any ideas about what he could do? (Call on individual students. Ideas: *Use the tape recorder; surprise the soldier with the flashlight.*)

> Tom put his hand over his face. He didn't remember that he had a flashlight in his hand. Without thinking, Tom turned it on.
> When the soldier saw the light, he stepped back. He put his sword on the ground. "On kon urub," he said very softly. The soldier got down on his hands and knees. "On kon urub," he said again.

2. Everybody, had that soldier ever seen a flashlight before? (Signal.) *No.*
2. Why not? (Call on a student. Idea: *They weren't made yet.*)
2. The way the soldier acted gives some clues about what the soldier was thinking. The soldier put his sword on the ground and said "On kon urub" very softly. What does that soldier think? (Call on a student. Idea: *That Tom is very special.*)

Eric said, "He thinks that you have some kind of great power. <u>Maybe</u> he thinks you are a <u>sun god</u>."

2. Why would the soldier think that? (Call on a student. Idea: *The flashlight seems like magic.*)

Tom smiled, "Maybe it will be fun to be a sun god."
Eric said, "Be careful, Tom."

1. Before, Eric was the one who was doing things that are dangerous. But now Tom is getting carried away. He'd better watch out.

Tom walked over to the soldier. "Take me to your <u>king</u>," he said. "The sun god wants to meet the king of Egypt." Tom pointed toward the middle of the city.

2. Who is the sun god that Tom is talking about? (Call on a student. Idea: *Himself.*)

The soldier stood up. He bowed three times. Then he started to lead the boys down the streets. Soon they came to a large palace that had hundreds of steps in front of it.
The soldier went up to three guards who were in front of the palace. The soldier talked and pointed to Tom. Then one guard walked up to the boys. The guard backed away and bowed three times.

2. Why are the soldiers bowing? (Call on a student. Idea: *They think Tom has special, magic powers.*)
2. Everybody, would they act that way if they thought that Tom was just another boy? (Signal.) *No.*
2. Get a picture in your mind of this next part.

Eric said, "I think he wants us to follow him."
So Tom and Eric followed the guard. Up the steps they went. Up, up, up to the great doors that led inside the palace.
"What a palace," Tom said. He had never been in a building so big. The hall seemed blocks and blocks long. And a soldier was standing every two yards on each side of the hall. There were hundreds of soldiers in that hall.

2. Everybody, how far apart were the soldiers? (Signal.) *Two yards.*
2. Were they on **one side** of the hall or **both sides**? (Signal.) *Both sides.*
2. Were there more than 100 soldiers in that hall? (Signal.) *Yes.*

The guard walked down the hall. Tom and Eric followed. At last they walked through another huge door. They were now inside a great room looking at an old man. He was sitting on the floor with a large chain around his neck. At the end of the chain was a large metal ball. The ball looked like the sun.

1. Do you think this old man is the king? (Call on a student. Student preference.)
1. We'll find out.

The soldier said something to the old man. The old man looked at the boys for a long time. Then he smiled and stood up. He walked over and held out his hand. "Ura bustu," he said.

1. Go back to the beginning of the story. Follow along while I read.
2. Read the rest of the story to yourself. Find out what the old man said when Tom turned the flashlight on. Raise your hand when you're finished.

> **"He wants the flashlight," Eric said. "Don't give it to him."**
>
> **"Don't worry," Tom said. Tom shook his head no. Then he pointed the flashlight at the sun on the old man's neck chain. Tom turned the flashlight on. The sun became bright.**
>
> **The old man held his hand over the sun. "On kon urub," he said. "On kon urub."**
>
> **Eric said, "Now he thinks that you're a sun god."**
> **MORE NEXT TIME**

2. (After all the students have raised their hand:) Earlier in the story, the soldier said, "On kon urub." When did the soldier say that? (Call on a student. Idea: *When Tom turned on the flashlight.*)
2. When did the old man say it? (Call on a student. Idea: *When Tom turned on the flashlight.*)
2. What do you think **on kon urub** means? (Call on a student. Ideas: *You are a god; I bow to you; you made light.*)

EXERCISE 5

PAIRED PRACTICE

You're going to read aloud to your partner. Today the **B** members will read first. Then the **A** members will read from the star to the end of the story.
(Observe students and give feedback.)

End-of-Lesson Activities

INDEPENDENT WORK

Now finish your independent work for lesson 133. Raise your hand when you're finished. (Observe students and give feedback.)

WORKCHECK

a. (Direct students to take out their marking pencils.)
• We're going to check your independent work. Remember, if you got an item wrong, make an **X** next to the item.
b. (For each item: Read the item. Call on a student to answer it. If the answer is wrong, say the correct answer. Refer to the Answer Key for the correct answers.)
c. Now use your pencil to fix up any items you got wrong. Remember, all mistakes must be fixed up before you hand in your work.

WRITING-SPELLING

(Present Writing-Spelling lesson 133 after completing Reading lesson 133. See Writing-Spelling Guide.)

LANGUAGE ARTS GUIDE

(Present Language Arts lesson 133 after completing Reading lesson 133. See Language Arts Guide.)

Lesson 134

EXERCISE 1

VOCABULARY REVIEW

a. You learned a sentence that tells what the police officers checked.
- Everybody, say that sentence. Get ready. (Signal.) *Police officers checked the ship's cargo.*
- (Repeat until firm.)

b. I'll say part of the sentence. When I stop, you say the next word. Listen: Police . . . Everybody, what's the next word? (Signal.) *Officers.*

c. Listen: Police officers checked the ship's . . . Everybody, what's the next word? (Signal.) *Cargo.*
- Say the whole sentence. Get ready. (Signal.) *Police officers checked the ship's cargo.*

EXERCISE 2

READING WORDS

Column 1

a. **Find lesson 134 in your textbook.** ✓
- Touch column 1. ✓
- (Teacher reference:)

1. ancient	4. bowl
2. mammoth	5. toaster
3. throne	6. electric

b. Word 1 is **ancient.** What word? (Signal.) *Ancient.*
- Spell **ancient.** Get ready. (Tap for each letter.) *A-N-C-I-E-N-T.*
- Things that are ancient are very, very old. Ancient rocks are rocks formed millions of years ago. An ancient city is a city that was formed thousands of years ago. What word means very, very old? (Signal.) *Ancient.*

c. Word 2 is **mammoth.** What word? (Signal.) *Mammoth.*
- Spell **mammoth.** Get ready. (Tap for each letter.) *M-A-M-M-O-T-H.*

d. Word 3. What word? (Signal.) *Throne.*
- Spell **throne.** Get ready. (Tap for each letter.) *T-H-R-O-N-E.*

e. Word 4. What word? (Signal.) *Bowl.*
- Spell **bowl.** Get ready. (Tap for each letter.) *B-O-W-L.*

f. Word 5. What word? (Signal.) *Toaster.*

g. Word 6. What word? (Signal.) *Electric.*

h. Let's read those words again, the fast way.
- Word 1. What word? (Signal.) *Ancient.*
- (Repeat for words 2–6.)

i. (Repeat step h until firm.)

Column 2

j. Find column 2. ✓
- (Teacher reference:)

1. **dish**washer	4. **in**sist
2. **app**liance	5. **tel**ephone
3. **gold**en	6. **tel**evision

- All these words have more than one syllable. The first syllable of each word is underlined.

k. Word 1. What's the first syllable? (Signal.) *dish.*
- What's the whole word? (Signal.) *Dishwasher.*

l. Word 2. What's the first syllable? (Signal.) *app.*
- What's the whole word? (Signal.) *Appliance.*

m. Word 3. What's the first syllable? (Signal.) *gold.*
- What's the whole word? (Signal.) *Golden.*

n. Word 4. What's the first syllable? (Signal.) *in.*
- What's the whole word? (Signal.) *Insist.*

o. Word 5. What's the first syllable? (Signal.) *tel.*
- What's the whole word? (Signal.) *Telephone.*

p. Word 6. What's the first syllable? (Signal.) *tel.*
- What's the whole word? (Signal.) *Television.*

q. Let's read those words again, the fast way.
- Word 1. What word? (Signal.) *Dishwasher.*
- (Repeat for words 2–6.)

r. (Repeat step q until firm.)

Column 3

s. Find column 3. ✓
   • (Teacher reference:)

1. spices	4. invention
2. bulbs	5. refrigerators
3. radios	6. computer

   • All these words have endings.
t. Word 1. What word? (Signal.) Spices.
u. Word 2. What word? (Signal.) *Bulbs.*
   • (Repeat for words 3–6.)
v. Let's read those words again.
   • Word 1. What word? (Signal.) *Spices.*
   • (Repeat for words 2–6.)
w. (Repeat step v until firm.)

Column 4

x. Find column 4. ✓
   • (Teacher reference:)

1. smashed	3. snapped
2. invented	4. pretended

   • All these words end with the letters **E-D.**
y. Word 1. What word? (Signal.)
   Smashed.
   • (Repeat for words 2–4.)
z. (Repeat step y until firm.)

Individual Turns

(For columns 1–4: Call on individual students, each to read one to three words per turn.)

EXERCISE 3

COMPREHENSION PASSAGE

a. Find part B in your textbook. ✓
   • You're going to read the next story about Eric and Tom. First you'll read the information passage. It gives some facts about inventing.
b. Everybody, touch the title. ✓
   • (Call on a student to read the title.) *[Inventing.]*
   • Everybody, what's the title? (Signal.) *Inventing.*
c. (Call on individual students to read the passage, each student reading two or three sentences at a time.)

Inventing

You live in a world that is filled with things that are made by humans. In this world are cars and airplanes and telephones and books. There are chairs and tables and stoves and dishes. There are thousands of things that you use every day.

Each of these things was <u>invented</u>. That means that somebody made the object for the first time.

• When a person invents something, what does that person do? (Call on a student. Idea: *Makes an object for the first time.*)

The person who made the first automobile invented the automobile. The person who made the first television invented the television. Remember, when somebody makes an object for the first time, the person invents that object. The object the person makes is called the invention. The first airplane was an invention. The first telephone was an invention.

• Everybody, what do we call the object that is made for the first time? (Signal.) *Invention.*
• When a person makes that object for the first time, what do we say the person did? (Signal.) *Invented the object.*
• Name some things that were invented. (Call on individual students. Ideas: *Car, refrigerator, telephone, light bulb,* etc.)

Everything that is made by humans was invented by somebody. At one time, there were no cars, light bulbs, or glass windows. People didn't know how to make these things, because nobody had invented them yet.

Most of the things that you use every day were invented after the year 1800. Here are just some of the things that people did not have before 1800: trains, trucks, cars, airplanes, bicycles, telephones, radios, televisions, movies, tape recorders, computers, electric appliances like washing machines, toasters, refrigerators, or dishwashers.

- Everybody, most of the things we use every day were invented after what year? (Signal.) *1800.*
- Name some of the things you wouldn't have if you lived before 1800. (Call on individual students. Ideas: *Radio, tape recorder, dishwasher,* etc.)

EXERCISE 4

STORY READING

a. Find part C in your textbook. ✓
- The error limit for group reading is 10. Read carefully.

b. Everybody, touch the title. ✓
- (Call on a student to read the title.) *[Eric and Tom Meet the King.]*
- Everybody, what's the title? (Signal.) *Eric and Tom Meet the King.*

c. (Call on individual students to read the story, each student reading two or three sentences at a time. Ask questions marked **1.**)

> - (Correct errors: Tell the word. Direct the student to reread the sentence.)
> - (If the group makes more than 10 errors, direct the students to reread the story.)

d. (After the group has read the selection making no more than 10 errors, read the story to the students and ask questions marked **2.**)

Eric and Tom Meet the King

Tom and Eric were in a huge palace. Tom had just convinced the old man with the golden sun that Tom was a sun god. The old man was holding his hand over the sun and saying, "On kon urub." Then the old man lifted the golden sun from around his neck and held it out for Tom. The old man bowed and said, "Ura, ura."

Eric said, "I think he wants you to have the golden sun."

Tom didn't want to take the sun, but the old man seemed to insist that he take it.

The sun was so heavy that Tom wondered how the old man could walk around with it hanging from his neck. Just as Tom put the chain around his neck, one of the guards handed him a pillow with a large gray cat sitting on it.

Eric said, "They think cats have special powers."

Tom felt silly with a large sun around his neck as he held a pillow with a gray cat on it.

Eric said, "I don't know about you, but I am very hungry."

Tom said, "Me, too." He handed the cat to the guard. Then he snapped his fingers. "Eat, eat," Tom said, and pretended to eat.

2. Everybody, show me how he would pretend to eat. ✓

"Hem stroo," the soldier said smiling. "Hem stroo." The soldier ran from the room and down the hall.

1. Do you think the soldier knew what Tom wanted? (Call on a student.) *[Yes.]*

Suddenly, many people came into the room. They were carrying all kinds of food. Tom looked at all of the food in front of him. He saw a large bowl. It had milk in it. Tom said, "I'll bet it's goat milk."

Eric tasted it. He made a face. "It's warm," he said. "Why don't they have <u>cold</u> milk?"

1. Do you know the answer? (Call on a student. Idea: *They had no refrigerators to keep food cold.*)

Tom said, "Their milk isn't cold because they don't have any way to keep it cold. Nobody had refrigerators until after the year 1800."

2. That year is 5000 years in the future for these people.

Tom and Eric ate and ate. Then the old man took Tom and Eric to their room. Tom put his flashlight in his pocket and went to sleep.

In the morning the old man took the boys to a great room at the end of the hall. Inside the room a young man sat on a throne. The throne was made of gold and silver.

1. Everybody, look at the picture. ✓
1. What is the **young** man sitting on? (Signal.) *A throne.*
1. What is the **old** man doing in the picture? (Signal.) *Bowing.*
1. Which one do you think is the king, **the old man** or **the young man?** (Call on a student.) *[The young man.]*

Eric said, "That young man must be the king."

"Hara uha <u>ho</u>," the king said. His voice was sharp.

2. Say it the way the king said it, with a sharp voice. (Call on a student. Student should read in a sharp, mean voice.)

Tom and Eric walked to the throne. The king stood up and walked to a window in the room. He pointed to the sunlight that was coming through the window. "Tasa u horu," he said. Then he pointed to Tom. "Umul hock a huck."

1. What did the king do at the window? (Call on a student. Idea: *He pointed to the sunlight coming in the window.*)
1. Everybody, then who did he point to? (Signal.) *Tom.*
1. What is he trying to say? (Call on a student. Idea: *He wants Tom to turn on the flashlight.*)

Tom knew what the king wanted. Tom pointed the flashlight at the king and pressed the button on the flashlight. But nothing happened. The flashlight did not go on. Tom pressed the button again. The outcome was the same.

1. What does that mean, the outcome was the same? (Call on a student. Ideas: *Nothing happened; the flashlight didn't work.*)
1. Go back to the beginning of the story. Follow along while I read.
2. Read the rest of the story to yourself. Find out what happened to the flashlight. Raise your hand when you're finished.

> "Aso uhuck," the king said. He snapped his fingers and two soldiers came forward. One of them grabbed Tom and the other grabbed Eric.
>
> The king grabbed the flashlight from Tom's hand and threw it to the floor. It smashed. Tom looked at the flashlight. Then he looked up into the face of the king. The king looked very, very mean.
>
> **MORE NEXT TIME**

2. (After all students have raised their hand:) What happened to the flashlight? (Call on a student. Ideas: *The king threw it on the floor; it got smashed.*)

2. The king snapped his fingers and said, "Aso uhuck." What happened after that? (Call on a student. Idea: *Two soldiers came forward and grabbed Tom and Eric.*)

2. What do you think **aso uhuck** could mean? (Call on a student. Idea: *Grab them.*)

EXERCISE 5

PAIRED PRACTICE

You're going to read aloud to your partner. Today the **A** members will read first. Then the **B** members will read from the star to the end of the story.

(Observe students and give feedback.)

End-of-Lesson Activities

INDEPENDENT WORK

Now finish your independent work for lesson 134. Raise your hand when you're finished. (Observe students and give feedback.)

WORKCHECK

a. (Direct students to take out their marking pencils.)

• We're going to check your independent work. Remember, if you got an item wrong, make an **X** next to the item.

b. (For each item: Read the item. Call on a student to answer it. If the answer is wrong, say the correct answer. Refer to the Answer Key for the correct answers.)

c. Now use your pencil to fix up any items you got wrong. Remember, all mistakes must be fixed up before you hand in your work.

WRITING-SPELLING

(Present Writing-Spelling lesson 134 after completing Reading lesson 134. See Writing-Spelling Guide.)

LANGUAGE ARTS GUIDE

(Present Language Arts lesson 134 after completing Reading lesson 134. See Language Arts Guide.)

Materials: You will need a globe for exercise 3. Each student will need their thermometer chart for exercise 5.

EXERCISE 1

VOCABULARY REVIEW

a. You learned a sentence that tells what the champions did. Everybody, say that sentence. Get ready. (Signal.) *The champions performed perfectly.*

b. I'll say part of the sentence. When I stop, you say the next word. Listen: The champions . . . Everybody, what's the next word? (Signal.) *Performed.*

c. Listen: The champions performed . . . Everybody, what's the next word? (Signal.) *Perfectly.*
  • Say the whole sentence. Get ready. (Signal.) *The champions performed perfectly.*

d. Listen: The . . . Everybody, what's the next word? (Signal.) *Champions.*

EXERCISE 2

READING WORDS

Column 1

a. **Find lesson 135 in your textbook.** ✓
  • Touch column 1. ✓
  • (Teacher reference:)

1. language	4. mammoth
2. argue	5. ancient
3. saber-toothed	

b. Word 1 is **language.** What word? (Signal.) *Language.*
  • Spell **language.** Get ready. (Tap for each letter.) L-A-N-G-U-A-G-E.

c. Word 2 is **argue.** What word? (Signal.) *Argue.*
  • Spell **argue.** Get ready. (Tap for each letter.) A-R-G-U-E.

d. Word 3 is **saber-toothed.** What word? (Signal.) *Saber-toothed.*

e. Word 4. What word? (Signal.) *Mammoth.*

• Spell **mammoth.** Get ready. (Tap for each letter.) M-A-M-M-O-T-H.

f. Word 5. What word? (Signal.) *Ancient.*
  • Spell **ancient.** Get ready. (Tap for each letter.) A-N-C-I-E-N-T.

g. Let's read those words again, the fast way.
  • Word 1. What word? (Signal.) *Language.*
  • (Repeat for words 2–5.)

h. (Repeat step g until firm.)

Column 2

i. Find column 2. ✓
  • (Teacher reference:)

1. spices	4. scratching
2. grain	5. replied
3. further	

j. Word 1. What word? (Signal.) *Spices.*

k. Word 2. What word? (Signal.) *Grain.*
  • Grain is the seed of grass or cereal plants. We get different kinds of grain from different plants—oats, wheat, corn. Bread, macaroni, and cereals are made from grain.

l. Word 3. What word? (Signal.) *Further.*
  • (Repeat for words 4 and 5.)

m. Let's read those words again.
  • Word 1. What word? (Signal.) *Spices.*
  • (Repeat for words 2–5.)

n. (Repeat step m until firm.)

Individual Turns

(For columns 1 and 2: Call on individual students, each to read one to three words per turn.)

EXERCISE 3

GLOBE

a. (Present a globe. Touch New York City.) Everybody, what's this place? (Signal.) *New York City.*
  • I'll show you where Greece is on the globe. (Trace the route from New York City to Greece.) Here's Greece. Your turn.

b. (Spin the globe.) Touch New York City. (Call on a student.)
- Touch Greece. ✓
- Touch Egypt. ✓
- (Repeat step b with other students.)

c. Everybody, what direction do you go to get from Turkey to Greece? (Signal.) *West.*
- What directions do you go to get from Egypt to Greece? (Signal.) *North and west.*

STORY READING

> **Note:** There is a reading checkout in this lesson; therefore, there is no second reading of the story and no paired practice.

a. Find part B in your textbook. ✓
- The error limit for group reading is 10. Read carefully.

b. Everybody, touch the title. ✓
- (Call on a student to read the title.) *[Eric and Tom Leave Egypt.]*
- Everybody, what's the title? (Signal.) *Eric and Tom Leave Egypt.*

c. (Call on individual students to read the story, each student reading two or three sentences at a time. Ask specified questions.)

> - (Correct errors: Tell the word. Direct the student to reread the sentence.)
> - (If the group makes more than 10 errors, direct the students to reread the story.)

Eric and Tom Leave Egypt

A soldier was holding Tom. The flashlight was on the floor. It was broken. Tom could not play sun god anymore.

1. What had happened to the flashlight? (Call on a student. Ideas: *It was broken; the batteries were dead.*)

The king was yelling at the old man. Suddenly, Tom got an idea. He reached into his pocket and took out the tape recorder. He pressed the button. The king was saying, "Ra hu hub haki."

1. If Tom makes a tape recording of the king's voice, what will the recorder say when Tom plays it back? (Call on a student.) *[Ra hu hub haki.]*

1. Why do you think the king is mad? (Call on a student. Ideas: *He thinks Tom and Eric are fakes; because the flashlight wouldn't work anymore.*)

Tom held the tape recorder up high and played back what he had recorded. "Ra hu hub haki." The king stopped yelling. He looked at Tom. The soldier let go of Tom. Tom ran the tape back and played it again. He played it as loud as it would go. "Ra hu hub haki."
The king smiled and bowed.

1. What does he think Tom is? (Call on a student. Idea: *A god.*)

Tom walked up to the king. He pressed the button so that the tape recorder would record again. Then he said, "I am the sun god, and I have your words on this tape."
The king bowed and said, "Un uh, run duh."
Tom played the tape back as loud as he could.

1. When Tom played it back, it said some things that Tom said and some things the king said. Tell me everything the recorder said this time. (Call on a student.) *[I am the sun god and I have your words on this tape. Un uh, run duh.]*

Eric said, "Tom, let's get out of here before the tape recorder breaks. Remember what happened to the flashlight."

Eric and Tom walked down the long, long hall. They did not look back. They walked through the great doors of the palace. Then they started to run.

1. How did they feel? (Call on a student. Ideas: *Scared; they wanted to get out of there.*)

They ran down the stairs—down, down. When they came to the bottom of the stairs, they kept on running. They ran down the streets of the city until they came to the river. Then they stopped. They were both tired. People around them were pointing at them and talking, but Tom and Eric felt safe here.

1. Why were people pointing at them? (Call on a student. Ideas: *They looked strange; they wore different clothes and hair styles.*)

Tom said, "That's the Nile River." He pointed to one of the huge rafts on the river. "That raft is carrying hundreds and hundreds of sacks of grain."

1. What do people do with grain? (Call on a student. Ideas: *Eat it; make bread out of it.*)

Tom continued, "One raft can carry as much grain as a hundred wagons could carry."

1. Everybody, which is the smarter way to move the grain, **by wagons** or **by raft?** (Signal.) *By raft.*
1. Why? (Call on a student. Idea: *It carries more.*)

"Why don't they use trucks?" Eric asked.

1. Tell him. (Call on a student. Idea: *They hadn't been invented yet.*)

Tom laughed. "Nobody will have trucks in Egypt for thousands of years."
Eric looked at the rafts on the river. They carried all kinds of things— animals, furs, spices, food, and even great big stones the size of a car. "What are they going to do with those stones?" he asked.
Tom said, "They will use them to build a pyramid. They need thousands of stones to build one pyramid."

1. What are they going to do with those stones? (Call on a student. Idea: *Build a pyramid with them.*)

Just then a soldier came up to Eric and Tom. He held out his sword. "Ra uh hack stuck," he said.

1. Everybody, is that soldier being friendly? (Signal.) *No.*
1. How do you know? (Call on a student. Idea: *He pointed his sword.*)

Tom held up the tape recorder and played back the soldier's words. "Ra uh hack stuck." The soldier backed away.

1. What is the soldier thinking now? (Call on a student. Idea: *He thinks the boys have magic powers.*)

Tom and Eric found a path that led up the mountain. They walked up and up. The mountain was very steep, and by the time they got to the time machine, they were tired and hungry.
They went inside the time machine. Tom sat down in the seat.

1. What happened then? (Call on a student. Idea: *The door closed.*)

> "This time," he said, "I'm going to make the handle go <u>up</u> so we can go <u>forward</u> in time."
>
> "I hope so," Eric said. "I don't want to go back any further in time."

1. Read the rest of the story to yourself. Find out what happened when the door of the time machine opened. Raise your hand when you're finished.

> Tom pushed up on the handle. It did not move. He moved in the seat. Then, suddenly, the handle moved up. Dials started to click and buzz. Lights went on and off. Tom felt the force against his face.
>
> Then everything was quiet except for a few dials that were clicking and buzzing. Tom heard something scratching on the outside of the time machine. He stood up. The door opened. And something started to walk inside the time machine. It was a great big yellow lion.
> **MORE NEXT TIME**

1. (After all students have raised their hand:) Everybody, did the handle go **up** or **down?** (Signal.) *Up.*
1. So did they go **forward** or **backward** in time? (Signal.) *Forward.*
1. What happened when the door of the time machine opened? (Call on a student. Idea: *A lion started to come inside.*)
1. I'll name some events. You tell me if each event happened in the part you read to yourself.
1. Tom heard something roaring outside the door. Everybody, did that happen? (Signal.) *No.*
1. Tom felt a great force against his face when the dials started to click and buzz. Did that happen? (Signal.) *Yes.*
1. Tom moved in the seat and the handle moved. Did that happen? (Signal.) *Yes.*

READING CHECKOUTS

a. Today is a reading-checkout day. While you're doing your independent work, I'm going to call on you one at a time to read part of the story from lesson 134. When I call you to come and do your checkout, bring your thermometer chart.
   • Remember, you pass the checkout by reading the passage in less than a minute without making more than 2 mistakes. And when you pass the checkout, you'll color the space for lesson 135 on your thermometer chart.
b. (Call on individual students to read the portion of story 134 marked with ⊙.)
   • (Time the student. Note words that are missed and number of words read.)
   • (Teacher reference:)

> ⊙ Suddenly, many people came into the room. They were carrying all kinds of food. Tom looked at all of the food in front of him. He saw a large bowl. It had milk in it. Tom said, "I'll bet it's goat milk."
>
> Eric tasted it. He made a face. "It's [50] warm," he said. "Why don't they have <u>cold</u> milk?"
>
> Tom said, "Their milk isn't cold because they don't have any way to keep it cold. [75] Nobody had refrigerators until after the year 1800."
>
> Tom and Eric ate and ate. Then the old man took Tom and Eric to their room. ⊙ [100]

   • (If the student reads the passage in one minute or less and makes no more than 2 errors, direct the student to color in the space for lesson 135 on the thermometer chart.)
   • (If the student makes any mistakes, point to each word that was misread and identify it.)
   • (If the student does not meet the rate-error criterion for the passage, direct the student to practice reading the story with the assigned partner.)

End-of-Lesson Activities

INDEPENDENT WORK

Now finish your independent work for lesson 135. Raise your hand when you're finished. (Observe students and give feedback.)

WORKCHECK

a. (Direct students to take out their marking pencils.)
 • We're going to check your independent work. Remember, if you got an item wrong, make an **X** next to the item.
b. (For each item: Read the item. Call on a student to answer it. If the answer is wrong, say the correct answer. Refer to the Answer Key for the correct answers.)

c. Now use your pencil to fix up any items you got wrong. Remember, all mistakes must be fixed up before you hand in your work.

WRITING-SPELLING

(Present Writing-Spelling lesson 135 after completing Reading lesson 135. See Writing-Spelling Guide.)

LANGUAGE ARTS GUIDE

(Present Language Arts lesson 135 after completing Reading lesson 135. See Language Arts Guide.)

Lessons 136–140 • Planning Page

	Lesson 136	Lesson 137	Lesson 138	Lesson 139	Lesson 140
Lesson Events	Vocabulary Review Reading Words Comprehension Passage Story Reading Paired Practice Independent Work Workcheck Writing-Spelling	Vocabulary Review Reading Words Comprehension Passage Story Reading Paired Practice Independent Work Workcheck Writing-Spelling	**Vocabulary Sentence** Reading Words Vocabulary Review Comprehension Passage Story Reading Paired Practice Independent Work Workcheck Writing-Spelling	Vocabulary Review Reading Words Comprehension Passages Story Reading Globe Review Paired Practice Independent Work Workcheck Writing-Spelling	Fact Game Reading Checkouts Test Marking the Test Test Remedies Literature Lesson
Vocabulary Sentence	#29: She paid the <u>correct</u> <u>amount</u>.	#30: <u>Perhaps</u> they will <u>reply</u> in a few days.	#33: The army was <u>soundly</u> <u>defeated</u> near the <u>village</u>.	#33: The army was <u>soundly</u> <u>defeated</u> near the <u>village</u>.	
Reading Words: Word Types	2-syllable words mixed words	modeled words –ing words words with endings mixed words	proper nouns mixed words multi-syllable words	multi-syllable words mixed words	
New Vocabulary	tame	English discover trumpeting tusks charged modern Spain	America Mexico Canada Viking Columbus		
Comprehension Passages	*A Queen Named Helen*	*Forty Thousand Years Ago*	*More About Time*	1) *More About Time* 2) *North America*	
Story	*Eric and Tom in Greece*	*Eric and Tom See Cave People*	*Eric and Tom in the City of the Future*	*Spain in 1492*	
Skill Items	Vocabulary Compare		Vocabulary		Test: Vocabulary Sentences #31, 32
Special Materials				Globe	Thermometer charts, dice, Fact Game 140, Fact Game Answer Key, scorecard sheets, *materials for literature project
Special Projects/ Activities					

* Literature anthology; blackline master 14A; lined paper, round plastic laundry basket; sheet or other fabric; materials for making badger head and tail (e.g. paper-mache for head, heavy rope for tail); materials for creating scenes

EXERCISE 1

VOCABULARY REVIEW

a. You learned a sentence that tells how much she paid.
- Everybody, say that sentence. Get ready. (Signal.) *She paid the correct amount.*
- (Repeat until firm.)

b. I'll say part of the sentence. When I stop, you say the next word. Listen: She paid the correct . . . Everybody, what's the next word? (Signal.) *Amount.*

c. Listen: She paid the . . . Everybody, what's the next word? (Signal.) *Correct.*
- Say the whole sentence. Get ready. (Signal.) *She paid the correct amount.*

EXERCISE 2

READING WORDS

Column 1

a. **Find lesson 136 in your textbook.** ✓
- Touch column 1. ✓
- (Teacher reference:)

1. **replied**	4. **language**
2. **argue**	5. **army**
3. **doorway**	

- All these words have more than one syllable. The first syllable of each word is underlined.

b. Word 1. What's the first syllable? (Signal.) *re.*
- What's the whole word? (Signal.) *Replied.*

c. Word 2. What's the first syllable? (Signal.) *ar.*
- What's the whole word? (Signal.) *Argue.*

d. Word 3. What's the first syllable? (Signal.) *door.*
- What's the whole word? (Signal.) *Doorway.*

e. Word 4. What's the first syllable? (Signal.) *lang.*
- What's the whole word? (Signal.) *Language.*

f. Word 5. What's the first syllable? (Signal.) *ar.*
- What's the whole word? (Signal.) *Army.*

g. Let's read those words again, the fast way.
- Word 1. What word? (Signal.) *Replied.*
- (Repeat for words 2–5.)

h. (Repeat step g until firm.)

Column 2

i. Find column 2. ✓
- (Teacher reference:)

1. **tame**	4. **spike**
2. **war**	5. **tusk**
3. **deal**	

j. Word 1. What word? (Signal.) *Tame.*
- **Tame** is the opposite of **wild.** Lions are wild; house cats are tame. Name some other animals that are tame. (Call on a student. Ideas: *Dogs, horses, chickens.*)

k. Word 2. What word? (Signal.) *War.*

l. Word 3. What word? (Signal.) *Deal.*
- (Repeat for words 4 and 5.)

m. Let's read those words again.
- Word 1. What word? (Signal.) *Tame.*
- (Repeat for words 2–5.)

n. (Repeat step m until firm.)

Column 3

o. Find column 3. ✓
- (Teacher reference:)

1. **gift**	3. **ancient**
2. **stared**	4. **trumpet**

p. Word 1. What word? (Signal.) *Gift.*
- (Repeat for words 2–4.)

q. Let's read those words again.
- Word 1. What word? (Signal.) *Gift.*
- (Repeat for words 2–4.)

r. (Repeat step q until firm.)

Individual Turns
(For columns 1–3: Call on individual students, each to read one to three words per turn.)

COMPREHENSION PASSAGE

a. Find part B in your textbook. ✓
- You're going to read the next story about Eric and Tom. First you'll read the information passage. It gives some facts about a war thousands of years ago.

b. Everybody, touch the title. ✓
- (Call on a student to read the title.) *[A Queen Named Helen.]*
- Everybody, what's the title? (Signal.) *A Queen Named Helen.*

c. (Call on individual students to read the passage, each student reading two or three sentences at a time.)

A Queen Named Helen

In today's story, you'll read more about the country of Greece three thousand years ago. At that time, part of Greece was at war with Troy. The war began because a Greek queen named Helen ran away with a man from Troy.

- Everybody, where was the queen from? (Signal.) *Greece.*
- What was her name? (Signal.) *Helen.*
- Where was the man from? (Signal.) *Troy.*
- How long ago did the war take place? (Signal.) *3,000 years ago.*

One thousand ships left Greece to go to war against Troy. The war lasted for ten years, but the Greek army could not get inside the walls around Troy.

- Everybody, how many ships went to war against Troy? (Signal.) *1,000.*
- How long did the war last? (Signal.) *Ten years.*
- What couldn't the Greek army do? (Call on a student. Idea: *Get inside the walls of Troy.*)

The war ended when the soldiers from Greece tricked the army from Troy. The Greek soldiers built a large horse and pretended to leave it as a gift. Then the army pretended to leave. The soldiers from Troy took the great horse inside the walls of the city. Greek soldiers were hiding inside the horse. That night, they came out, opened the gates, and let the army from Greece inside the city.

- Everybody, which side won the war, Greece or Troy? (Signal.) *Greece.*
- What did the Greek army build? (Signal.) *A horse.*
- What was inside the horse? (Signal.) *Soldiers.*
- What did the soldiers inside the horse do that night? (Call on a student. Ideas: *Let the rest of the army into the city; opened the gates.*)

STORY READING

a. Find part C in your textbook. ✓
- The error limit for group reading is 12. Read carefully.

b. Everybody, touch the title. ✓
- (Call on a student to read the title.) *[Eric and Tom in Greece.]*
- Everybody, what's the title? (Signal.) *Eric and Tom in Greece.*
- What country are Eric and Tom going to? (Signal.) *Greece.*

c. (Call on individual students to read the story, each student reading two or three sentences at a time. Ask questions marked **1.**)

- (Correct errors: Tell the word. Direct the student to reread the sentence.)
- (If the group makes more than 12 errors, direct the students to reread the story.)

d. (After the group has read the selection making no more than 12 errors, read the story to the students and ask questions marked **2.**)

Eric and Tom in Greece

A lion was in the doorway of the time machine. The lion was walking toward Tom. Tom could see the muscles in the lion's legs as it walked.

1. Everybody, get a picture of how Tom must feel. The door opens and a lion walks in. A lion is so strong that it can kill a horse with no trouble at all.

Suddenly, a man came through the doorway of the time machine. He was wearing a long white robe. He stared at the lights and dials. The man put his hand on the lion's back. The lion looked up at the man.

1. Everybody, does that lion seem wild? (Signal.) *No.*

"That lion is tame," Eric said.
The man said something to Tom and Eric, but they could not understand the man's language. The man pointed toward the door of the time machine and then walked out of the time machine. Tom and Eric followed him.
The time machine was in a place that looked like a park. There were trees and grass. A few young men were standing and talking. Tom said, "I think we are in a school of long, long ago. I think we are in ancient Greece."
Eric said, "I thought we went forward in time."
Tom said, "Maybe we did, but not far enough."

2. Why did Eric think they went forward in time? (Call on a student. Idea: *Because the handle moved up.*)

The man in the robe said something and then pointed to a large table covered with food.
"He wants us to eat," Tom said.
"Good deal," Eric said. "I'm really hungry. I don't even care if they give us warm milk."

2. Where did they have warm milk before? (Call on a student. Idea: *In Egypt.*)

After Tom and Eric ate, they watched the young men and their teacher. The teacher sat on a stone bench. The young men sat on the ground around him. The teacher asked questions. The young men would try to answer the questions. The teacher asked more questions.

2. Everybody, touch the teacher in the picture. ✓
2. What is the teacher wearing? (Call on a student. Ideas: *A long robe; sandals; a crown of leaves.*)
2. What is the teacher holding? (Call on a student. Ideas: *A scroll; paper.*)
2. Why do you think the teacher keeps asking questions? (Call on a student. Idea: *He is teaching them.*)
2. Tom doesn't know the language the teacher speaks, but Tom knows that the teacher is asking questions. How could he tell each time the teacher asks a question? (Call on a student. Ideas: *His voice changes; the young men answer.*)

Tom said, "I think they're learning how to argue. They argue so they can learn to think clearly. The teacher wants to show them that they don't know as much as they think they know."
"Why is he doing that?" Eric asked.
Tom replied, "So they will think about things."

2. What do you do when you argue with someone? (Call on a student. Idea: *You disagree.*)

2. Why are they learning how to argue?
(Call on a student. Idea: *So they will think about things.*)

Just then a man on a horse rode to the top of a hill near the school. Then he called to the teacher. The teacher walked up the hill. Tom and Eric followed. Tom could see the ocean from the top of the hill. The man on the horse pointed to hundreds of ships on the ocean.

Tom and Eric looked at the ships. Eric said, "I have never seen so many ships in one place before. Where do you think they're going?"

Tom said, "I think we're in Greece three thousand years ago. A queen of one city in Greece ran away with somebody from Troy. So part of Greece went to war and sent a thousand ships into battle." Tom pointed to the ships below. "I think those are the ships that are going to Troy."

Some ships were loaded with soldiers and horses. Others carried large machines for throwing rocks through the air. Tom said, "Thousands of men will die in the battle with Troy. And that battle will go on for many years."

2. Everybody, what was the name of the queen? (Signal.) *Helen.*
2. How many years will the battle with Troy last? (Signal.) *Ten years.*
2. Who will win that battle? (Signal.) *Greece.*
2. How will they win it? (Call on a student. Idea: *With the big wooden horse.*)

In the distance, Tom and Eric could hear the sounds of soldiers singing. Tom and Eric watched for a few minutes. The teacher standing next to them shook his head. He looked very sad.

2. Why? (Call on a student. Ideas: *He doesn't like war; he knows many people will die in the war.*)

"I think we'd better get out of here," Tom said. "I want to get back home."

Tom and Eric started to walk back to the time machine. The teacher and the young men were still on the hill.

1. Go back to the beginning of the story. Follow along while I read.
2. Read the rest of the story to yourself. Find out what happened to the handle in the time machine. Raise your hand when you're finished.

Tom and Eric went inside the time machine. Tom sat down in the seat. The door closed. Then Tom said, "I wish I knew how to make this time machine work right."

Eric said, "Let <u>me</u> try. You didn't do very well the last time <u>you</u> tried."

Eric reached for the handle. Tom tried to push Eric's hand away, but Eric had a good grip on the handle. Suddenly, the handle moved down— almost all the way down. Before Tom could pull the handle back up, he felt the force against his face and ears.

"Oh, no!" Eric yelled. Then everything seemed to go dark.
MORE NEXT TIME

2. (After all students have raised their hand:) What happened to the handle in the time machine? (Call on a student. Idea: *It went almost all the way down.*)
2. Everybody, if the handle went down almost all the way, did they go **forward** in time or **backward**? (Signal.) *Backward.*
2. They're already three thousand years back in time. How far back in time do you think they are going this time? (Call on a student. Accept a response that is much more than three thousand years.)

PAIRED PRACTICE

You're going to read aloud to your partner. Today the **B** members will read first. Then the **A** members will read from the star to the end of the story.

(Observe students and give feedback.)

End-of-Lesson Activities

INDEPENDENT WORK

Now finish your independent work for lesson 136. Raise your hand when you're finished. (Observe students and give feedback.)

WORKCHECK

a. (Direct students to take out their marking pencils.)
- We're going to check your independent work. Remember, if you got an item wrong, make an **X** next to the item.
b. (For each item: Read the item. Call on a student to answer it. If the answer is wrong, say the correct answer. Refer to the Answer Key for the correct answers.)

c. Now use your pencil to fix up any items you got wrong. Remember, all mistakes must be fixed up before you hand in your work.

WRITING-SPELLING

(Present Writing-Spelling lesson 136 after completing Reading lesson 136. See Writing-Spelling Guide.)

LANGUAGE ARTS GUIDE

(Present Language Arts lesson 136 after completing Reading lesson 136. See Language Arts Guide.)

Lesson 137

EXERCISE 1

VOCABULARY REVIEW

a. You learned a sentence that tells when they might reply.

- Everybody, say that sentence. Get ready. (Signal.) *Perhaps they will reply in a few days.*
- (Repeat until firm.)

b. Everybody, what is the **first** word of the sentence? (Signal.) *Perhaps.*

c. I'll say part of the sentence. When I stop, you say the next word. Listen: Perhaps they will . . . Everybody, what's the next word? (Signal.) *Reply.*

- Say the whole sentence. Get ready. (Signal.) *Perhaps they will reply in a few days.*

EXERCISE 2

READING WORDS

Column 1

a. **Find lesson 137 in your textbook.** ✓
- Touch column 1. ✓
- (Teacher reference:)

1. **English**	4. **brought**
2. **discover**	5. **village**
3. **future**	6. **defeat**

b. Word 1 is **English.** What word? (Signal.) *English.*
- Spell **English.** Get ready. (Tap for each letter.) *E-N-G-L-I-S-H.*
- English is the name of the language that people speak in the United States. Everybody, what's the name of the language spoken in the United States? (Signal.) *English.*

c. Word 2 is **discover.** What word? (Signal.) *Discover.*
- Spell **discover.** Get ready. (Tap for each letter.) *D-I-S-C-O-V-E-R.*
- The person who is the first to find something is the person who discovers that thing. The person who first found America was the person who discovered America. What's another way to describe the person who first found gold in Alaska? (Call on a student.) *[The person who discovered gold in Alaska.]*

d. Word 3 is **future.** What word? (Signal.) *Future.*
- Spell **future.** Get ready. (Tap for each letter.) *F-U-T-U-R-E.*

e. Word 4 is **brought.** What word? (Signal.) *Brought.*
- Spell **brought.** Get ready. (Tap for each letter.) *B-R-O-U-G-H-T.*

f. Word 5 is **village.** What word? (Signal.) *Village.*

g. Word 6 is **defeat.** What word? (Signal.) *Defeat.*

h. Let's read those words again, the fast way.
- Word 1. What word? (Signal.) *English.*
- (Repeat for words 2–6.)

i. (Repeat step h until firm.)

Column 2

j. Find column 2. ✓
- (Teacher reference:)

1. **trumpeting**	4. **closing**
2. **snorting**	5. **crunching**
3. **breathing**	

- All these words end with the letters **I-N-G.**

k. Word 1. What word? (Signal.) *Trumpeting.*
- A trumpeting sound is something that sounds like it comes from a musical instrument called a trumpet. Elephants make a trumpeting sound.

l. Word 2. What word? (Signal.) *Snorting.*
- (Repeat for words 3–5.)

m. Let's read those words again.
- Word 1. What word? (Signal.) *Trumpeting.*
- (Repeat for words 2–5.)

n. (Repeat step m until firm.)

Column 3

o. Find column 3. ✓
- (Teacher reference:)

1. **tusks**	3. **ponies**
2. **charged**	4. **blinked**

- All these words have an ending.
- p. Word 1. What word? (Signal.) *Tusks.*
- q. Word 2. What word? (Signal.) *Charged.*
  - When an animal charges, it puts its head down and runs at something as fast as it can go. Everybody, what do we call it when an animal runs at something as fast as it can? (Signal.) *Charging.*
- r. Word 3. What word? (Signal.) *Ponies.*
- s. Word 4. What word? (Signal.) *Blinked.*
- t. Let's read those words again.
  - Word 1. What word? (Signal.) *Tusks.*
  - (Repeat for: **2. charged, 3. ponies, 4. blinked.**)
- u. (Repeat step t until firm.)

Column 4

- v. Find column 4. ✓
  - (Teacher reference:)

1. **curved**	4. **modern**
2. **tigers**	5. **Spain**
3. **spikes**	

- w. Word 1. What word? (Signal.) *Curved.*
  - Word 2. What word? (Signal.) *Tigers.*
  - Word 3. What word? (Signal.) *Spikes.*
- x. Word 4. What word? (Signal.) *Modern.*
  - **Modern** is the opposite of **old-fashioned.** What's the opposite of old-fashioned clothes? (Signal.) *Modern clothes.*
  - What's the opposite of an old-fashioned movie? (Signal.) *Modern movie.*
- y. Word 5. What word? (Signal.) *Spain.*
  - Spain is a country that is near Italy. Look at the map on page 281 of your textbook. ✓

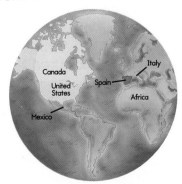

  - Touch Spain. It's just west of Italy. ✓
- z. Turn back to page 258 in your textbook. ✓
- a. Let's read the words in column 4 again.
  - Word 1. What word? (Signal.) *Curved.*
  - (Repeat for words 2–5.)
- b. (Repeat step a until firm.)

Individual Turns

(For columns 1–4: Call on individual students, each to read one to three words per turn.)

EXERCISE 3

COMPREHENSION PASSAGE

- a. Find part B in your textbook. ✓
  - You're going to read the next story about Eric and Tom. First you'll read the information passage. It gives some facts about what it was like forty thousand years ago.
- b. Everybody, touch the title. ✓
  - (Call on a student to read the title.) *[Forty Thousand Years Ago.]*
  - Everybody, what's the title? (Signal.) *Forty Thousand Years Ago.*
- c. (Call on individual students to read the passage, each student reading two or three sentences at a time.)

Forty Thousand Years Ago

Things looked very different forty thousand years ago. There were no buildings or streets. The humans who lived then were a little different from the humans who live today. Some of them wore animal skins and lived in caves.

- Touch the human in the picture. ✓
- That person was shorter than people who live today, but that person was very strong.

Many kinds of animals that you see today were around forty thousand years ago, but some of the animals from that time were different. The picture shows a saber-toothed tiger, a horse, a human, and a kind of elephant called a mammoth.

The saber-toothed tiger had a short tail and teeth like spikes.

- Touch the tiger's teeth. ✓

- Those teeth are longer than the teeth of tigers that live today.
- Touch the tiger's tail. ✓
- That tail is shorter than tiger tails of today.

> **The horse was much smaller than most horses of today.**
> **The mammoth had long hair and long, curved tusks.**

- Elephants that live today have tusks, but not huge ones like the mammoth had. Also, the elephants that live today don't have long hair.

EXERCISE 4

STORY READING

a. Find part C in your textbook. ✓
- The error limit for group reading is 10. Read carefully.

b. Everybody, touch the title. ✓
- (Call on a student to read the title.) *[Eric and Tom See Cave People.]*
- Everybody, what's the title? (Signal.) *Eric and Tom See Cave People.*

c. (Call on individual students to read the story, each student reading two or three sentences at a time. Ask questions marked **1**.)

- (Correct errors: Tell the word. Direct the student to reread the sentence.)
- (If the group makes more than 10 errors, direct the students to reread the story.)

d. (After the group has read the selection making no more than 10 errors, read the story to the students and ask questions marked **2**.)

> **Eric and Tom See Cave People**
>
> **The force was so great that Tom's ears began ringing. He had trouble breathing. He couldn't talk.**

2. Why was the force so much greater this time than it had been before? (Call on a student. Ideas: *Because they were going so far back in time; because the handle moved almost all the way down.*)

Then things inside the time machine looked brighter again. The dials and lights blinked and flashed.

"I hate to look outside," Eric said. His voice sounded funny.

Tom rubbed his eyes. "That handle went down almost all the way," Tom said.

Eric stood up and the door opened. The air was cool, and the trees outside looked a little different from any Tom had ever seen.

Eric and Tom stood outside the time machine for a few minutes. They looked in all directions, but they couldn't see any people. At first they didn't see any animals either. But then they heard a terrible roar.

A moment later, three very small horses charged down a hill. They were no bigger than ponies, but they looked different.

The horses ran through the long grass. Another animal was running behind them. It was very fast, but not as tall as the horses. Tom could see it leaping through the tall grass, but he couldn't get a good look at it. Suddenly, the horses turned and ran downhill. The animal that had been chasing them stopped and stood on top of a mound. Now Tom and Eric could see the animal clearly.

Eric said, "Do you see what I see?"

Tom didn't take his eyes from the animal. "Yes," he said.

The animal had a short tail, and two long teeth that stuck down like spikes. Tom said, "I think we've gone back about forty thousand years from our time. I think we're looking at a saber-toothed tiger."

1. Everybody, how far back in time are they now? (Signal.) *40,000 years.*

1. What's the name of the animal that's standing on the mound? (Signal.) *Saber-toothed tiger.*
1. It has two teeth that stick down like spikes. Everybody, touch them. ✓
1. What kind of tail does it have? (Call on a student. Idea: *Short.*)

> Tom said, "Those other animals were horses that lived forty thousand years ago."
> Just as Eric started to say something, a loud snorting noise came from the other side of the time machine.

2. Make a loud, snorting noise. (Call on a student.)

> The boys turned around. The animal making the noise was a giant mammoth—an elephant with long fur and great tusks.

1. Everybody, what's the name of the animal making the snorting noise? (Signal.) *A mammoth.*

> It held its trunk high in the air. Its eyes were bright and it didn't look friendly. "Let's get out of here," Tom said. The boys ducked inside the time machine. Tom ran to the seat and sat down, but just as the door was closing, the mammoth charged into it. It made a terrible crunching sound. And the door wouldn't close.

2. What made the crunching sound? (Call on a student. Idea: *The mammoth charging into the time machine door.*)
2. Why do you think the door wouldn't close? (Call on a student. Idea: *The mammoth bent the door.*)

> The door was open about a foot.

2. Everybody, show me how far the door was open. ✓

> The mammoth stuck its trunk through the open door and let out a great trumpeting sound.

2. Make that sound. (Call on a student.)

> The mammoth suddenly backed up and began to run. Some humans were running down the hill. The humans were dressed in animal skins. They were shouting as they ran.

2. Everybody, what was coming down the hill? (Signal.) *Humans.*

> The mammoth ran downhill. "Let's get out of here," Tom said.
> The humans were coming closer to the time machine. They were about fifty yards away. They were shouting and growling. Tom had picked up a long branch. He was trying to bend the door so that it would close.

1. Go back to the beginning of the story. Follow along while I read.
2. Why was the door bent? (Call on a student. Idea: *The mammoth had hit it.*)
2. Read the rest of the story to yourself. Find out if they closed the door. Raise your hand when you're finished.

> Two men were running toward the door. "Push on the door," Tom yelled. He was trying to bend the bottom of the door with the branch.
> The men were only a few yards from the door now. Tom could smell them. "Push," Tom said. "Push."
> "Blump." One of the men had thrown a rock and hit the side of the time machine. "Blump, blump, blump." More rocks.
> One of the men grabbed the door. Tom could see his face and his teeth.
> **MORE NEXT TIME**

2. (After all students have raised their hand:) Everybody, did the boys close the door? (Signal.) *No.*
2. How did they try to close it? (Call on a student. Idea: *By pushing on it and bending the bottom of it with a branch.*)
2. Everybody, what did the men throw at the time machine? (Signal.) *Rocks.*

2. Let me read the last part of the story to you. Close your eyes and get a picture of what's happening.

The mammoth suddenly backed up and began to run. Some humans were running down the hill. The humans were dressed in animal skins. They were shouting as they ran.

The mammoth ran downhill. "Let's get out of here," Tom said.

The humans were coming closer to the time machine. They were about fifty yards away. They were shouting and growling. Tom had picked up a long branch. He was trying to bend the door so that it would close.

Two men were running toward the door. "Push on the door," Tom yelled. He was trying to bend the bottom of the door with the branch.

The men were only a few yards from the door now. Tom could smell them. "Push," Tom said. "Push."

"Blump." One of the men had thrown a rock and hit the side of the time machine. "Blump, blump, blump." More rocks.

One of the men grabbed the door. Tom could see his face and his teeth.

EXERCISE 5
PAIRED PRACTICE

You're going to read aloud to your partner. Today the **A** members will read first. Then the **B** members will read from the star to the end of the story.
(Observe students and give feedback.)

INDEPENDENT WORK

Now finish your independent work for lesson 137. Raise your hand when you're finished.
(Observe students and give feedback.)

WORKCHECK

a. (Direct students to take out their marking pencils.)
  • We're going to check your independent work. Remember, if you got an item wrong, make an **X** next to the item.
b. (For each item: Read the item. Call on a student to answer it. If the answer is wrong, say the correct answer. Refer to the Answer Key for the correct answers.)
c. Now use your pencil to fix up any items you got wrong. Remember, all mistakes must be fixed up before you hand in your work.

WRITING-SPELLING

(Present Writing-Spelling lesson 137 after completing Reading lesson 137. See Writing-Spelling Guide.)

LANGUAGE ARTS GUIDE

(Present Language Arts lesson 137 after completing Reading lesson 137. See Language Arts Guide.)

EXERCISE 1

VOCABULARY

a. **Find page 342 at the back of your textbook.** ✓
- Touch sentence 33. ✓
- This is a new vocabulary sentence. It says: The army was soundly defeated near the village. Everybody, read that sentence. Get ready. (Signal.) *The army was soundly defeated near the village.*
- Close your eyes and say the sentence. Get ready. (Signal.) *The army was soundly defeated near the village.*
- (Repeat until firm.)

b. The sentence says that the army was **defeated. Defeated** is another word for **beaten.** What's **a beaten army?** (Signal.) *A defeated army.*
- What's **a beaten fighter?** (Signal.) *A defeated fighter.*

c. The sentence says that the army was **soundly** defeated. That means the army was **completely** beaten. Everybody, what's another way of saying **completely beaten?** (Signal.) *Soundly defeated.*

d. The army was soundly defeated near the **village. A village** is a **small town.** What's another way of saying **She lived in a small town?** (Signal.) *She lived in a village.*

e. Listen: The army was soundly defeated near the village. Everybody, say the sentence. Get ready. (Signal.) *The army was soundly defeated near the village.*

f. What word means **small town?** (Signal.) *Village.*
- What word means **beaten?** (Signal.) *Defeated.*
- What word means **completely** or **really?** (Signal.) *Soundly.*
- (Repeat step f until firm.)

EXERCISE 2

READING WORDS

Column 1

a. Find lesson 138 in your textbook. ✓
- Touch column 1. ✓

- (Teacher reference:)

1. America	4. Viking
2. Mexico	5. Columbus
3. Canada	

- All these words begin with a capital letter.
b. Word 1 is **America.** What word? (Signal.) *America.*
- Spell **America.** Get ready. (Tap for each letter.) *A-M-E-R-I-C-A.*
- America is a large part of the world. America has many countries in it.
c. Word 2 is **Mexico.** What word? (Signal.) *Mexico.*
- Spell **Mexico.** Get ready. (Tap for each letter.) *M-E-X-I-C-O.*
- Mexico is one of the countries of America.
d. Word 3 is **Canada.** What word? (Signal.) *Canada.*
- Spell **Canada.** Get ready. (Tap for each letter.) *C-A-N-A-D-A.*
- Canada is one of the countries of America.
e. Word 4 is **Viking.** What word? (Signal.) *Viking.*
- Spell **Viking.** Get ready. (Tap for each letter.) *V-I-K-I-N-G.*
- The Vikings were people who lived far north of Spain and Italy. The Vikings sailed all around the world and made war with many other countries. Everybody, what's the name of the warriors who lived far north of Spain and Italy? (Signal.) *Vikings.*
f. Word 5 is **Columbus.** What word? (Signal.) *Columbus.*
- The name of the man who sailed across the ocean and discovered America is Columbus. Everybody, who discovered America? (Signal.) *Columbus.*
g. Let's read those words again, the fast way.
- Word 1. What word? (Signal.) *America.*
- (Repeat for words 2–5.)
h. (Repeat step g until firm.)

Column 2

i. Find column 2. ✓
- (Teacher reference:)

1. modern   3. future

2. brought   4. languages

j. Word 1. What word? (Signal.) *Modern.*
 • (Repeat for words 2–4.)
k. (Repeat step j until firm.)

Column 3

l. Find column 3. ✓
 • (Teacher reference:)

1. defeated   3. discovered

2. village   4. English

m. Word 1. What word? (Signal.) *Defeated.*
 • (Repeat for words 2–4.)
n. (Repeat step m until firm.)

Individual Turns

(For columns 1–3: Call on individual students, each to read one to three words per turn.)

EXERCISE 3

VOCABULARY REVIEW

a. Here's the new vocabulary sentence: The army was soundly defeated near the village.
 • Everybody, say the sentence. Get ready. (Signal.) *The army was soundly defeated near the village.*
 • (Repeat until firm.)
b. What word means **beaten?** (Signal.) *Defeated.*
 • What word means **small town?** (Signal.) *Village.*
 • What word means **completely** or **really?** (Signal.) *Soundly.*

EXERCISE 4

COMPREHENSION PASSAGE

a. Find part B in your textbook. ✓
 • You're going to read the next story about Eric and Tom. First you'll read the information passage.
b. Everybody, touch the title. ✓
 • (Call on a student to read the title.) *[More About Time.]*
 • Everybody, what's the title? (Signal.) *More About Time.*
c. (Call on individual students to read the passage, each student reading two or three sentences at a time.)

More About Time

Look at the time line. Touch dot B.

• (Teacher reference:)

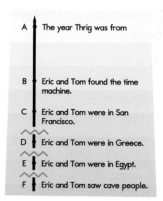

A	The year Thrig was from
B	Eric and Tom found the time machine.
C	Eric and Tom were in San Francisco.
D	Eric and Tom were in Greece.
E	Eric and Tom were in Egypt.
F	Eric and Tom saw cave people.

• Everybody, do it. ✓

That dot shows when Eric and Tom started their trip. What year was that?

• Everybody, what's the answer? (Signal. Accept current year.)

Touch dot A.

• Everybody, do it. ✓

That dot shows the year that Thrig was from. What year was that?

• Everybody, what's the answer? (Signal.) *2400.*

Touch dot C.

• Everybody, do it. ✓

That dot shows when Eric and Tom were in San Francisco. What year was that?

• Everybody, what's the answer? (Signal.) *1906.*

Touch dot D.

• Everybody, do it. ✓

That dot shows when Eric and Tom were in Greece. How long ago was that?

• Everybody, what's the answer? (Signal.) *3,000 years ago.*

Touch dot E.

- Everybody, do it. ✓

That dot shows when Eric and Tom were in Egypt. How long ago was that?

- Everybody, what's the answer? (Signal.) *5,000 years ago.*

Touch dot F.

- Everybody, do it. ✓

That dot shows when Eric and Tom saw the cave people. How long ago was that?

- Everybody, what's the answer? (Signal.) *40,000 years ago.*

EXERCISE 5

STORY READING

a. Find part C in your textbook. ✓
- The error limit for group reading is 11. Read carefully.
b. Everybody, touch the title. ✓
- (Call on a student to read the title.) *[Eric and Tom in the City of the Future.]*
- Everybody, what's the title? (Signal.) *Eric and Tom in the City of the Future.*
- Everybody, what year are we in now? (Signal. Accept current year.)
- Name a year that is in the future. (Call on individual students. Accept appropriate responses.)
- The title tells us that Tom and Eric go **into the future.** So they are going **ahead** of the year that we live in now.
c. (Call on individual students to read the story, each student reading two or three sentences at a time. Ask questions marked **1.**)

- (Correct errors: Tell the word. Direct the student to reread the sentence.)
- (If the group makes more than 11 errors, direct the students to reread the story.)

d. (After the group has read the selection making no more than 11 errors, read the story to the students and ask questions marked **2.**)

Eric and Tom in the City of the Future

"Push," Tom yelled.

1. Everybody, who's he yelling to? (Signal.) *Eric.*
1. What are they trying to do? (Call on a student. Idea: *Close the door.*)
1. Why are they trying to close the door? (Call on a student. Ideas: *So they can get out of there; to keep out the cave people.*)

Just then a large rock hit the door. And suddenly the door closed. The rock must have straightened the door so that it could close again.

2. What did that rock do? (Call on a student. Idea: *Straightened the door.*)

The door started to open again. "Quick," Tom said. "Sit in the chair so the door closes."
Eric ran to the seat and sat down. The door stayed closed now.
"Blump, blump." Rocks were hitting the side of the time machine.
"Push the handle up," Tom said. Eric bounced around in the seat and pushed on the handle. Rocks continued to hit the time machine.
Suddenly, the handle went up—far up. Tom almost fell down from the force. Then he almost passed out.

1. Everybody, which way did the handle go? (Signal.) *Up.*
1. So are they going to go **forward** or **backward** in time? (Signal.) *Forward.*
1. Is the force **very great** or **not so great?** (Signal.) *Very great.*
1. So what does that tell you about how far forward they are going in time? (Call on a student. Idea: *A long way.*)

After a few moments, the force died down. Eric stood up, and the door opened.
The time machine was next to a huge building—the tallest building that Tom had ever seen. There were buildings all around. Tom could not see the sun, only buildings. There were no streets and no cars—just buildings.
People were walking near the time machine. They wore funny clothes that seemed to shine.
Eric said, "We must have gone into the future."

2. What clues were there to make Eric think that they had gone into the future? (Call on individual students. Ideas: *The people wore funny clothes that seemed to shine; there were lots of huge buildings; no cars or streets.*)

A young man walked by the time machine. Tom said, "Can you help us?" The man looked at Tom and said, "Sellip." Then he walked away.

Sellip.

2. Everybody, did the man speak a language that Tom understands? (Signal.) *No.*
2. What did the man say? (Signal.) *Sellip.*
2. Look at the picture. Name some things in that picture that are different from the things that you see in the city today. (Call on individual students. Ideas: *The buildings look different; people's clothes look different; the people look different.*)

Tom and Eric stopped person after person. But every person said, "Sellip," and walked away. Finally, Tom stopped an old man. "Can you help us?" Tom asked.
The old man smiled. Very slowly he said, "I . . . will . . . try."
Tom and Eric grinned.

2. Why did they feel happy? (Call on a student. Ideas: *Someone could speak English; someone was going to help them.*)

Tom said, "Can you help us work our time machine?"
The old man made a face. Then he said, "Talk . . . slower."
Tom said, "Can . . . you . . . help . . . us . . . work . . . this . . . machine?"

The old man said, "No. We . . . have . . . machines . . . that . . . fix . . . machines. People . . . do . . . not . . . fix machines."

2. Everybody, what do they use to fix machines? (Signal.) *Machines.*

Tom said, "Can . . . you . . . get . . . a machine . . . to help . . . us . . . work . . . our . . . time machine?"
The old man said, "That . . . time machine . . . is too old. We do not have . . . machines . . . that work . . . on such . . . old . . . time machines."

2. Everybody, could the old man help them? (Signal.) *No.*
2. Why not? (Call on a student. Ideas: *Their time machine is too old; there are no machines to fix an old time machine.*)
2. Everybody, what year did Thrig come from? (Signal.) *2400.*
2. So what year was the time machine from? (Signal.) *2400.*
2. The man that Tom and Eric are talking to thinks that the time machine is very, very old. So were Tom and Eric farther in the future than 2400? (Call on a student.) *Yes.*

Tom felt sad. He and Eric would have to figure out how to work the machine by themselves.

2. Why would they have to figure it out by themselves? (Call on a student. Idea: *Because no one else could help them.*)

The old man made a face. He thought for a few moments. Then he said, "What . . . year . . . are you . . . from?" Eric told him.
The old man thought and thought. "We . . . are . . . four thousand years . . . after your . . . time."

2. Everybody, how far in the future are the boys now? (Signal.) *4,000 years.*

Eric said, "Why . . . do you speak . . . English? Nobody else . . . speaks . . . English."

> The old man said, "I study . . . old, old languages. You . . . are very . . . lucky . . . to find me. No . . . other . . . people in the city . . . know . . . your language."

2. Everybody, what language do Tom and Eric speak? (Signal.) *English.*
2. Why does the old man know their language? (Call on a student. Idea: *He studies old languages.*)
2. Everybody, how many other people in the city of the future know English? (Signal.) *None.*

> Eric asked, "What does . . . sellip . . . mean?"
>
> The old man said, "Sellip . . . means this: I am . . . very sorry . . . that I cannot . . . help you. I . . . do not understand . . . your words. Good day."
>
> Tom said, "Do you mean . . . that . . . one little . . . word . . . like sellip . . . means all that?"
>
> "Yes," the old man said. "People . . . who live . . . in this time . . . do not have . . . to think . . . very much. So . . . the language . . . that they use . . . is very . . . simple. They . . . let the machines . . . do all . . . of their . . . thinking . . . for them.

1. Go back to the beginning of the story. Follow along while I read.
2. Why do the people have a very simple language? (Call on a student. Idea: *They don't think much so they don't talk much.*)
2. Read the rest of the story to yourself. Find out what Tom saw when the door of the time machine opened. Raise your hand when you're finished.

> Eric and Tom got into the time machine. Tom sat down and the door closed. Tom pulled the handle about halfway down. The dials buzzed. Lights went on and off. The force pushed against Tom's ears. Then it died down.
>
> Tom stood up. The door opened. And outside the door, Tom could see water. On that water was a ship. But it wasn't a modern ship. It was an old-time sailing ship.
> **MORE NEXT TIME**

2. (After all students have raised their hand:) Everybody, did Tom move the handle **up** or **down?** (Signal.) *Down.*
2. How far down? (Call on a student. Idea: *Halfway down.*)
2. Everybody, if the handle went halfway down, did the boys go **forward** in time or **backward?** (Signal.) *Backward.*
2. What did Tom see when the door of the time machine opened? (Call on a student. Idea: *Water and a ship.*)
2. Everybody, was the ship they saw a **modern ship** or an **old-time ship?** (Signal.) *Old-time ship.*

EXERCISE 6

PAIRED PRACTICE

You're going to read aloud to your partner. Today the **B** members will read first. Then the **A** members will read from the star to the end of the story.
(Observe students and give feedback.)

INDEPENDENT WORK

Now finish your independent work for lesson 138. Raise your hand when you're finished.
(Observe students and give feedback.)

WORKCHECK

a. (Direct students to take out their marking pencils.)
• We're going to check your independent work. Remember, if you got an item wrong, make an **X** next to the item.
b. (For each item: Read the item. Call on a student to answer it. If the answer is wrong, say the correct answer. Refer to the Answer Key for the correct answers.)
c. Now use your pencil to fix up any items you got wrong. Remember, all mistakes must be fixed up before you hand in your work.

WRITING-SPELLING

(Present Writing-Spelling lesson 138 after completing Reading lesson 138. See Writing-Spelling Guide.)

LANGUAGE ARTS GUIDE

(Present Language Arts lesson 138 after completing Reading lesson 138. See Writing-Spelling Guide.)

Lesson 139

Material: You will need a globe for exercise 5.

EXERCISE 1
VOCABULARY REVIEW

a. Here's the new vocabulary sentence: The army was soundly defeated near the village.
 • Everybody, say the sentence. Get ready. (Signal.) *The army was soundly defeated near the village.*
 • (Repeat until firm.)

b. What word means **beaten?** (Signal.) *Defeated.*
 • What word means **completely** or **really?** (Signal.) *Soundly.*
 • What word means **small town?** (Signal.) *Village.*

EXERCISE 2
READING WORDS

Column 1

a. **Find lesson 139 in your textbook.** ✓
 • Touch column 1. ✓
 • (Teacher reference:)

1. Mexico	4. angry
2. discovered	5. countries
3. America	6. Vikings

b. Word 1. What word? (Signal.) *Mexico.*
 • (Repeat for words 2–6.)
c. Let's read those words again.
 • Word 1. What word? (Signal.) *Mexico.*
 • (Repeat for words 2–6.)
d. (Repeat step c until firm.)

Column 2

e. Find column 2. ✓
 • (Teacher reference:)

1. Columbus	4. crouch
2. brought	5. Spain
3. Canada	6. crouched

f. Word 1. What word? (Signal.) *Columbus.*
 • (Repeat for words 2–6.)

g. Let's read those words again.
 • Word 1. What word? (Signal.) *Columbus.*
 • (Repeat for words 2–6.)
h. (Repeat step g until firm.)

Individual Turns
(For columns 1 and 2: Call on individual students, each to read one to three words per turn.)

EXERCISE 3
COMPREHENSION PASSAGES

Passage B

a. Find part B in your textbook. ✓
 • You're going to read the next story about Eric and Tom. First you'll read two information passages.
b. Everybody, touch the title. ✓
 • (Call on a student to read the title.) *[More About Time.]*
 • Everybody, what's the title? (Signal.) *More About Time.*
c. (Call on individual students to read the passage, each student reading two or three sentences at a time.)

More About Time

• **Look at the time line. Touch dot C.**

• (Teacher reference:)

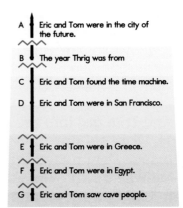

A	Eric and Tom were in the city of the future.
B	The year Thrig was from
C	Eric and Tom found the time machine.
D	Eric and Tom were in San Francisco.
E	Eric and Tom were in Greece.
F	Eric and Tom were in Egypt.
G	Eric and Tom saw cave people.

• Everybody, do it. ✓

That dot shows when Eric and Tom started their trip. What year was that?

- Everybody, what's the answer? (Signal. Accept current year.)

Touch dot A.

- Everybody, do it. ✓

That dot shows when Eric and Tom were in the city of the future. How far in the future was that?

- Everybody, what's the answer? (Signal.) *4,000 years in the future.*

Touch dot B.

- Everybody, do it. ✓

That dot shows the year that Thrig was from. What year was that?

- Everybody, what's the answer? (Signal.) *2400.*

Touch dot D.

- Everybody, do it. ✓

That dot shows when Eric and Tom were in San Francisco. What year was that?

- Everybody, what's the answer? (Signal.) *1906.*

Touch dot E.

- Everybody, do it. ✓

That dot shows when Eric and Tom were in Greece. How long ago was that?

- Everybody, what's the answer? (Signal.) *3,000 years ago.*

Touch dot F.

- Everybody, do it. ✓

That dot shows when Eric and Tom were in Egypt. How long ago was that?

- Everybody, what's the answer? (Signal.) *5,000 years ago.*

Touch dot G.

- Everybody, do it. ✓

That dot shows when Eric and Tom saw the cave people. How long ago was that?

- Everybody, what's the answer? (Signal.) *40,000 years ago.*

Passage C

d. Find part C in your textbook. ✓
e. Everybody, touch the title. ✓
- (Call on a student to read the title.) *[North America.]*
- Everybody, what's the title? (Signal.) *North America.*
f. (Call on individual students to read the passage, each student reading two or three sentences at a time.)

North America

In today's story, you will read about North America. Here are some countries that are in North America: Canada, the United States, and Mexico.

See if you can name those three countries that are in North America.

- Name those countries. (Call on a student.) *[Canada, the United States, and Mexico.]*

Touch each country on the map.

- Everybody, touch Canada. ✓
- Touch the United States. ✓
- Touch Mexico. ✓
- There are also smaller countries in North America.

Remember, the United States is part of North America. But North America is bigger than the United States.

- Everybody, which is bigger, the United States or North America? (Signal.) *North America.*
- The United States is one country in North America. Name two other countries that are in North America. (Signal.) *Canada, Mexico.*

EXERCISE 4

STORY READING

a. Find part D in your textbook. ✓
- The error limit for group reading is 9. Read carefully.

b. Everybody, touch the title. ✓
- (Call on a student to read the title.) *[Spain in 1492.]*
- Everybody, what's the title? (Signal.) *Spain in 1492.*
- The title tells the year Eric and Tom went to next. Everybody, what year? (Signal.) *1492.*
- In what time were they before going to 1492? (Call on a student. Idea: *4,000 years in the future.*)

c. (Call on individual students to read the story, each student reading two or three sentences at a time. Ask questions marked **1.**)

- (Correct errors: Tell the word. Direct the student to reread the sentence.)
- (If the group makes more than 9 errors, direct the students to reread the story.)

d. (After the group has read the selection making no more than 9 errors, read the story to the students and ask questions marked **2.**)

Spain in 1492

Tom and Eric were near an ocean. In the distance they could see an old-time sailing ship.

1. For Tom and Eric, the sailing ship was old-time. But it wasn't old-time for the people in 1492. It was modern for them.

There was a shack near the shore. Tom and Eric started down the hill toward the shack. A fat man standing next to the shack was wearing funny pants and a long cape.

2. Everybody, touch the shack in the picture. ✓
2. Look at the man. Those were the kind of clothes men wore in 1492.
2. Everybody, touch the sailing ship. ✓

The man called out to Tom, but Tom couldn't understand what he said.

1. Why not? (Call on a student. Idea: *He was speaking another language.*)

Tom called, "Do you speak English?"
The man replied, "Yes."
Tom walked down to the shack. Eric followed him. Tom said, "What year is it?"
The man said, "1492."
Eric said, "Wasn't that the year that Columbus discovered America?"
"Yes," Tom said. "Columbus discovered America in 1492."

2. That's an important fact. I'll read that fact again: Columbus discovered America in 1492.
- Everybody, say that fact. Get ready. (Signal.) *Columbus discovered America in 1492.*
- (Repeat until firm.)
2. Name 3 countries that are in North America. (Call on a student.) *[Canada, the United States, Mexico.]*
2. Everybody, who discovered America? (Signal.) *Columbus.*
2. When did Columbus discover America? (Signal.) *1492.*
2. Remember the fact about Columbus. Columbus discovered America in 1492. Everybody, say that fact one more time. Get ready. (Signal.) *Columbus discovered America in 1492.*

The man became angry. "Did you say Columbus?" The man pointed to the ship at the dock. "That ship belongs to Columbus. Columbus is a crazy person."

1. Everybody, does the fat man think that Columbus is a great person? (Signal.) *No.*
- I wonder why.

The man went into his shack. Tom and Eric followed. On the walls were many maps, but they did not look like any maps that Tom and Eric had ever seen.

The man touched a spot on the largest map. "We are here in Spain. Columbus plans to sail his ships off the end of the world. He says that the world is round, but it is flat. If the world was round, we would roll off."

2. Everybody, what country are Eric and Tom in now? (Signal.) *Spain.*
2. Is the world really **round** or **flat?** (Signal.) *Round.*
2. What does the fat man think will happen to Columbus if he tries to sail from Spain to America? (Call on a student. Idea: *He'll fall off the edge of the world.*)

Eric said, "Everybody knows that the world is round."

The man shouted, "You lie. I am going to call the soldiers."

2. Everybody, does the man want to listen to Eric? (Signal.) *No.*

Tom took out the tape recorder. Then he said to the man, "Say something. Say anything at all."

The man said, "I will take you to the soldiers."

Tom played back what the man had said. "I will take you to the soldiers."

The man looked around the room. "Who said that?" He looked at the recorder. "A voice without a man!"

Tom explained the tape recorder. Then Eric said, "That big thing on the hill is our time machine. It brought us here."

The man shook his head. Then he said, "You know things that I do not know. Why does the world look so flat if it is round?"

2. Everybody, is the man willing to listen to Tom and Eric now? (Signal.) *Yes.*
2. What made him change his mind? (Call on a student. Idea: *The tape recorder.*)
2. Listen to his question again: Why does the world look so flat if it is round?

Tom pointed to a ship that was far out on the ocean. "Look at that ship. All you can see is the top part of it."

The man looked at the ship. "You are right," he said. "I cannot see the bottom part of the ship."

Tom said, "You cannot see the bottom part of the ship because the earth is round. If the earth were flat, you would be able to see the whole ship. The earth looks flat because it is very, very big. You see just a small part of it."

1. Everybody, touch the ship in the picture. ✓
1. Can you see the bottom part of the ship? (Signal.) *No.*
1. How much of the ship would you be able to see if the world was flat? (Call on a student. Idea: *All of it.*)
1. You can't see all of it. So what do you know about the shape of the world? (Call on a student. Idea: *It's round.*)
1. Go back to the beginning of the story. Follow along while I read.
2. Did Tom give a good explanation? (Call on a student. Idea: *Yes.*)

2. Read the rest of the story to yourself. Find out why Eric and Tom had to hurry back to the time machine. Raise your hand when you're finished.

> **Then Eric said, "Tom, I just saw something go into our time machine."**
>
> **"What was it?" Tom asked.**
>
> **Eric replied, "It looked like a big white dog."**
>
> **The man hit his fist on the table. "I would like to kill that dog. He is mean. And he always comes around my shack. He bit one of my men the other day."**
>
> **Eric said, "What if that dog bumps against the handle? We'll never get home."**
>
> **Eric and Tom ran from the shack. They ran up the hill to the time machine. The fat man was right behind them.**
>
> **MORE NEXT TIME**

2. (After all students have raised their hand:) Why did Eric and Tom have to hurry back to the time machine? (Call on a student. Idea: *A dog went inside.*)

2. Everybody, did the fat man like the dog? (Signal.) *No.*

2. Why not? (Call on a student. Ideas: *Because the dog was always around the man's shack; the dog was mean; the dog had bitten one of the man's men.*)

2. What could that dog do to make the time machine disappear? (Call on a student. Idea: *Bump into the handle.*)

2. What were Tom and Eric doing at the end of this story? (Call on a student. Idea: *Running up the hill toward the time machine.*)

2. What was the fat man doing? (Call on a student. Ideas: *Following Tom and Eric; running toward the time machine.*)

EXERCISE 5

GLOBE REVIEW

a. (Present a globe. Touch New York City.) Everybody, what's this place? (Signal.) *New York City.*

• I'll show you where Spain is on the globe. (Trace the route from New York City to Spain.) Here's Spain. Your turn.

b. (Spin the globe. Call on a student.) Touch New York City. ✓
• Touch Spain. ✓
• Touch Egypt. ✓
• Touch Greece. ✓
• (Repeat step b with other students.)

EXERCISE 6

PAIRED PRACTICE

You're going to read aloud to your partner. Today the **A** members will read first. Then the **B** members will read from the star to the end of the story.
(Observe students and give feedback.)

INDEPENDENT WORK

Now finish your independent work for lesson 139. Raise your hand when you're finished.
(Observe students and give feedback.)

WORKCHECK

a. (Direct students to take out their marking pencils.)
• We're going to check your independent work. Remember, if you got an item wrong, make an **X** next to the item.

b. (For each item: Read the item. Call on a student to answer it. If the answer is wrong, say the correct answer. Refer to the Answer Key for the correct answers.)

c. Now use your pencil to fix up any items you got wrong. Remember, all mistakes must be fixed up before you hand in your work.

> *Note:* Before presenting lesson 140, you will need to:
> • Reproduce blackline masters for the Fact Game;
> • Preview Literature lesson 14, secure materials and reproduce blackline masters. (See the Literature Guide.)

WRITING-SPELLING

(Present Writing-Spelling lesson 139 after completing Reading lesson 139. See Writing-Spelling Guide.)

LANGUAGE ARTS GUIDE

(Present Language Arts lesson 139 after completing Reading lesson 139. See Language Arts Guide.)

Materials: Each student will need their thermometer chart for exercise 2.

EXERCISE 1

FACT GAME

Fact Game

For each team (4 or 5 students):
- pair of number cubes (or dice)
- copy of Fact Game 140

For each student:
- their copy of the scorecard sheet

For each monitor:
- a pencil
- Fact Game 140 Answer Key (at end of textbook C)

Reading Checkout
- Each student needs their thermometer chart

Literature Lesson 14
- See Literature Guide for the materials you will need

a. (Divide students into groups of four or five. Assign monitors.)
b. You'll play the game for 10 minutes. (Circulate as students play the game. Comment on groups that are playing well.)
c. (At the end of 10 minutes, have all students who earned more than 10 points stand up.)
- (Tell the monitor of each game that ran smoothly:) Your group did a good job.

EXERCISE 2

READING CHECKOUTS

a. Today is a test day and a reading-checkout day. While you're writing answers, I'm going to call on you one at a time to read part of the story we read in lesson 139. When I call you to come and do your checkout, bring your thermometer chart.
- Remember, you pass the checkout by reading the passage in less than a minute without making more than 2

mistakes. And when you pass the checkout, you color the space for lesson 140 on your thermometer chart.
b. (Call on individual students to read the portion of story 139 marked with ◦.)
- (Time the student. Note words that are missed and number of words read.)
- (Teacher reference:)

◦ **The man became angry. "Did you say Columbus?" The man pointed to the ship at the dock. "That ship belongs to Columbus. Columbus is a crazy person."**

The man went into his shack. Tom and Eric followed. On the walls were many maps, but they did not look like any [50] maps that Tom and Eric had ever seen.

The man touched a spot on the largest map. "We are here in Spain. Columbus plans to [75] sail his ships off the end of the world. He says that the world is round, but it is flat. If the world was round, ◦ [100] we would roll off."

- (If the student reads the passage in one minute or less and makes no more than 2 errors, direct the student to color in the space for lesson 140 on the thermometer chart.)
- (If the student makes any mistakes, point to each word that was misread and identify it.)
- (If the student does not meet the time-error criteria for the passage, direct the student to practice reading the story with the assigned partner.)

EXERCISE 3

TEST

a. **Find page 283 in your textbook.** ✓
- This is a test. You'll work items you've done before.
b. Work carefully. Raise your hand when you've completed all the items.
(Observe students but do not give feedback on errors.)

MARKING THE TEST

a. (Check students' work before beginning lesson 141. Refer to the Answer Key for the correct answers.)

b. (Record all test 14 results on the Test Summary Sheet and the Group Summary Sheet. Reproducible Summary Sheets are at the back of the Teacher's Guide.)

TEST REMEDIES

• (Provide any necessary remedies for test 14 before presenting lesson 141. Test remedies are discussed in the Teacher's Guide.)

Test 14 Firming Table

Test Item	Introduced in lesson	Test Item	Introduced in lesson	Test Item	Introduced in lesson
1	131	13	135	25	129
2	131	14	134	26	128
3	131	15	136	27	132
4	131	16	136	28	133
5	132	17	136	29	136
6	132	18	136	30	132
7	132	19	137	31	137
8	134	20	137	32	127
9	135	21	139	33	131
10	135	22	139	34	131
11	135	23	139	35	127
12	135	24	138	36	131

LITERATURE

(Present Literature lesson 14 after completing Reading lesson 140. See Literature Guide.)

LANGUAGE ARTS GUIDE

(Present Language Arts lesson 140 after completing Reading lesson 140. See Language Arts Guide.)

	Lesson 141	Lesson 142	Lesson 143	Lesson 144	Lesson 145
Lesson Events	Vocabulary Review Reading Words Comprehension Passage Story Reading Paired Practice Independent Work Workcheck Writing-Spelling	Vocabulary Review Reading Words Comprehension Passage Story Reading Paired Practice Independent Work Workcheck Writing-Spelling	Vocabulary Review Reading Words Comprehension Passage Story Reading Paired Practice Independent Work Workcheck Writing-Spelling	Vocabulary Review Reading Words Comprehension Passage Story Reading Paired Practice Independent Work Workcheck Optional Activity Writing-Spelling	Reading Words Comprehension Passage Story Reading Reading Checkouts Independent Work Workcheck Writing-Spelling End-of-Program Test Marking the Test Test Remedies
Vocabulary Sentence	sentence #31 sentence #32 sentence #33	#31: The palace guards spoke different languages.	#32: His argument convinced them to buy an appliance.	#33: The army was soundly defeated near the village.	
Reading Words: Word Types	modeled words words with endings mixed words	modeled words	words with endings mixed words	modeled words multi-syllable words words with endings mixed words	mixed words
New Vocabulary	probably attack Concord president			microphone wrapped spy lad	confused
Comprehension Passages	*More About Time*	*Vikings*	*More About Time*	*Facts About the United States*	*More About Time*
Story	*The Dog and the Time Machine*	*The Land of the Vikings*	*Trying to Get Home*	*Concord*	*Home*
Skill Items	Vocabulary Sentence	Vocabulary Sentences Vocabulary	Compare		Test: Vocabulary Sentences #32, 33
Special Materials					Thermometer charts; *materials for literature project; **materials for special project 1; drawing materials for Activity
Special Projects/ Activities			Project after lesson 143	Project after lesson 144	Activity and 2 projects after End-of-Program test

* Literature anthology; blackline masters 15A, 15B; lined paper.

** Large butcher paper or poster board (at least 2 feet by 5 feet); colored markers; crayons; paints; scissors; and other construction materials.

Lesson 141

EXERCISE 1

VOCABULARY REVIEW

a. You learned a sentence that tells about the palace guards.
- Everybody, say that sentence. Get ready. (Signal.) *The palace guards spoke different languages.*
- (Repeat until firm.)

b. You learned a sentence that tells what his argument did.
- Everybody, say that sentence. Get ready. (Signal.) *His argument convinced them to buy an appliance.*
- (Repeat until firm.)

c. Here's the last sentence you learned: The army was soundly defeated near the village.
- Everybody, say that sentence. Get ready. (Signal.) *The army was soundly defeated near the village.*
- (Repeat until firm.)

d. Everybody, what word means **small town?** (Signal.) *Village.*
- What word means **completely** or **really?** (Signal.) *Soundly.*
- What word means **beaten?** (Signal.) *Defeated.*
- (Repeat step d until firm.)

e. Once more. Say the sentence that tells where the army was soundly defeated. Get ready. (Signal.) *The army was soundly defeated near the village.*

EXERCISE 2

READING WORDS

Column 1

a. **Find lesson 141 in your textbook.** ✓
- Touch column 1. ✓
- (Teacher reference:)

1. **George Washington**	4. **Concord**
2. **probably**	5. **president**
3. **attack**	

b. Number 1 is a name: **George Washington.** What name? (Signal.) *George Washington.*

c. Word 2 is **probably.** What word? (Signal.) *Probably.*

- Spell **probably.** Get ready. (Tap for each letter.) *P-R-O-B-A-B-L-Y.*
- If something will probably happen, you are pretty sure it will happen. It will most likely happen. Everybody, what's another way of saying **The weather will most likely be cloudy?** (Signal.) *The weather will probably be cloudy.*
- What's another way of saying **We will most likely go to the movies?** (Signal.) *We will probably go to the movies.*

d. Word 3 is **attack.** What word? (Signal.) *Attack.*
- Spell **attack.** Get ready. (Tap for each letter.) *A-T-T-A-C-K.*
- When people attack, they do something to start a fight or a battle. If a dog attacks a mail carrier, the dog goes after the mail carrier and starts a fight. Everybody, what word means **start a fight** or **battle?** (Signal.) *Attack.*

e. Word 4 is **Concord.** What word? (Signal.) *Concord.*
- Spell **Concord.** Get ready. (Tap for each letter.) *C-O-N-C-O-R-D.*
- Concord is the name of one of the first towns in the United States.

f. Word 5 is **president.** What word? (Signal.) *President.*
- The president of a country is the person who has the most power to run that country. Who is the president of the United States now? (Call on a student. Accept appropriate response.)
- That person has the most power to run the United States.

g. Let's read those words again, the fast way.
- Number 1. What name? (Signal.) *George Washington.*
- Word 2. What word? (Signal.) *Probably.*
- (Repeat for words 3–5.)

h. (Repeat step g until firm.)

Column 2

i. Find column 2. ✓
- (Teacher reference:)

1. **dirty**	3. **beaten**
2. **banging**	4. **sniffed**

- All these words have endings.
- j. Word 1. What word? (Signal.) *Dirty.*
  - (Repeat for: **2. banging, 3. beaten, 4. sniffed.**)
- k. Let's read those words again.
  - Word 1. What word? (Signal.) *Dirty.*
  - (Repeat for words 2–4.)
- l. (Repeat step k until firm.)

Column 3

m. Find column 3. ✓
- (Teacher reference:)

1. **Viking**	4. **doesn't**
2. **whispered**	5. **yelp**
3. **crouched**	

- n. Word 1. What word? (Signal.) *Viking.*
  - (Repeat for words 2–5.)
- o. Let's read those words again.
  - Word 1. What word? (Signal.) *Viking.*
  - (Repeat for words 2–5.)
- p. (Repeat step o until firm.)

Individual Turns

(For columns 1–3: Call on individual students, each to read one to three words per turn.)

EXERCISE 3

COMPREHENSION PASSAGE

a. Find part B in your textbook. ✓
- You're going to read the next story about Eric and Tom. First you'll read the information passage. It gives some more facts about time.
b. Everybody, touch the title. ✓
- (Call on a student to read the title.) *[More About Time.]*
- Everybody, what's the title? (Signal.) *More About Time.*
c. (Call on individual students to read the passage, each student reading two or three sentences at a time.)

More About Time

- (Teacher reference:)

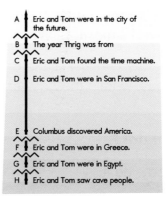

A Eric and Tom were in the city of the future.
B The year Thrig was from
C Eric and Tom found the time machine.
D Eric and Tom were in San Francisco.
E Columbus discovered America.
F Eric and Tom were in Greece.
G Eric and Tom were in Egypt.
H Eric and Tom saw cave people.

Look at the time line. Touch dot C.

- Everybody, do it. ✓

That dot shows when Eric and Tom started their trip. What year was that?

- Everybody, what's the answer? (Signal.) (Accept appropriate response.)

Touch dot A.

- Everybody, do it. ✓

That dot shows when Eric and Tom were in the city of the future. When was that?

- Everybody, what's the answer? (Signal.) *4,000 years in the future.*

Touch dot B.

- Everybody, do it. ✓

That dot shows the year that Thrig was from. What year was that?

- Everybody, what's the answer? (Signal.) *2400.*

Touch dot D.

- Everybody, do it. ✓

That dot shows when Eric and Tom were in San Francisco. What year was that?

- Everybody, what's the answer? (Signal.) *1906.*

Touch dot E.

- Everybody, do it. ✓

That dot shows when Columbus discovered America. What year was that?

- Everybody, what's the answer? (Signal.) *1492.*

Touch dot F.

- Everybody, do it. ✓

That dot shows when Eric and Tom were in Greece. How long ago was that?

- Everybody, what's the answer? (Signal.) *3,000 years ago.*

Touch dot G.

- Everybody, do it. ✓

That dot shows when Eric and Tom were in Egypt. How long ago was that?

- Everybody, what's the answer? (Signal.) *5,000 years ago.*

Touch dot H.

- Everybody, do it. ✓

That dot shows when Eric and Tom saw the cave people. How long ago was that?

- Everybody, what's the answer? (Signal.) *40,000 years ago.*

EXERCISE 4

STORY READING

a. Find part C in your textbook. ✓
- The error limit for group reading is 11. Read carefully.
b. Everybody, touch the title. ✓
- (Call on a student to read the title.) *[The Dog and the Time Machine.]*
- Everybody, what's the title? (Signal.) *The Dog and the Time Machine.*
c. (Call on individual students to read the story, each student reading two or three sentences at a time. Ask questions marked **1.**)

- (Correct errors: Tell the word. Direct the student to reread the sentence.)
- (If the group makes more than 11 errors, direct the students to reread the story.)

d. (After the group has read the selection making no more than 11 errors, read the story to the students and ask questions marked **2.**)

The Dog and the Time Machine

Tom and Eric ran up the hill to the time machine.

1. Who remembers why they were running? (Call on a student. Idea: *They were afraid the dog would bump the handle on the time machine.*)

Tom looked inside. The big white dog was crouched down near the handle.

1. Why could that be trouble? (Call on a student. Idea: *If the dog bumped the handle, the machine might leave.*)

"Grrrrrr," the dog said, and Tom could see his teeth. The dog was very dirty and very skinny.
Eric looked inside and then whispered, "Tom, he's right next to the handle. If he bumps into that handle, the machine might disappear and we'll never get back home."
The fat man pushed past Tom and Eric. He was holding a big stick.

1. What do you think he wanted to do with that stick? (Call on a student. Idea: *Hit the dog.*)
1. Why? (Call on a student. Idea: *He didn't like the dog.*)

"Let me at that dog," the man said. "I will give him a beating he will remember."
"No," Tom said and grabbed the man's arm. "Don't scare him."
The man looked at the inside of the time machine. He looked at the dials. He watched the lights go on and off. Suddenly, he looked very frightened. "I have never seen such a thing as this machine," he said softly.

2. How do you think he feels seeing the inside of the time machine? (Call on a student. Ideas: *Surprised, curious, afraid, amazed.*)

> **Tom hardly heard what the man said.**

2. Why? (Call on a student. Ideas: *He was worried that the dog might bump the handle; because the man was talking so softly.*)

> **Tom held out his hand. "Come here, boy," he said very softly.**
> **"Grrrrrr," the dog said and showed his teeth again.**
> **Tom turned to the man. "Do you have some food we can give the dog?" Tom asked.**
> **"No, no," the man said. "I do not want to be around that dog or that machine." The man started to run back down the hill.**

2. Why doesn't that man want to be around the time machine? (Call on a student. Idea: *He's afraid of the machine.*)

> **Eric said, "That dog doesn't like you, Tom. Let me talk to him."**
> **Tom stepped out of the doorway. Eric went inside and moved toward the dog very slowly. The dog crouched lower and lower as Eric moved toward him. "Don't be afraid of me," Eric said softly.**
> **The dog did not show his teeth. Slowly, Eric reached out and patted the dog on his head. The dog's tail wagged a little.**

1. Listen: The dog's tail wagged a little. What does that mean? (Call on a student. Ideas: *He likes Eric; he feels friendly.*)

> **Eric said, "You are a very nice dog."**
> **Eric backed away from the dog. "Come here," he said softly.**

1. What is Eric trying to do? (Call on a student. Idea: *Get the dog away from the handle.*)

> **The dog stood up. His back was only about a centimeter from the handle.**

2. Everybody, show me how far his back was from the handle. ✓

> **Tom could hardly watch. "Come here," Eric said again.**
> **The dog took another step. Then he wagged his tail. His tail banged against the handle. "Oh, no," Tom said to himself.**
> **But the dog's tail did not move the handle. The dog walked up to Eric. The dog jumped up on Eric and licked his face.**

1. Everybody, who did the dog like? (Signal.) *Eric.*

> **"Tom, he likes me," Eric said.**
> **Tom patted the dog's head.**

2. Everybody, is the dog still ready to fight Tom? (Signal.) *No.*

> **Then Tom looked outside the time machine. The fat man was near his shack, talking to three soldiers. The fat man pointed toward the time machine.**

2. What do you think he was telling the soldiers? (Call on a student. Idea: *To attack the time machine.*)

> **Tom said, "We'd better get out of here. Take the dog outside."**
> **"No," Eric said. "Those men might hurt him. We've got to take him with us."**
> **The soldiers started running up the hill. Tom ran over to the seat and sat down. Swwwwwsssssh—the door closed.**
> **A few moments later, a soldier was yelling and banging on the door. BOOM, BOOM.**
> **Eric said, "Hurry up, Tom, before he breaks the door."**
> **BOOM, BOOM, BOOM.**
> **Tom grabbed the handle and pulled on it. It didn't move. The dog was crouched in front of the door. "Grrrrrr," the dog growled.**

2. Who was he growling at? (Call on a student. Idea: *The soldier.*)

> **Tom pulled on the handle. The handle moved.**

1. Go back to the beginning of the story. Follow along while I read.
2. Read the rest of the story to yourself. Find out the mistake that Tom made. Raise your hand when you're done.

> **The dials clicked and buzzed. The dog let out a little yelp. Then, as the force died down, the dog sniffed the air.**
>
> **Eric said, "Tom, you pulled down on the handle. You should have pushed up."**
>
> **Tom stood up and the door opened. The dog jumped back. The time machine was on another hill above water. And there was a ship down below them near the shore. The air outside was cool.**
>
> **Tom pointed to the ship. "That is a Viking ship."**
>
> **The Viking ship moved slowly along the shore of the ocean.**
> **MORE NEXT TIME**

2. (After all students have raised their hand, call on a student:) What mistake did Tom make? (Call on a student. Idea: *He pulled down on the handle.*)
2. Everybody, so where did they go in time, **forward** or **backward?** (Signal.) *Backward.*
2. Are they **closer** to the year we are now or **farther away?** (Signal.) *Farther away.*

2. What kind of ship did they see at the end of the story? (Signal.) *A Viking ship.*
2. Touch the Viking ship in the picture. ✓
2. That ship has oars for rowing and a sail. Everybody, point your finger to show which way the ship is moving. ✓

EXERCISE 5

PAIRED PRACTICE

You're going to read aloud to your partner. Today the **B** members will read first. Then the **A** members will read from the star to the end of the story.
(Observe students and give feedback.)

INDEPENDENT WORK

Now finish your independent work for lesson 141. Raise your hand when you're finished.
(Observe students and give feedback.)

WORKCHECK

---

a. (Direct students to take out their marking pencils.)
  • We're going to check your independent work. Remember, if you got an item wrong, make an **X** next to the item.
b. (For each item: Read the item. Call on a student to answer it. If the answer is wrong, say the correct answer. Refer to the Answer Key for the correct answers.)
c. Now use your marking pencil to fix up any items you got wrong. Remember, all mistakes must be fixed up before you hand in your work.

WRITING-SPELLING

(Present Writing-Spelling lesson 141 after completing Reading lesson 141. See Writing-Spelling Guide.)

EXERCISE 1

VOCABULARY REVIEW

a. You learned a sentence that tells about palace guards.

- Everybody, say that sentence. Get ready. (Signal.) *The palace guards spoke different languages.*
- (Repeat until firm.)

b. I'll say part of the sentence. When I stop, you say the next word. Listen: The palace . . . Everybody, what's the next word? (Signal.) *Guards.*

c. Listen: The . . . Everybody, what's the next word? (Signal.) *Palace.*

- Say the whole sentence. Get ready. (Signal.) *The palace guards spoke different languages.*

d. Listen: The palace guards spoke different . . . Everybody, what's the next word? (Signal.) *Languages.*

EXERCISE 2

READING WORDS

a. **Find lesson 142 in your textbook.** ✓

- Touch word 1. ✓
- (Teacher reference:)

1. **wrestle**	4. **fighters**
2. **helmet**	5. **village**
3. **voices**	6. **probably**

b. Word 1 is **wrestle.** What word? (Signal.) *Wrestle.*

- Spell **wrestle.** Get ready. (Tap for each letter.) *W-R-E-S-T-L-E.*

c. Word 2. What word? (Signal.) *Helmet.*

- Spell **helmet.** Get ready. (Tap for each letter.) *H-E-L-M-E-T.*

d. Word 3. What word? (Signal.) *Voices.*

- Spell **voices.** Get ready. (Tap for each letter.) *V-O-I-C-E-S.*

e. Word 4. What word? (Signal.) *Fighters.*

- Spell **fighters.** Get ready. (Tap for each letter.) *F-I-G-H-T-E-R-S.*

f. Word 5. What word? (Signal.) *Village.*

- Spell **village.** Get ready. (Tap for each letter.) *V-I-L-L-A-G-E.*

g. Word 6. What word? (Signal.) *Probably.*

h. Let's read those words again, the fast way.

- Word 1. What word? (Signal.) *Wrestle.*
- (Repeat for words 2–6.)

i. (Repeat step h until firm.)

EXERCISE 3

COMPREHENSION PASSAGE

a. Find part B in your textbook. ✓

- You're going to read the next story about Eric and Tom. First you'll read the information passage. It gives some facts about Vikings.

b. Everybody, touch the title. ✓

- (Call on a student to read the title.) *[Vikings.]*
- Everybody, what's the title? (Signal.) *Vikings.*

c. (Call on individual students to read the passage, each student reading two or three sentences at a time.)

> **Vikings**
>
> **In today's story you will read about Vikings. Here are some facts about Vikings:**
> **Vikings were great fighters.**

- Everybody, say that fact. Get ready. (Signal.) *Vikings were great fighters.*
- (Repeat until firm.)

> **Vikings sailed across the ocean to America before Columbus did.**

- Everybody, who sailed to America first, the Vikings or Columbus? (Signal.) *Vikings.*

> **Vikings lived far north of Italy and Spain. The map shows where the Vikings lived.**

- Everybody, touch Spain on the map. ✓
- Touch Italy. ✓
- Now move your finger to the Land of the Vikings. ✓
- Everybody, in which direction did you have to go from Italy to reach the Land of the Vikings? (Signal.) *North.*

The Vikings lived where the winters are very long and cold.

- What do you know about the winters in the Land of the Vikings? (Call on a student. Idea: *They were long and cold.*)

EXERCISE 4

STORY READING

a. Find part C in your textbook. ✓
- The error limit for group reading is 11. Read carefully.
b. Everybody, touch the title. ✓
- (Call on a student to read the title.) *[The Land of the Vikings.]*
- Everybody, what's the title? (Signal.) *The Land of the Vikings.*
c. (Call on individual students to read the story, each student reading two or three sentences at a time. Ask questions marked **1.**)

> - (Correct errors: Tell the word. Direct the student to reread the sentence.)
> - (If the group makes more than 11 errors, direct the students to reread the story.)

d. (After the group has read the selection making no more than 11 errors, read the story to the students and ask questions marked **2.**)

The Land of the Vikings

Tom and Eric were standing on the top of a hill looking at a Viking ship on the ocean below them. Tom figured that he and Eric were probably close to the year 1000.

1. Everybody, what year were Eric and Tom in? (Signal.) *1000.*
1. What year had they been in when they were in Spain? (Signal.) *1492.*
- So they had gone back in time from 1492 to about 1000.

The Viking ship was moving slowly along the shore. Tom could hear the voices of the men on the ship as they sang. But he could not understand the words of the song.

2. Why not? (Call on a student. Idea: *It was in a different language.*)

As Tom watched the Viking ship, it turned and went out to sea. Eric asked, "Didn't the Vikings go to America before Columbus did?"
Tom said, "The Vikings sailed to America long before Columbus did."

2. Everybody, when did Columbus discover America? (Signal.) *1492.*
- The Vikings may have gone to America around the year 1000.

Suddenly, the dog turned around and started to growl.

1. What would that mean? (Call on a student. Idea: *Someone was coming.*)

Tom turned around. A very big man was behind them. The man was dressed in a robe made of animal skins. He wore a helmet with horns on either side.

1. Everybody, look at the picture. What is the Viking holding? (Signal.) *A sword.*
1. Do you think that Viking is friendly? (Call on a student. Student preference.)

> "Grrrr," the dog growled.
> The Viking looked at the dog and smiled. "Nur su urf," he said.

1. Everybody, does the Viking want to fight? (Signal.) *No.*
1. What do you think **nur su urf** might mean? (Call on a student. Ideas: *Who are you?; I like your dog.*)

> Tom said, "We can't understand your language."
> The Viking pointed to the dog and smiled again. "Su urf," he said.
> Eric said, "I think he's trying to tell us that he likes our dog."
> The Viking touched Tom's shirt. "Su urf," he said. Then he pointed to the time machine. Again he said, "Su urf."

1. What do you think **su urf** means? (Call on a student. Idea: *I like.*)
1. Name some things the Viking likes. (Call on a student. Ideas: *The shirt, the dog, the time machine.*)

> Eric said, "I think he likes everything, Tom."
> The Viking waved his hand and then pointed. "Ul fas e mern," he said.
> "He wants us to come with him," Eric said.
> So Tom, Eric, and the dog followed the Viking into a grove of trees.

1. Would you want to follow that Viking? (Call on a student. Student preference.)

> They walked down a hill on the other side of the grove. At last they came to a little village. There were many huts and many dogs. The dogs started to bark.
> The white dog growled at the other dogs.

> People came from their huts and looked at Tom and Eric. The Viking who was walking with them told the people something and the people smiled.
> A big gray dog came up to Eric and Tom's dog. Suddenly, the dogs started to fight and the Vikings started to cheer. Eric said, "Tom, stop them."
> Tom moved toward the dogs, but a Viking grabbed his arm and shook his head. "In sing e tool," he said.
> The dogs continued to fight. The gray dog was as big as the white dog, and he looked stronger than the white dog. But the white dog was a little faster. Again and again the gray dog jumped at the white dog, but the white dog got out of the way. Both dogs became tired. The white dog had a cut on his neck. The gray dog's leg was hurt. Suddenly, the gray dog stopped fighting. He was about a yard from the white dog. He crouched down. The white dog started to move toward him, and the gray dog turned away.
> All the people cheered.

2. Which dog won the fight? (Call on a student. Idea: *The white dog.*)
2. How do you know? (Call on a student. Idea: *The gray dog turned away.*)
2. Everybody, were the people mad at the white dog for winning the fight? (Signal.) *No.*

> A woman ran over to the white dog. He growled at her, and everybody cheered again.

2. What kind of dogs do the Vikings like? (Call on a student. Ideas: *Winners; brave dogs; dogs that are good fighters.*)

> Then she gave him a great big bone.

1. Everybody, look at the picture. Do the Vikings look happy or sad? (Signal.) *Happy.*

Tom said, "I think our dog just beat their best dog."

Three Vikings came over and patted Tom and Eric on the back. They led Tom and Eric to a large building.

2. Everybody, go back to the picture on page 299. Touch that large building. ✓
2. You can also see some huts in the background. Touch a hut. ✓

It was very dark inside the building. There were no windows, but there were many dogs and many tables. And it smelled bad.

1. Go back to the beginning of the story. Follow along while I read.
2. The buildings were built for the kind of winters the Vikings had. What kind of winters were those? (Call on a student. Ideas: *Long, cold, snowy.*)
2. What would happen during the winters if there were a lot of open windows in the building? (Call on a student. Ideas: *It would get very cold inside the building; the snow would come in.*)
2. Why do you think it smelled bad? (Call on a student. Ideas: *The people didn't wash; food rotted on the floor; there were no windows so there was no fresh air; there were lots of dogs.*)
2. Read the rest of the story to yourself. Find out whether the Vikings finished their meal. Raise your hand when you're done.

The Vikings sat down at one of the tables. Tom and Eric sat next to them. Then some Viking women brought in great pieces of cooked meat. Each Viking took his knife and cut off a big piece. One of the Vikings cut pieces for Tom and Eric.

Eric said, "How are we supposed to eat? We don't have any forks."

Tom pointed to the Vikings. "Just eat the way they are eating." The Vikings were eating with their hands.

Suddenly, the dogs outside began to bark again. All the Vikings stopped eating. A boy ran into the building. "Left ingra," he yelled. The Vikings grabbed their knives and ran out of the building.

MORE NEXT TIME

2. (After all students have raised their hand:) Everybody, did the Vikings finish their meal? (Signal.) *No.*
2. What first made the Vikings stop eating? (Call on a student. Idea: *The dogs outside started barking.*)
2. A boy came in and yelled, "Left ingra." What did the Vikings do then? (Call on a student. Idea: *They grabbed their knives and ran outside.*)
2. What do you think **left ingra** could mean? (Call on a student. Ideas: *Danger; someone's coming.*)
2. I'll name some events. You tell me if each event happened in the part you read to yourself. The Vikings cut off pieces of meat for Tom and Eric. Everybody, did that happen? (Signal.) *Yes.*
2. The Vikings gave Tom and Eric the largest forks they had. Did that happen? (Signal.) *No.*
2. Tom and Eric sat on the floor. Did that happen? (Signal.) *No.*
2. The Vikings were eating with their hands. Did that happen? (Signal.) *Yes.*

EXERCISE 5

PAIRED PRACTICE

You're going to read aloud to your partner. Today the **A** members will read first. Then the **B** members will read from the star to the end of the story.

(Observe students and give feedback.)

End-of-Lesson Activities

Now finish your independent work for lesson 142. Raise your hand when you're finished. (Observe students and give feedback.)

WORKCHECK

a. (Direct students to take out their marking pencils.)
  • We're going to check your independent work. Remember, if you got an item wrong, make an **X** next to the item.

b. (For each item: Read the item. Call on a student to answer it. If the answer is wrong, say the correct answer. Refer to the Answer Key for the correct answers.)

c. Now use your marking pencil to fix up any items you got wrong. Remember, all mistakes must be fixed up before you hand in your work.

WRITING-SPELLING

(Present Writing-Spelling lesson 142 after completing Reading lesson 142. See Writing-Spelling Guide.)

Lesson 143

EXERCISE 1

VOCABULARY REVIEW

a. You learned a sentence that tells what his argument did. Everybody, say the sentence. Get ready. (Signal.) *His argument convinced them to buy an appliance.*

b. I'll say part of the sentence. When I stop, you say the next word. Listen: His argument . . . Everybody, what's the next word? (Signal.) *Convinced.*

c. Listen: His . . . Everybody, what's the next word? (Signal.) *Argument.*

• Say the whole sentence. Get ready. (Signal.) *His argument convinced them to buy an appliance.*

d. Listen: His argument convinced them to buy an . . . Everybody, what's the next word? (Signal.) *Appliance.*

EXERCISE 2

READING WORDS

Column 1

a. **Find lesson 143 in your textbook.** ✓

• Touch column 1. ✓

• (Teacher reference:)

| 1. snowing | 3. flakes |
| 2. attacked | 4. marching |

• All these words have endings.

b. Word 1. What word? (Signal.) *Snowing.*

• (Repeat for words 2–4.)

c. (Repeat step b until firm.)

Column 2

d. Find column 2. ✓

• (Teacher reference:)

1. wrestle	4. outside
2. church	5. puzzle
3. beard	

e. Word 1. What word? (Signal.) *Wrestle.*

• Spell **wrestle.** Get ready. (Tap for each letter.) W-R-E-S-T-L-E.

f. Word 2. What word? (Signal.) *Church.*

• Spell **church.** Get ready. (Tap for each letter.) C-H-U-R-C-H.

g. Word 3. What word? (Signal.) *Beard.*

• Spell **beard.** Get ready. (Tap for each letter.) B-E-A-R-D.

h. Word 4. What word? (Signal.) *Outside.*

i. Word 5. What word? (Signal.) *Puzzle.*

j. Let's read those words again, the fast way.

• Word 1. What word? (Signal.) *Wrestle.*

• (Repeat for words 2–5.)

k. (Repeat step j until firm.)

Individual Turns

(For columns 1 and 2: Call on individual students, each to read one to three words per turn.)

EXERCISE 3

COMPREHENSION PASSAGE

a. Find part B in your textbook. ✓

• You're going to read the next story about Eric and Tom. First you'll read the information passage. It gives some more facts about time.

b. Everybody, touch the title. ✓

• (Call on a student to read the title.) [*More About Time.*]

• Everybody, what's the title? (Signal.) *More About Time.*

c. (Call on individual students to read the passage, each student reading two or three sentences at a time.)

More About Time

• (Teacher reference:)

A — Eric and Tom were in the city of the future.

B — The year Thrig was from

C — Eric and Tom found the time machine.

D — Eric and Tom were in San Francisco.

E — Columbus discovered America.

F — Eric and Tom were in the Land of the Vikings.

G — Eric and Tom were in Greece.

H — Eric and Tom were in Egypt.

I — Eric and Tom saw cave people.

Look at the time line. Touch dot C.

- Everybody, do it. ✓

That dot shows when Eric and Tom started their trip. What year was that?

- Everybody, what's the answer? (Signal. Accept appropriate response.)

Touch dot A.

- Everybody, do it. ✓

That dot shows when Eric and Tom were in the city of the future. When was that?

- Everybody, what's the answer? (Signal.) *4,000 years in the future.*

Touch dot B.

- Everybody, do it. ✓

That dot shows the year that Thrig was from. What year was that?

- Everybody, what's the answer? (Signal.) *2400.*

Touch dot D.

- Everybody, do it. ✓

That dot shows when Eric and Tom were in San Francisco. What year was that?

- Everybody, what's the answer? (Signal.) *1906.*

Touch dot E.

- Everybody, do it. ✓

That dot shows when Columbus discovered America. What year was that?

- Everybody, what's the answer? (Signal.) *1492.*

Touch dot F.

- Everybody, do it. ✓

That dot shows when Eric and Tom were in the Land of the Vikings. What year was that?

- Everybody, what's the answer? (Signal.) *1000.*

Touch dot G.

- Everybody, do it. ✓

That dot shows when Eric and Tom were in Greece. How long ago was that?

- Everybody, what's the answer? (Signal.) *3,000 years ago.*

Touch dot H.

- Everybody, do it. ✓

That dot shows when Eric and Tom were in Egypt. How long ago was that?

- Everybody, what's the answer? (Signal.) *5,000 years ago.*

Touch dot I.

- Everybody, do it. ✓

That dot shows when Eric and Tom saw the cave people. How long ago was that?

- Everybody, what's the answer? (Signal.) *40,000 years ago.*

EXERCISE 4

STORY READING

a. Find part C in your textbook. ✓
- The error limit for group reading is 12. Read carefully.
b. Everybody, touch the title. ✓
- (Call on a student to read the title.) *[Trying to Get Home.]*
- Everybody, what's the title? (Signal.) *Trying to Get Home.*
c. (Call on individual students to read the story, each student reading two or three sentences at a time. Ask questions marked 1.)

- (Correct errors: Tell the word. Direct the student to reread the sentence.)
- (If the group makes more than 12 errors, direct the students to reread the story.)

d. (After the group has read the selection making no more than 12 errors, read the story to the students and ask questions marked **2**.)

Trying to Get Home

Tom and Eric were inside the dark Viking building. Suddenly, the Vikings were fighting outside.

1. What had the Vikings been doing before they ran outside? (Call on a student. Idea: *Eating.*)
1. What made them run outside? (Call on a student. Ideas: *A boy came in shouting; the dogs were barking.*)

The Vikings were using big, heavy swords and knives. Vikings from another village had attacked. These Vikings wore bands around their arms. Their leader was a huge man with a red beard.

2. Everybody, look at the picture. ✓
2. How can you tell which Vikings are from another village? (Call on a student. Ideas: *They wore bands around their arms; their clothes were different.*)
2. Everybody, touch the leader of the Vikings from the other village. ✓
2. Who started this fight, the Vikings Tom and Eric were visiting, or the Vikings from another village? (Call on a student. Idea: *The Vikings from another village.*)

Tom said, "I've got an idea." He started his tape recorder and ran outside. "Stop fighting! I am the god of sounds!" he yelled.

1. What did Tom say he was? (Call on a student. Idea: *The god of sounds.*)
1. When did Tom do this trick before? (Call on a student. Idea: *In Egypt.*)
1. Do you think it will work? (Call on a student. Student preference.)

A Viking looked at him. "Un sur," he yelled.
Tom quickly played back the tape.

2. Say everything the tape recorder played back. (Call on a student.) *[Stop fighting, I am the god of sounds. Un sur.]*

Some of the Vikings stopped fighting. They looked at Tom. Now more Vikings stopped fighting. Tom played the recording again and again. Soon all of the Vikings were looking at Tom.
One Viking raised his sword. His voice boomed out, "Esen trala."

1. Say that the way he yelled it. (Call on a student. Student should sound mean, loud, and threatening.)

Tom played back the Viking's voice: "Esen trala."
The Viking dropped his sword and stared at Tom. Then he turned to some of the other Vikings and said, "Su urf."

1. The first Viking the boys met kept saying **su urf**. What does **su urf** mean? (Call on a student. Idea: *I like that.*)

The Vikings smiled. Then they started to laugh. They laughed and laughed. Some of them laughed so hard they almost fell over. The leader of the Vikings came over and grabbed Tom. He lifted Tom high into the air. All the Vikings held up their swords. "Sorta groob!" they shouted. "Sorta groob!"

2. What does **sorta groob** mean? (Call on a student. Ideas: *Let's quit fighting; this is great; he's a magician.*)

The Vikings carried Eric and Tom into the dark building. All the Vikings sat down—the Vikings from both villages.

2. Who was in the building now? (Call on a student. Ideas: *Vikings from both villages, Tom and Eric, dogs.*)

There was shouting and yelling and dogs barking. Everybody ate and drank. For a long time, the Vikings sang and the dogs barked.

Then the Vikings went outside. Two Vikings started to wrestle. The other Vikings cheered, and the dogs barked. The two great Vikings rolled over and over on the ground.

Finally, the smaller Viking won. All the Vikings cheered. The Viking who lost stood up, smiled, and put one arm around the neck of the other Viking.

2. Everybody, was that Viking a good loser? (Signal.) *Yes.*

Later in the evening, Tom, Eric, and the dog walked back to the time machine. The Vikings followed. They sang. Some of the Vikings looked inside the time machine. Then Tom motioned so that the Vikings would move away from the time machine.

2. Show me how Tom motioned for the Vikings to move back. (Call on a student.)

Tom sat down in the seat. The door closed.

Eric said, "Let's try to get to our year. I'm tired of going through time."

1. Everybody, what year are Eric and Tom in? (Signal.) *1000.*
1. What year do they want to get to? (Signal. Accept appropriate response.)
1. So do they have to go **forward** or **backward** in time? (Signal.) *Forward.*
1. Which way should they move the handle? (Signal.) *Up.*

Tom pushed up on the handle. Dials started to click. Lights went on and off. Tom felt the force push against his ears. Then the force died down.

Tom stood up. The door opened. A blast of cold air came into the time machine. Outside it was snowing. The snow started to blow into the time machine.

Eric said, "Tom, let's get out of here. It's too cold out there."

Tom said, "How are we going to know where we are if we don't go outside and look around?"

1. What year are the boys in now? (Call on a student. Accept any year beyond 1000.)
1. How would you find out? (Call on a student. Ideas: *Go out and look around; ask people.*)

Eric said, "But Tom, we'll freeze out there."

The time machine was on the top of a hill. The snow was coming down so hard that Tom could not see very far. He could see a grove of trees in the distance, but he couldn't see beyond.

2. What could he see? (Call on a student. Idea: *A grove of trees.*)

Tom said, "I'll run to the grove and take a look. Maybe I can find somebody who can tell us the date. I'll be right back."

1. What was Tom going to look for? (Call on a student. Idea: *A person.*)
1. How far was he going to go? (Call on a student. Idea: *As far as the grove.*)

Tom ran from the time machine. He ran through the snow. It was deep and cold. His shoes filled up with snow. The cold wind cut through his shirt. Tom ran to the trees and looked into the distance. He didn't see anything.

1. Go back to the beginning of the story. Follow along while I read.

2. Everybody, was Tom dressed well for this kind of weather? **(Signal.)** *No.*

2. What was he wearing? **(Call on a student. Idea:** *A shirt and pants and shoes.)*

2. What should he be wearing in weather like this? **(Call on a student. Ideas:** *Boots, a coat, a sweater, etc.)*

2. Read the rest of the story to yourself. Find out why Tom called to Eric. Raise your hand when you're done.

> **But then Tom heard something. It sounded like a bell, very far away. So he ran through the trees toward the sound of the bell. He still couldn't see anything. And he was getting very cold. "I'd better get back to the time machine," he said to himself. He started to run back. The snow was coming down much harder now. Big fluffy flakes filled the air.**
>
> **Tom ran back through the trees. Then he stopped and looked. He could not see the time machine. He called out, "Eric!" Then he listened. No answer. Tom was lost. The cold was cutting into his fingers and ears.**
> **MORE NEXT TIME**

2. **(After all students have raised their hand:)** Why couldn't Tom find his way back to the time machine? **(Call on a student. Idea:** *He couldn't see through the snow.)*

2. When Tom ran from the time machine, he left clues that showed where he went. What clues are those? **(Call on a student. Idea:** *His footprints.)*

2. Why didn't he just look for his footprints and walk back to the time machine? **(Call on a student. Idea:** *His footprints had filled up with snow.)*

PAIRED PRACTICE

You're going to read aloud to your partner. Today the **B** members will read first. Then the **A** members will read from the star to the end of the story.
(Observe students and give feedback.)

End-of-Lesson Activities

INDEPENDENT WORK

Now finish your independent work for lesson 143. Raise your hand when you're finished.
(Observe students and give feedback.)

WORKCHECK

a. **(Direct students to take out their marking pencils.)**
• We're going to check your independent work. Remember, if you got an item wrong, make an **X** next to the item.
b. **(For each item: Read the item. Call on a student to answer it. If the answer is wrong, say the correct answer. Refer to the Answer Key for the correct answers.)**
c. Now use your marking pencil to fix up any items you got wrong. Remember, all mistakes must be fixed up before you hand in your work.

WRITING-SPELLING

(Present Writing-Spelling lesson 143 after completing Reading lesson 143. See Writing-Spelling Guide.)

Special Project

Note: After completing lesson 143, do this special project with the students. You may do the project during another part of the school day.

a. Everybody, find page 312 in your textbook. ✓
   - (Call on individual students to read two or three sentences.)
   - (Teacher reference:)

   ### Special Project

   A story that tells about a real person and that reports things that are true is called a **biography.** You may be able to find biographies of several Vikings. One is Leif Ericson; another is Eric the Red.

   Look for a biography about one of these men and write three important things about his life.

b. Everybody, what do we call a story that is true and that tells about the life of one person? (Signal.) *A biography.*
   - You're going to look for a biography about Leif Ericson or Eric the Red. How will you find that biography? (Call on a student. Idea: *Go to the library.*)
   - You're going to write something after you find the biography. What are you going to write? (Call on a student. Idea: *Three important things about his life.*)

c. (Assign students to work in teams of three or four. After they write their reports, arrange a time when the groups present what they found out to the rest of the class or to another class.)

Lesson 144

EXERCISE 1

VOCABULARY REVIEW

a. You learned a sentence that tells where the army was soundly defeated.
 • Everybody, say that sentence. Get ready. (Signal.) *The army was soundly defeated near the village.*

b. I'll say part of the sentence. When I stop, you say the next word. Listen: The army was soundly defeated near the . . . Everybody, what's the next word? (Signal.) *Village.*

c. Listen: The army was . . . Everybody, what's the next word? (Signal.) *Soundly.*
 • Say the whole sentence. Get ready. (Signal.) *The army was soundly defeated near the village.*

d. Listen: The army was soundly . . . Everybody, what's the next word? (Signal.) *Defeated.*

EXERCISE 2

READING WORDS

Column 1

a. **Find lesson 144 in your textbook.** ✓
 • Touch column 1. ✓
 • (Teacher reference:)

1. **August**	4. **valley**
2. **character**	5. **puzzled**
3. **microphone**	

b. Word 1 is **August.** What word? (Signal.) *August.*
 • Spell **August.** Get ready. (Tap for each letter.) *A-U-G-U-S-T.*

c. Word 2 is **character.** What word? (Signal.) *Character.*

d. Word 3 is **microphone.** What word? (Signal.) *Microphone.*
 • A microphone is a tool that picks up sounds. A telephone has a part that is a microphone. You speak into that part. Tape recorders have a microphone. You speak into the microphone to record what you want to record. Everybody, what's the part of a recorder that picks up your voice? (Signal.) *Microphone.*

e. Word 4. What word? (Signal.) *Valley.*
 • Word 5. What word? (Signal.) *Puzzled.*

f. Let's read those words again, the fast way.
 • Word 1. What word? (Signal.) *August.*
 • (Repeat for words 2–5.)

g. (Repeat step f until firm.)

Column 2

h. Find column 2. ✓
 • (Teacher reference:)

1. <u>**marching**</u>	4. <u>**fire**</u>**place**
2. <u>**pres**</u>**ident**	5. <u>**Con**</u>**cord**
3. <u>**Rob**</u>**ert**	

 • All these words have more than one syllable. The first syllable in each word is underlined.

i. Word 1. What's the first syllable? (Signal.) *march.*
 • What's the whole word? (Signal.) *Marching.*

j. Word 2. What's the first syllable? (Signal.) *pres.*
 • What's the whole word? (Signal.) *President.*

k. Word 3. What's the first syllable? (Signal.) *rob.*
 • What's the whole word? (Signal.) *Robert.*

l. Word 4. What's the first syllable? (Signal.) *fire.*
 • What's the whole word? (Signal.) *Fireplace.*

m. Word 5. What's the first syllable? (Signal.) *con.*
 • What's the whole word? (Signal.) *Concord.*

n. Let's read those words again, the fast way.
 • Word 1. What word? (Signal.) *Valley.*
 • (Repeat for words 2–5.)

o. (Repeat step n until firm.)

Column 3

p. Find column 3. ✓
 • (Teacher reference:)

1. **wrapped**	4. **studied**
2. **dying**	5. **shooting**
3. **losing**	

 • All these words have endings.

q. Word 1. What word? (Signal.)
Wrapped.
- When you wrap a package with paper, you put paper around it. When you wrap yourself in a blanket, you put a blanket around you.
r. Word 2. What word? (Signal.) *Dying.*
- (Repeat for: **3. losing, 4. studied, 5. shooting.**)
s. Let's read those words again.
- Word 1. What word? (Signal.) *Wrapped.*
- (Repeat for: **2. dying, 3. losing, 4. studied, 5. shooting.**)
t. (Repeat step s until firm.)

Column 4

u. Find column 4. ✓
- (Teacher reference:)

1. George Washington	3. lad
2. spy	4. church

v. Number 1. What name? (Signal.)
George Washington.
- Word 2. What word? (Signal.) *Spy.*
- A spy is a person who gives important information to the enemy. A spy pretends to be somebody who would not do something like that. Everybody, what do we call a person who gives important information to the enemy? (Signal.) *Spy.*
- Word 3. What word? (Signal.) *Lad.*
- A **lad** is a **young man.** Everybody, what's another way of saying **He was a smart young man?** (Signal.) *He was a smart lad.*
- What's another way of saying **Thank you, young man?** (Signal.) *Thank you, lad.*
- Word 4. What word? (Signal.) *Church.*
w. Let's read those words again.
- Number 1. What name? (Signal.) *George Washington.*
x. Word 2. What word? (Signal.) *Spy.*
- (Repeat for words 3 and 4.)
y. (Repeat steps w and x until firm.)

Individual Turns

(For columns 1–4: Call on individual students, each to read one to three words per turn.)

COMPREHENSION PASSAGE

a. Find part B in your textbook. ✓
- You're going to read the next story about Eric and Tom. First you'll read the information passage. It gives some facts about the United States.
b. Everybody, touch the title. ✓
- (Call on a student to read the title.) *[Facts About the United States.]*
- Everybody, what's the title? (Signal.) *Facts About the United States.*
c. (Call on individual students to read the passage, each student reading two or three sentences at a time.)

Facts About the United States

Here are facts about things that happened when the United States became a country:
    The United States had been part of another country called England.

- Everybody, the United States had been part of which country? (Signal.) *England.*

In 1776, the United States announced that it was a new country. England said the United States could not be a new country and went to war with the United States.

- Which two countries went to war? (Call on a student.) *England and the United States.*
- Why did England go to war with the United States? (Call on a student. Idea: *Because the United States announced that it was a new country.*)

The leader of the United States Army was George Washington.

- Everybody, who was the leader of the army during this war? (Signal.) *George Washington.*

The United States won the war with England.

- Everybody, which country won the war? (Signal.) *United States.*

**George Washington became the
first president of the United States.**

- Everybody, who was the first president?
  (Signal.) *George Washington.*
- Raise your hand if you know who the
  president is today. (Call on a student.
  Accept appropriate response.)

STORY READING

a. Find part C in your textbook. ✓
- The error limit for group reading is 11.
  Read carefully.
b. Everybody, touch the title. ✓
- (Call on a student to read the title.)
  [Concord.]
- Everybody, what's the title? (Signal.)
  Concord.
c. (Call on individual students to read the
  story, each student reading two or three
  sentences at a time. Ask questions
  marked **1.**)

- (Correct errors: Tell the word. Direct
  the student to reread the sentence.)
- (If the group makes more than 11 errors,
  direct the students to reread the story.)
---

d. (After the group has read the selection
  making no more than 11 errors, read the
  story to the students and ask questions
  marked **2.**)

Concord

**"I must keep moving," Tom said to
himself.**

1. Where was he? (Call on a student.
   Ideas: *Concord; in a snowstorm in a
   grove of trees.*)
1. What would happen to him if he stopped
   moving? (Call on a student. Idea: *He'd
   freeze to death.*)

**He was afraid. He started running
through the deep snow. He could
see his breath, but no footprints.**

1. Whose footprints was he looking for?
   (Call on a student. Idea: *His own.*)
1. What would he do if he found footprints?
   (Call on a student. Idea: *Follow them
   back to the time machine.*)

**The snow had almost stopped. The
cold air cut through his shirt. He ran
and he ran.**

   **Suddenly, he stopped. In a valley
below there was a little village.
There was a horse and rider moving
slowly down the street. A few people
were standing in front of a church.
The church bell was ringing—"gong,
gong, gong." The village looked very
peaceful.**

1. Everybody, what year did Tom and Eric
   want to get to? (Signal. Accept
   appropriate response.)
1. Everybody, look at the picture. What
   things in the picture tell you that they are
   not in that year? (Call on a student.
   Ideas: *The houses are different; there
   are horses; there are no cars; there are
   no electric streetlights; old-fashioned
   clothing.*)
1. What would you see in the village if Tom
   was in the right year? (Call on individual
   students. Ideas: *Cars, buses, cement,
   neon lights,* etc.)

**Tom ran down the hill and into the
village. Tom ran toward the people
who were standing in front of the
church. A man said, "You should be
wearing a coat."**

1. Everybody, what language is the man
   speaking? (Signal.) *English.*
1. So where do you think Tom is? (Call on
   a student. Ideas: *The United States;
   Canada; England.*)

   Tom said, "I'm . . . lost."

2. Why is he talking slowly? (Call on a
   student. Ideas: *He's cold, confused,
   tired, out of breath.*)

Another man said, "Come inside, lad."

The men took Tom into the church. Tom sat down near a fireplace. The heat felt good. Tom rubbed his hands together. Slowly, the cold feeling in his hands and feet started to go away.

Tom turned to one of the men and said, "What year is it?"

The man smiled. "Everyone knows what year this is. This is 1777."

1. Everybody, what year? (Signal.) *1777.*
1. Why did the man think that everybody knew the year? (Call on a student. Idea: *He thought Tom was from that year.*)
1. If Tom is in 1777, something very important happened one year before. What happened? (Call on a student. Idea: *The United States became a country.*)
1. Everybody, in what year did the United States become a country? (Signal.) *1776.*
1. So Tom was in the village one year after the United States became a country.

Tom said to himself, "1777." Then he asked, "And where am I?"

"You are in the town of Concord."

Tom thought for a moment. The United States became a country in 1776. It was a year later now, and the United States was at war with England. The United States was losing the war.

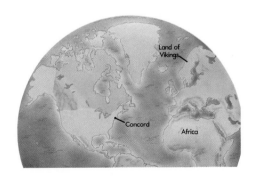

2. Everybody, who was the United States at war with? (Signal.) *England.*
2. Which country was winning that war so far? (Signal.) *England.*
2. Which country ended up winning the war? (Signal.) *United States.*

2. Look at the map on the next page. It shows where Tom and Eric were before going to Concord. It also shows where Concord is. Everybody, tell me where they were before going to Concord. (Signal.) *The Land of the Vikings.*
2. Touch the Land of the Vikings on the map. ✓
2. Touch Concord on the map. ✓
2. What country is Concord in? (Signal.) *The United States.*

Just then, Tom heard a dog barking outside the church. The white dog was standing in the middle of the street. Tom ran up to the dog. "Where's Eric?" Tom asked.

The dog barked and ran down the street.

1. What was the dog trying to show by barking and running down the street? (Call on a student. Idea: *Where Eric was.*)

Tom started to run after him. A man caught up to Tom and said, "Here." He handed Tom a big coat. It was made of fur. Tom put it on as he ran. The coat was very warm. The man who ran with Tom was tall and skinny. He took great big steps, and Tom had trouble keeping up with him.

"My name is Robert," the man said as they ran along.

They followed the dog up a hill and down the other side. Then they saw Eric. He was sitting in the snow, crying. He looked very cold. Robert took off his coat and wrapped it around Eric. Eric said, "I . . . I got lost." The dog licked his face. Eric patted the dog on the head.

Eric, Tom, and Robert started walking back to town. Eric studied Robert's clothes and said, "We are not in the right year, are we?"

2. Everybody, look at the picture. Name some things about Robert's clothes that let Eric know they were not in the right year. (Call on a student. Ideas: *He has on short pants; a ruffled shirt; a strange scarf; a strange hat; buckled shoes.*)

> Tom said to Eric, "I'll tell you about the year we're in. Right now, George Washington and his army are sick and hungry. Many of them are dying."

2. Who was George Washington? (Call on a student. Ideas: *The leader of the U.S. Army; the first president; a general.*)

> Robert said, "And Washington will not be able to make it through the winter. The English are going to win the war."
>
> "No," Tom said. "The United States will win."

2. Everybody, who was right? (Signal.) *Tom.*

> Robert laughed. "You talk like a fool. Some of Washington's men don't have shoes. They don't have food. How can they win a battle?"
>
> Just as Tom was going to answer Robert's question, he noticed the town below them. He could see English soldiers marching into the town. They wore red coats. Robert said, "The English are looking for spies. If they find a spy, they shoot him."

1. Go back to the beginning of the story. Follow along while I read.

2. What are the English soldiers doing? (Call on a student. Idea: *Looking for spies.*)
2. What will they do to spies they find? (Call on a student. Idea: *Shoot them.*)
2. Everybody, what were the English soldiers wearing? (Signal.) *Red coats.*
2. Read the rest of the story to yourself. Find out why Tom yelled, "Let's get out of here." Raise your hand when you're done.

> Just then a shot sounded through the hills. One of the English soldiers dropped to the snow. Another shot sounded. The soldiers ran this way and that way.
>
> Robert said, "Some of Washington's men are shooting at the English."
>
> "Kazinnnnng." Something hit a tree next to Eric. Tom said, "Hey, the English are shooting at us."
>
> "Zuuuuuuump." Another shot hit the snow near Tom. Tom yelled, "Let's get out of here."
> **MORE NEXT TIME**

2. (After all students have raised their hand:) Why did Tom yell, "Let's get out of here"? (Call on a student. Idea: *Because the English soldiers were shooting at them.*)
2. Everybody, who started the shooting, the English soldiers or Washington's men? (Signal.) *Washington's men.*
2. Why were the English soldiers shooting at Tom, Eric, and Robert? (Call on a student. Ideas: *The soldiers thought they were spies; thought they were enemy soldiers.*)

EXERCISE 5

PAIRED PRACTICE

You're going to read aloud to your partner. Today the **A** members will read first. Then the **B** members will read from the star to the end of the story.
(Observe students and give feedback.)

End-of-Lesson Activities

Now finish your independent work for lesson 144. Raise your hand when you're finished.

(Observe students and give feedback.)

WORKCHECK

a. (Direct students to take out their marking pencils.)
- We're going to check your independent work. Remember, if you got an item wrong, make an **X** next to the item.
b. (For each item: Read the item. Call on a student to answer it. If the answer is wrong, say the correct answer. Refer to the Answer Key for the correct answers.)

c. Now use your marking pencil to fix up any items you got wrong. Remember, all mistakes must be fixed up before you hand in your work.

OPTIONAL ACTIVITY

(Sing the song "Yankee Doodle" with the students.)

WRITING-SPELLING

(Present Writing-Spelling lesson 144 after completing Reading lesson 144. See Writing-Spelling Guide.)

Special Project

Note: After completing lesson 144, do this special project with the students. You may do the project during another part of the school day.

a. Everybody, find page 321 in your textbook. ✓
- (Call on individual students to read two or three sentences.)
- (Teacher reference:)

> You have learned about what a biography is. There are biographies of George Washington.
> Find a biography about George Washington and write three important things about his life. Don't write about anything that you've already read about in your textbook.

b. Everybody, what do we call a story that is true and that tells about the life of one person? (Signal.) *A biography.*
- You're going to find a biography about George Washington. How will you find that biography? (Call on a student. Idea: *Go to the library.*)
- You're going to write something after you find the biography. What are you going to write? (Call on a student. Idea: *Three important things about his life.*)
c. (Assign students to work in teams of three or four. After they write their reports, arrange a time when the groups present what they found out to the rest of the class or to another class.)

Lesson 145

Materials: Each student will need their thermometer chart for exercise 4.

EXERCISE 1

READING WORDS

Column 1

a. **Find lesson 145 in your textbook.** ✓
- (Teacher reference:)

1. puzzled	3. cracked
2. creaked	4. August

- Touch column 1. ✓
b. Word 1. What word? (Signal.) *Puzzled.*
- Another word for **confused** is **puzzled.** Everybody, what's another way of saying **The message confused her?** (Signal.) *The message puzzled her.*
c. Word 2. What word? (Signal.) *Creaked.*
d. Word 3. What word? (Signal.) *Cracked.*
e. Word 4. What word? (Signal.) *August.*
f. Let's read those words again.
- Word 1. What word? (Signal.) *Puzzled.*
- (Repeat for words 2–4.)
g. (Repeat step f until firm.)

Column 2

h. Find column 2. ✓
- (Teacher reference:)

1. described	4. voice
2. dashboard	5. character
3. microphone	

i. Word 1. What word? (Signal.) *Described.*
- (Repeat for words 2–5.)
j. Let's read those words again.
- Word 1. What word? (Signal.) *Described.*
- (Repeat for words 2–5.)
k. (Repeat step j until firm.)

Individual Turns

(For columns 1 and 2: Call on individual students, each to read one to three words per turn.)

EXERCISE 2

COMPREHENSION PASSAGE

a. Find part B in your textbook. ✓
- You're going to read the last story about Eric and Tom. First you'll read the information passage. It gives some more facts about time.
b. Everybody, touch the title. ✓
- (Call on a student to read the title.) *[More About Time.]*
- Everybody, what's the title? (Signal.) *More About Time.*
c. (Call on individual students to read the passage, each student reading two or three sentences at a time.)

More About Time

- (Teacher reference:)

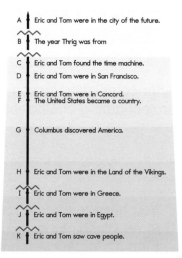

Look at the time line. Touch dot C.

- Everybody, do it. ✓

That dot shows when Eric and Tom started their trip. What year was that?

- Everybody, what's the answer? (Signal. Accept appropriate response.)

Touch dot A.

- Everybody, do it. ✓

That dot shows when Eric and Tom were in the city of the future. When was that?

• Everybody, what's the answer? (Signal.) *4,000 years in the future.*

Touch dot B.

• Everybody, do it. ✓

That dot shows the year that Thrig was from. What year was that?

• Everybody, what's the answer? (Signal.) *2400.*

Touch dot D.

• Everybody, do it. ✓

That dot shows when Eric and Tom were in San Francisco. What year was that?

• Everybody, what's the answer? (Signal.) *1906.*

Touch dot E.

• Everybody, do it. ✓

That dot shows when Eric and Tom were in Concord. What year was that?

• Everybody, what's the answer? (Signal.) *1777.*

Touch dot F.

• Everybody, do it. ✓

That dot shows when the United States became a country. What year was that?

• Everybody, what's the answer? (Signal.) *1776.*

Touch dot G.

• Everybody, do it. ✓

That dot shows when Columbus discovered America. What year was that?

• Everybody, what's the answer? (Signal.) *1492.*

Touch dot H.

• Everybody, do it. ✓

That dot shows when Eric and Tom were in the Land of the Vikings. What year was that?

• Everybody, what's the answer? (Signal.) *1000.*

Touch dot I.

• Everybody, do it. ✓

That dot shows when Eric and Tom were in Greece. How long ago was that?

• Everybody, what's the answer? (Signal.) *3,000 years ago.*

Touch dot J.

• Everybody, do it. ✓

That dot shows when Eric and Tom were in Egypt. How long ago was that?

• Everybody, what's the answer? (Signal.) *5,000 years ago.*

Touch dot K.

• Everybody, do it. ✓

That dot shows when Eric and Tom saw the cave people. How long ago was that?

• Everybody, what's the answer? (Signal.) *40,000 years ago.*

STORY READING

> *Note:* There is a reading checkout in this lesson; therefore, there is no second reading of the story and no paired practice.

a. Find part C in your textbook. ✓
- The error limit for group reading is 12. Read carefully.

b. Everybody, touch the title. ✓
- (Call on a student to read the title.) *[Home.]*
- Everybody, what's the title? (Signal.) *Home.*
- What do you think will happen in this story? (Call on a student. Idea: *Tom and Eric will get home.*)

c. (Call on individual students to read the story, each student reading two or three sentences at a time. Ask specified questions.)

> - (Correct errors: Tell the word. Direct the student to reread the sentence.)
> - (If the group makes more than 12 errors, direct the students to reread the story.)

Home

Tom, Eric, and Robert were running from the English soldiers. After they ran about a mile, Tom stopped and said, "We don't know where we're going." He turned around. "But the dog knows." Tom bent down next to the dog. "Take us back to the time machine," Tom said.

1. How would the dog know how to get there? (Call on a student. Idea: *He can smell it.*)

Tom gave the dog a little push. The dog sniffed the air and then started to run. He stopped to sniff some animal tracks. He stopped to eat snow. But then he started to run in a straight line over the hills.

1. What do you think it means when he goes in a straight line? (Call on a student. Idea: *He knows where he's going.*)

So Tom, Eric, and Robert followed the dog. Just when Tom began to think the dog didn't know where he was going, Robert said, "What is that thing ahead of us?"

1. What do you think Robert sees? (Call on a student. Idea: *The time machine.*)

Tom looked through the trees. "That's it. That's our time machine." Tom, Eric, and Robert ran up to the time machine. Robert looked very puzzled.

1. Why? (Call on a student. Idea: *He'd never seen a time machine before.*)
1. Everybody, show me a puzzled look. ✓

The door to the time machine was open, and the time machine was filled with snow. There was so much snow inside that the seat was covered.

1. The snow by the seat could cause a problem. How? (Call on a student. Ideas: *It could close the door; it could mess up the machine.*)

Tom and Eric started to dig through the snow. They pushed most of it out of the time machine.
Then Tom turned to Robert. Tom said, "You'd better come with us. If the English soldiers find you, they'll kill you."
"No," Robert said. "I am going to fight the English. I will join Washington's army."

1. Whose side of the war will Robert fight on? (Call on a student. Idea: *The United States.*)

Eric took off Robert's coat and handed it to him. "You will need this," he said.
Tom took off his coat. He said, "And you can give this to one of the other soldiers."

1. Why would the soldiers need coats? (Call on a student. Ideas: *It's cold; the U. S. Army doesn't have money to buy coats.*)

Robert took the coats. He put one on and threw the other over his shoulder. "Good luck," he said.

Robert started running down the hill. Soon he had disappeared into the woods. Three soldiers in red coats were coming from the other direction.

1. Everybody, which army were the red-coated soldiers from? (Signal.) *England.*

Tom sat down in the seat. The door did not close. Tom said, "The seat must be frozen." He bounced up and down. The English soldiers were very close. The dog was standing in the doorway growling at them. One soldier came up to the doorway. "Come out of there," he yelled.

Eric pushed on the seat. Tom bounced up and down. Suddenly, the seat creaked and—swwwwsh—the door closed.

"Bong! Bong!"

1. What's making that bong-bong sound? (Call on a student. Idea: *Soldiers pounding on the door.*)

"I hope the handle works," Tom said. He pulled on the handle, but it seemed to be frozen.

1. If the handle seemed to be frozen, what did it do? (Call on a student. Idea: *It didn't move.*)

Tom banged on the dashboard. Suddenly, a door opened and a microphone popped out.

1. Everybody, look back at the picture on page 325. Touch the dashboard. ✓
1. Touch the door that opened. ✓

1. Touch the microphone. ✓

A voice said, "What year and month do you wish to go to?"

1. What did the voice ask? (Call on a student.) *[What year and month do you wish to go to?]*
1. Whose voice do you think that is? (Call on individual students. Student preference.)
1. What is the microphone for? (Call on a student. Idea: *Telling the machine where to go.*)
1. Eric and Tom have been working the time machine the wrong way. How do you think you are supposed to go from one time to another? (Call on a student. Idea: *Talk into the microphone and tell the machine where to go.*)

Eric and Tom looked at each other. "The month we want is August," Eric said. Then he told the year.

1. Everybody, what year? (Signal. Accept appropriate response.)

The handle moved. Several dials lit up.

1. Everybody, did anyone have to touch the handle to make it move? (Signal.) *No.*
1. What made it move? (Call on a student. Idea: *A computer.*)

Then the voice said, "What date in August?"

Eric said, "The 19th. It is a Saturday."

Again the end of the handle moved, and several more dials lit up.

1. What made it move again? (Call on a student. Ideas: *A computer; new information.*)

The voice said, "What time on August 19th?"

Tom said, "Make it about the time the sun goes down."

The voice said, "What place do you wish to go to on August 19th?"

Eric described the place.

1. I'll read the next sentence:
   The voice said, "On August 19th, the sun sets at 8:32 P.M. in that place."
1. Now you read that sentence. (Call on a student.)

> The voice said, "On August 19th, the sun sets at 8:32 P.M. in that place."
>   Eric asked Tom, "Who are we talking to?"
>   The voice said, "I am the computer that runs this time machine."

1. Eric asked Tom, "Who are we talking to?" Everybody, did Tom answer the question? (Signal.) *No.*
1. Who answered it? (Signal.) *The computer.*

> Suddenly, the force pushed against Tom. Then the force died down. Slowly, Tom stood up and the boys went outside.
>   The time machine was on the mountain where Tom and Eric had found it. Thrig was standing next to the time machine. He told the boys, "I feel better now. I think I can make the trip back to the year 2400." He got in the time machine. The door closed, and a moment later, the time machine disappeared. Eric said, "I hope he makes it."
>   Tom said, "Me, too." Then he looked down the mountain and could see the other kids walking home down the path below.
>   "Let's get out of here," Tom said. Tom yelled out to the other kids, "Hey wait for us!"

1. Read the rest of the story to yourself. Find out who was named Columbus. Raise your hand when you're done.

> Tom, Eric, and the dog caught up to the other kids. Someone asked, "Hey, where did you get the dog?"
>   Tom smiled. "You wouldn't believe me if I told you."
>   Another kid asked, "What's the dog's name?"
>   Eric said, "Columbus."
>   "That's a silly name for a dog," one kid said.

> Eric said, "It's not a silly name for <u>this</u> dog."
>   One of the girls said, "Let's go home. We've got a long way to go."
>   Tom laughed. "We don't have very far to go at all." Eric laughed too.
>   "Wow!" Tom said. "It sure feels good to be home." He patted Columbus on the head. Columbus wagged his tail. The lights were going on all over the town below. That town sure looked good.
> **The End**

1. (After all students have raised their hand:) Who was named Columbus? (Call on a student. Idea: *The dog.*)
1. One of the kids said, "That's a silly name for a dog." Why wasn't that a silly name for the white dog? (Call on a student. Ideas: *Because the dog came from the time of Columbus; because the dog left Spain in 1492 and came to America.*)
1. A girl said, "Let's go home. We've got a long way to go." What did Tom say to her? (Call on a student. Idea: *That they didn't have very far to go at all.*)
1. Why didn't Tom think home was very far away? (Call on a student. Idea: *Because they'd gone so far.*)
1. Let me read the last part of this story. Everybody, close your eyes and get a picture of it.
   The time machine was on the mountain where Tom and Eric had found it. Thrig was standing next to the time machine. He told the boys, "I feel better now. I think I can make the trip back to the year 2400." He got in the time machine. The door closed, and a moment later, the time machine disappeared. Eric said, "I hope he makes it."
   Tom said, "Me, too." Then he looked down the mountain and could see the other kids walking home down the path below.
   "Let's get out of here," Tom said. Tom yelled out to the other kids, "Hey wait for us!"
   Tom, Eric, and the dog caught up to the other kids. Someone asked, "Hey, where did you get the dog?"
   Tom smiled. "You wouldn't believe me if I told you."
   Another kid asked, "What's the dog's name?"

Eric said, "Columbus."

"That's a silly name for a dog," one kid said.

Eric said, "It's not a silly name for this dog."

One of the girls said, "Let's go home. We've got a long way to go."

Tom laughed. "We don't have very far to go at all." Eric laughed too.

"Wow!" Tom said. "It sure feels good to be home." He patted Columbus on the head. Columbus wagged his tail. The lights were going on all over the town below. That town sure looked good.

THE END

EXERCISE 4

READING CHECKOUTS

a. Today is a reading-checkout day. While you're doing your independent work, I'm going to call on you one at a time to read part of the story from lesson 144. When I call you to come and do your checkout bring your thermometer chart.

• Remember, you pass the checkout by reading the passage in less than a minute without making more than 2 mistakes. And when you pass the checkout, you'll color the space for lesson 145 on your thermometer chart.

b. (Call on individual students to read the portion of story 144 marked with ☀.)

• (Time the student. Note words that are missed and number of words read.)

• (Teacher reference:)

☀ **The dog barked and ran down the street. Tom started to run after him. A man caught up to Tom and said, "Here."**
He handed Tom a big coat. It was made of fur. Tom put it on as he ran. The coat was very warm. The man who ran [50] **with Tom was tall and skinny. He took great big steps, and Tom had trouble keeping up with him.**

"My name is Robert," the man [75] **said as they ran along.**

They followed the dog up a hill and down the other side. Then they saw Eric. He was sitting in ☀ [100] **the snow, crying.**

• (If the student reads the passage in one minute or less and makes no more than 2 errors, direct the student to color in the space for lesson 145 on the thermometer chart.)

• (If the student makes any mistakes, point to each word that was misread and identify it.)

• (If the student does not meet the rate-error criterion for the passage, direct the student to practice reading the story with the assigned partner.)

End-of-Lesson Activities

INDEPENDENT WORK

Now finish your independent work for lesson 145. Raise your hand when you're finished. (Observe students and give feedback.)

WORKCHECK

a. (Direct students to take out their marking pencils.)

• We're going to check your independent work. Remember, if you got an item wrong, make an **X** next to the item.

b. (For each item: Read the item. Call on a student to answer it. If the answer is wrong, say the correct answer. Refer to the Answer Key for the correct answers.)

c. Now use your marking pencil to fix up any items you got wrong. Remember, all mistakes must be fixed up before you hand in your work.

Note: Administer End-of Program Test before doing Special Projects 1 and 2.

WRITING-SPELLING

(Present Writing-Spelling lesson 145 after completing Reading lesson 145. See Writing-Spelling Guide.)

ACTIVITY

(Present Activity 39 after completing Reading lesson 145. See Activities Across the Curriculum.)

Test 15

END-OF-PROGRAM TEST

EXERCISE 1

TEST

a. **Find page 331 in your textbook.** ✓
- This lesson is a test. You'll work items you've done before.
b. Work carefully. Raise your hand when you've completed all the items.
   (Observe students but do not give feedback on errors.)

EXERCISE 2

MARKING THE TEST

a. (Check students' work. Refer to the Answer Key for the correct answers.)
b. (Record all test 15 results on the Test Summary Sheet and the Group Summary Sheet. Reproducible Summary Sheets are at the back of the Teacher's Guide.)

EXERCISE 3

TEST REMEDIES

- (Provide any necessary remedies for test 15. Test remedies are discussed in the Teacher's Guide.)

Test 15 Firming Table

Test Item	Introduced in lesson	Test Item	Introduced in lesson	Test Item	Introduced in lesson
1	138	11	144	21	132
2	131	12	144	22	132
3	138	13	135	23	131
4	138	14	135	24	145
5	131	15	139	25	132
6	142	16	142	26	139
7	144	17	144	27	142
8	144	18	139	28	136
9	144	19	139	29	132
10	144	20	138	30	137

LITERATURE

(Present Literature lesson 15 after completing Reading lesson 145. See Literature Guide.)

Special Projects

Project 1

Note: After completing lesson 145, do these special projects with the students. You may do these projects during another part of the school day.

Materials: Large butcher paper or poster board (at least 2 feet by 5 feet), colored markers, crayons, paints, scissors, and other construction materials.

a. Find page 336 in your textbook. ✓
• This section tells about a special project we're going to do.
• (Call on individual students to read two or three sentences at a time.)
• (Teacher reference:)

Special Project

Make a time line that shows facts about your school and some of the people in it. Show the following events on your time line:

1. When the youngest student in your class was born.
2. When the oldest student in your class was born.
3. When you will enter high school.
4. When you will graduate from high school.
5. When your teacher or principal was born.
6. When your school was built.

You may want to show pictures of the people or things named on your time line. You may want to add other events that are important to your school or the students in your class.

b. (Divide students into two groups, each of which is responsible for part of the project:
• Group 1 is responsible for items that refer to students in the class (items 1–4 specified in the project description);
• Group 2 is responsible for items that refer to people or things other than students in the class.)
c. (Each group is to get the information and create the entries on the time line. Each entry has a date and a description of an event. Some entries may also have illustrations.)

Purpose: To explore oral and cultural traditions.

a. You've read about how people who live in different times and in different places look at things differently. Eric and Tom went to places where people spoke languages that are different from our language and believed things that we don't believe.

- We're going to invite somebody to our class who comes from a place that is very different from where we live. That person will tell us about where they live, about their favorite stories and songs, about how they celebrate birthdays and other holidays. The person will show us how to say different things in the language of the place the person came from.

b. (Ask students if they know a family that comes from a place where they speak a different language. If no students can identify a family, ask students how the class could go about finding a person who is from a culture different from theirs. Suggestions: Call a community college, the Chamber of Commerce, churches, university, public library, the police department, INS [immigration and naturalization service—listed in phone directory.])

- (Once a speaker is identified, refer to the globe and identify the country the person came from. Make up a fact sheet that students are to memorize—for example, distance from the United States, at least two major cities, rough population of the country.)

- (The class is to generate a list of questions the speaker is to answer. Among the items students should find out about are how to say different things in the native language, the person's favorite children's story or story character, how the people from that country celebrate holidays, how much things cost, what kinds of foods they eat, a simple song that the students could learn, what kind of work the people in the family had.)

- (Students are to ask the speaker assigned questions and spontaneous questions.)

- (Following the discussion, students are to write about the three most interesting things they learned.)